REVOLUTIONARIES
AND FUNCTIONARIES

OTHER BOOKS BY RICHARD FALK

Legal Order in a Violent World

This Endangered Planet

Crimes of War

A Study of Future Worlds

A Global Approach to National Policy

Human Rights and State Sovereignty

Indefensible Weapons: The Political and Psychological Case Against Nuclearism
(with Robert Jay Lifton)

The End of World Order

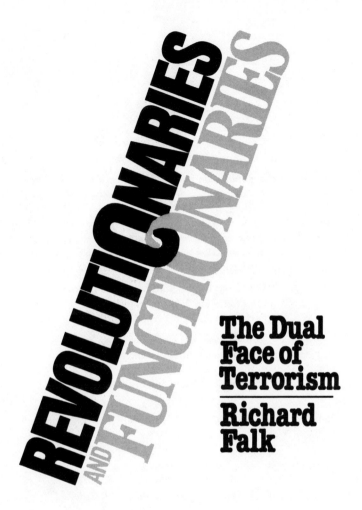

REVOLUTIONARIES AND FUNCTIONARIES

The Dual Face of Terrorism

Richard Falk

E. P. DUTTON NEW YORK

Written under the auspices of the
Center of International Studies,
Princeton University

Published in the United States by E. P. Dutton,
a division of NAL Penguin Inc.,
2 Park Avenue, New York, N.Y. 10016.

Published simultaneously in Canada
by Fitzhenry and Whiteside Limited, Toronto.

Library of Congress Cataloging-in-Publication Data

Falk, Richard A.
Revolutionaries and functionaries: the dual face of terrorism /
Richard Falk.
p.   cm.
Bibliography: p.
Includes index.
1. Terrorism.   2. Revolutionists.   I. Title.
HV6431.F35   1988
303.6'25—dc19   87-25198
                                                              CIP

ISBN: 0-525-24604-5

Designed by REM Studios

1 3 5 7 9 10 8 6 4 2

First Edition

For my daughter Kate
with love

and the dream of a
postterrorist world

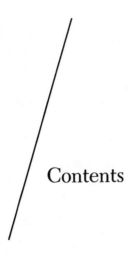

Contents

vii

Acknowledgments

In an important sense, every book is a kind of covert operation. There are many secret collaborators, some supportive, others antagonistic. Perhaps, because of the subject matter, I am more than usually conscious of this covertness, and I want to dilute it somewhat by acknowledging a few of the hidden hearts and minds.

I have been helped throughout by the exceptional scholarly auspices provided at Princeton University's Center of International Studies and by the encouragement of its director and my friend, Henry Bienen. In the foreground of support have been my devoted and talented secretary, June Garson, and the generally efficient Center staff. I have benefited, especially, from the good fortune of a diligent and energetic research assistant, Philomena Fischer.

Mary Kaldor unwittingly is responsible for the whole undertaking. It was her urgent request for an instant essay on the topic in the immediate aftermath of the American attack on Libya in April 1986 that got me started thinking about the varieties of terrorism that combat each other in a spirit of mindless self-righteousness.

Testing some of these ideas in the classroom has been of great help to me. I want to thank several groups of Princeton students for their tough questions and critical reactions. Contrary to some impressions on the political Right, it is often the teacher who learns, the students who teach. Higher education at its best involves an interactive process of inquiry rather than a linear transmission of knowledge, much less ideology, from the relatively old expert to the relatively young novice.

Of specific help to me have been several colleagues who read and perceptively commented on the manuscript in detail: Kader Asmal, Leif Haase, Samuel Kim, Mary Morris, Paul Wapner. Each response altered my thinking, but not sufficiently, I am sure, to address the range of their concerns. Helpful general reactions to an earlier draft were also provided by Rev. Elisabeth Gerle, Catherine Keller, and Peri Pamir. Further in the background have been those who through their works and lives have over the years influenced my understanding of the shape and character of political violence in the world, both by governments and by their most radical opponents. In this regard I would mention, especially, the following: Eqbal Ahmad, Fouad Ajami, Richard Barnet, Noam Chomsky, Ramsey Clark, Giri Deshingkar, Jim and Shelley Douglass, Daniel Ellsberg, Mansour Farhang, Michael Klare, Rajni Kothari, Robert Jay Lifton, Saul Mendlovitz, Marcus Raskin, Edward Said, Gene Sharp, E. P. Thompson, and Howard Zinn. Still further in the background are those shaping voices, in my case especially Camus, Gandhi, Jesus, King, Tolstoy. The Select Bibliography indicates some additional influences active in the writing process.

I want, also, to thank my editor, Paul De Angelis, for his exceptional patience, sensitivity, and general intelligence. To the degree my argument coheres and convinces, he deserves much of the credit. Finally, my agent, Ellen Levine, has been supportive throughout well beyond the line of duty.

The approach taken and the subject matter are such that it is hardly necessary to absolve others from responsibility for the views set forth, but I do so anyway, to remove any doubt that those acknowledged necessarily share my assessments of the terrorist menace.

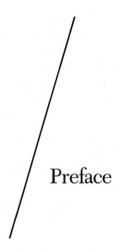

Preface

*The deeper unsatisfied war beneath
and behind the declared war.*

ROBERT DUNCAN, "Achilles Song"

This book argues that to act effectively against terrorism, we must first learn to think clearly about what it is. It also contends that there exists great confusion, some genuine, some insidious, about the true character of terrorism in our world. As well, there are several strange, even startling, inconsistencies between what our government in Washington tells us as citizens about terrorism and the actual policies it pursues.

So far, the subject matter of terrorism has been dominated, with a few notable exceptions, by polemical treatments of the topic that encourage the illusion that terrorism is something alien to American patterns of conduct in the world, that it is done unto us, and that what we do violently unto others is legitimate counterterrorism, or, in the language of the polemics, "fighting back."

The general view is that the deepest roots of terrorism involve some mixture of desperation and depravity within dispossessed political extremists, especially those on the Left. My claim is that this mainstream image of terrorism is dangerously misleading. It overlooks the often calculating character of recourse to wanton and indiscriminate political violence from a variety of sources, including the deepest recesses of governmental bureaucracy operating in an entirely cool, calculating, rational style.

My argument is that it is futile and hypocritical self-deception to suppose that we can use the word *terrorism* to establish a double standard pertaining to the use of political violence. Unless we are consistent and self-critical in our use of language we invite the very violence we deplore.

Terrorism, then, is used here to designate any type of political violence that lacks an adequate moral and legal justification, regardless of whether the actor is a revolutionary group or a government. Of course, such a definition is open to interpretation. The word *adequate* suggests that legal and moral judgments are unavoidably somewhat subjective and that the process of justification is necessarily grounded in the realms of private morality and partisan ideology. To justify political violence adequately means seeking a generally persuasive and objective interpretation of prevailing community norms as embodied in international law and in a shared ethos that restricts political violence to a defensive role and unconditionally protects those who are innocent. Seeking such an objective interpretation is not easy in a world of rival belief systems and cultural backgrounds, but neither is it impossible.

A pitfall of repudiating terrorism is the question of its effectiveness, especially in war. So long as terrorist methods are relied upon by states to avoid defeat or hasten victory in war, bolstered by the claim of saving lives, terrorists of all persuasions gain validation, provided only that they express some plausible justification that an indiscriminate attack or a sacrifice of innocent lives is reasonably consonant with their political goals. Programs of counterterrorism must renounce certain forms of political violence even if they seem effective and even if they are selected by leaders of governments or battlefield commanders in the heat of war.

It is foolish moralism to suppose that revolutionary groups would be prepared to follow a higher morality than that accepted by states. And it is hypocritical to insist that they do so; besides, it has no effect, except possibly as an example of self-deluding propaganda. On occasion, revolutionary groups adopt a higher morality, either renouncing violence altogether or being much more careful than their governmental adversaries about the protection of innocence. A comparison between the tactics of the African National Congress and the South African government over the course of several decades discloses such a persistent normative gap favorable to the revolutionary group in relation to the role of political violence in the South African struggle. Similar claims have been advanced on behalf of the conduct of the Sendero Luminoso ("shining path") in Peru, both as to its care in confining violence to appropriate targets given the reality of revolutionary struggle and its relatively greater care as to the protection of innocence as compared to the government of Peru, especially during the period of Fernando Belaúnde Terry's presidency (1980–1985).[1]

Similarly, we cannot argue conclusively that terrorism never works, and that therefore its renunciation on all sides could be undertaken as a practical political step. It is true that terroristic methods often harden opposition and alienate the perpetrators from the citizenry. But it is also true that acts of terrorism under certain circumstances focus attention on grievances and may induce an adversary to back down. Arguably, the British decisions to quit Ireland after World War I and Palestine and Cyprus after World War II were influenced by the terrorist tactics of their opponents, and surely the French defeat in Algeria was a consequence, in part, of terrorist challenges by revolutionary nationalists. Similarly the Allied powers in World War II may have weakened the will of Germany and Japan to resist by large-scale indiscriminate air attacks against heavy concentrations of the civilian population on cities.

The embodiment of terrorism in the modern war-fighting mentality is, at present, a fact of international life. Without using the word *terrorism,* Thomas Schelling accurately and typically associates the essence of military strategy with calculated recourse to terrorism:

> Military strategy can no longer be thought of, as it could for some countries in some eras, as the science of military victory. It is now equally, if not more, the art of coercion, of intimidation and deterrence. The instruments of war are more punitive than acquisitive. Military strategy, whether we like it or not, has become the diplomacy of violence.[2]

The essence of our problem is that terrorism has been routinized on every side of the main political equations of our day.

In various forms, terrorism is as old as government and armed struggle, and as pervasive. The modern torment over terrorism arises because our lives and societies are more interconnected than ever before through mass media and because we live in an era of pervasive turmoil and high-technology weaponry that threaten the very idea of a human future.

It is too easy to blame the terrorist menace on the evil other. To end terrorism, in my view, requires a cultural resolve to avoid indiscriminate and unjustified political violence and to respect the integrity of civilian life at all costs. As soon as the choice of violent means is entrusted to human evaluations of effectiveness in supporting a political cause in a given setting, a terrorist ethos is bound to hold sway in circumstances of crisis and pressure.

Another strong temptation is to turn from terrorism to pacifism. After all, our world is saturated with violence, and we seem locked into a series of cultural patterns that sustain spirals of violence within and between nations. To move from violence to nonviolence is also to solve the problem of ambiguity. We do away with the dilemmas of assessment if we agree that violence is *never* justified. And further, nonviolence enjoys a strong mandate in several leading world religions, including Christianity and Buddhism, providing a basis for challenging the war system at a time of great jeopardy to the entire human species.

Yet pure nonviolence is not the course proposed here. For one thing, the opposite of terrorism is not nonviolence, but permissible violence. In other words, we don't want to claim that a war fought in self-defense is an instance of terrorism. That would be an abuse of language as damaging as that of now associating terrorism only with the political violence of enemies while reserving to ourselves the right to engage in comparable practice.

Furthermore, given the way the world is organized—repressive governments, aggressive foreign policies—it is unrealistic and arrogant to insist that victims acquiesce in injustice. We may be exceedingly skeptical about violent strategies, and yet there does not seem to be either an ethical basis or a political structure that could sustain an invariable practice of nonviolence.

What we can do, and need to try, although it is difficult, is to oppose at the very least those forms of political violence that seek to gain their ends by striking fear into hearts and minds and that refuse to respect the innocence of civilian life. Such a position demands a lot, including the practice of warfare in a principled way. But unless we demand this much we are fooling ourselves if we think we are opposing terrorism. How can we claim to be antiterrorists unless we have ourselves renounced terrorism?

In writing this book, I am taking such a question seriously, reacting to mainstream attempts to muddle our understanding of the real challenge of terrorism. There are three main elements: first, a reaction to the effort to mobilize Americans for political violence overseas under the banner of counterterrorism; second, a reaction to a related effort to induce Americans to accept or ignore cruel and savage uses of violence by those fighting against Communists, radicals, and revolutionary nationalists in various Third World settings; third, a reaction to elaborate official attempts to hide indiscriminate and frightening forms of political violence behind the protective cover of "national security" and "nuclear deterrence." There are even indications that support for "Star Wars"—the Strategic Defense Initiative (SDI)—increasingly rests on a counterterrorist rationalization. The latest reasoning is that even if the shield will never protect us against Soviet missiles, it can realistically defend against some future attack by a terrorist state such as Qaddafi's Libya or against a revolutionary group that gains control over some nuclear missiles. The evocation of terrorism is apparently so powerful that it has the alchemical capacity to endow even the most implausible undertaking with a certain plausibility.

Let me illustrate the confusion that exists at the highest levels of government. During his congressional testimony at the Iran/Contra hearings, Rear Admiral John Poindexter, the former national security adviser, recounts that President Reagan was reading, with evident approval, Benjamin Netanyahu's *Terrorism: How the West Can Win* on the plane to and from the Tokyo economic summit in May 1986. This book of essays on terrorism by various authors and edited by the Israeli ambassador represents a prime example of the polemical literature of counterterrorism that associates the terrorist threat almost exclusively with Third World radicals, especially in the Mediterranean region, and their supposed masters in the Kremlin. Poindexter reports Reagan's looking up from the book, saying: "Look, I don't want to pull out our support for the Contras for any reason. This would be an unacceptable option. Isn't there something that I could do unilaterally?"[3]

What is so bewitching about this incident is the apparent sincerity of the president's confusion: a self-righteous condemnation on every conceivable ground of those elements in the Third World who oppose our interests and, simultaneously, an equally self-righteous endorsement of those who favor our objectives. What creates incoherence, and undermines our diplomatic stature as a leader among nations, is that we commit ourselves ardently to the very kinds of political violence we deplore if used by those who are seen as pursuing goals hostile to our foreign policy interests. We confuse ourselves and others about the issue of violence at a time in history when human survival may ultimately depend on clarity and coherence.

There is another preliminary issue. In a democracy, especially, we depend very much on trust among the citizenry and between the citizens and their government. Secrecy, public lies, and state propaganda exact a high cost in the quality of government, as we have seen recently in the course of sorting out the Iran/Contra disclosures. But also crucial is the integrity of language and public discourse on the great issues of the day. As is so often observed, the media shape our image of the world, and disinformation contaminates our capacity to think, feel, and act. For this reason it is vital to regard an assault upon language as a threat to the body politic itself and to recognize that such an assault has distorted the public's perception of terrorism and thus has undermined the strength and well-being of our society.

From this perspective, the unfortunate character of the existing counterterrorist consensus, the Irangate disclosures can be viewed as a kind of blessing. The very boldness of the bureaucratic style exhibited by operatives at the National Security Council and the CIA reveals that there's far more to counterterrorism than had hitherto met the public eye. At the very least, there are at least two counterterrorist policies, often proceeding at cross-purposes: There is open warfare against those who are associated with various revolutionary causes, especially in the Mediterranean region, and then there is a secret diplomacy that seeks to lure fundamentalists into the Western camp and is prepared to trade arms for American hostages even when that entails arming a government that has organized, financed, and otherwise encouraged the most militant and gross forms of anti-American terrorism. Such is the tapestry of deceit and contradiction, including "the neat idea" of diverting funds to the Contras so as to finance their right-wing terrorist activities. To paraphrase Talleyrand's quip about intervention, terrorism and counterterrorism are two ways to describe the same activity.

Yet with Congress baffled, the public disturbed, the media agitated, Reagan's leadership tarnished, the stage is set for a wider, more helpful debate about terrorism and counterterrorism. A less self-assured and self-righteous counterterrorist consensus exists at the present time. The sincerity and coherence of the United States program of counterterrorism have been drawn into question for the first time since the Vietnam policy went sour.

Recalling the Vietnam debate is suggestive in another sense. For many years there was a prointerventionist consensus at the national level that similarly dominated and bounded discussion. Throughout the early and mid-1960s opponents were marginalized, their views ignored, even castigated. Opposition to the war was commonly treated as disloyalty, evidence of a lack of patriotism. Then in early 1968 the Tet offensive shattered with a single tactical blow most of the illusions that had sustained support at the center for the prolonged, failed, dirty war effort that was proving so costly in lives and resources. The Tet offensive stripped away the pretense of success that had been orchestrated over the years by a compulsively optimistic, bipartisan cold war interpretation of what was actually happening in Vietnam. The credibility of prowar elements suffered severely when the National Liberation Front, supposedly waning and crippled, mounted its surprise multiple attack on the main cities in South Vietnam at Tet in February 1968. All the doubts and objections to the war, so effectively dismissed by the media and representative institutions, became respectable grounds for questioning, even opposing, the wisdom as well as the propriety of the policy. Although some prowar analysts continue to claim that the outcome of the Tet offensive was a jolting military defeat for the National Liberation Front, the actual impact was a decisive political defeat for prowar forces. The immediate effect was to release establishment skeptics from the closet. Senator Gene

McCarthy spoke out only after Tet, but then made Vietnam policy the basis for a strong movement of opposition to Lyndon Johnson's leadership of the country and the Democratic party that climaxed at the Democratic Party Convention in summer 1968 when Americans watched on TV as the Chicago police were beating up young, radical, violent antiwar activists in the streets of the city.

It would be a mistake to push this analogy too far. The terrorist issue is an important one, but it lacks the objective centrality that Vietnam possessed at the height of the war when hundreds of Americans were dying each month. Also, Ronald Reagan is a gifted, if now weakened, president who knows how to dodge bullets and has a residue of support associated with the appearance of economic recovery and the celebration of conservative virtue. Furthermore, opposition to official propagandist packaging of counterterrorism is so far ambivalent and lacks the mandate of a mass movement in the streets and on the campuses. As matters stand, the counter-terrorist consensus remains stable, but the Iran/Contra disclosures have temporarily expanded the boundaries of responsible discussion and reflection. Even this gain could be surprisingly short-lived if further revolutionary activity sends new terrorist shivers through American society.

My argument responds to the debate on terrorist policy that has swirled around the White House during the Reagan years. It was after all President Reagan himself and his first secretary of state, Alexander Haig, who early announced that counterterrorism would be the hallmark of U.S. foreign policy. And they meant it, although in their own way. Partly, it was a costly exaggeration of revolutionary violence that both tempted hostile forces to take advantage of the salience their activities were being given and a means of mobilizing American public opinion for an activist foreign policy that was bound to produce anxiety among the citizenry and feelings of frustration among foreign policy professionals who were aware of their limited capabilities to carry out such an antiterrorist policy. But the neoconservative mood in Washington was receptive. In this setting, a whole genre of counterterrorist literature surfaced to lend a helping hand.

The fever chart on the menace from revolutionary terrorism reveals a disturbing instability. Leaders and pundits in the United States exaggerated the menace early in this decade when it served their purposes. More recently, especially since the Iran/Contra disclosures, the problem of terrorism has been officially downplayed for equally political purposes. Claims have been made that the tough United States stand on counterterrorism has had its effect, especially the punitive air attack on Libya in April 1986. The media tends to reflect faithfully the official mood on such matters, and public attitudes of panic or complacency largely follow the lead of media treatment. For instance, after the counterterrorist media blitz, millions of American tourists stayed away from Europe in the summer of 1986 only to return in record numbers the following summer, apparently feeling reassured by a calmer atmosphere.

True, there have been no anti-American terrorist spectaculars of the *Achille Lauro* or TWA Flight 847 (June 1985) variety in the last year or so, but the underlying conditions, attitudes, personnel, frustrations, and vulnerabilities remain essentially unchanged. The overall international incidence of revolutionary terrorist attacks has actually increased in the last year or so, but the form has changed, and the locus has shifted to Latin America and Asia to a certain extent.[4]

There is another point here. What Washington officialdom and the media identify as terrorism is far narrower than the terrorist menace depicted in this book. My argument is that when governments, in times of war and peace, deliberately direct their violence at innocent civilians or, for that matter, detained soldiers, these governments are engaged in terrorist activity, and that this pattern has not diminished. The willingness to employ violence indiscriminately for political goals remains an underlying and largely unchallenged feature of our overall situation. As a result, the brunt of the terrorist challenge remains a modern constant even if the selective manipulation of information can make public concern rise and fall virtually at will.

This book is a response to the counterterrorist campaign as mounted by Washington in recent years. As such it concentrates on the interaction between revolutionary violence and the United States government, as well as of closely allied governments, especially Israel. An accurate reading of the arguments presented here, however, suggests that standard tactics and weaponry used by all sides of political conflict in the world today possess a terrorist character. Soviet tactics in Afghanistan have been clearly terrorist in character, as have Soviet preparations for nuclear war. The focus on Washington rather than Moscow reflects my view as an American that a propagandistic depiction of terrorism to mobilize counterterrorist militancy is particularly destructive of our capacity as citizens to grasp and respond to a far more threatening disregard of limits in relation to political violence.

In the end there are two principal ways to frame the debate on terrorism: the mainstream focus on the political violence of revolutionary groups and their supporters and the emphasis of this book on impermissible forms of political violence, regardless of the identity of the actor. The attempt here is to persuade readers of the importance of moving from the narrow to the broader conception of terrorism.

REVOLUTIONARIES
AND FUNCTIONARIES

ONE

The Two Sources
of Terrorism

Three years ago in Los Angeles I gave a talk on behalf of the
Armenian Assembly at an event organized to reflect upon the
continuing injustice of the unacknowledged Turkish genocide
carried out against the Armenian people, largely in 1915.[1] I
was struck then by the deep feeling of emotion that seemed
to be experienced by Armenians of all ages despite the sev-
enty-year lapse of time since these deliberate mass killings
occurred. Unacknowledged injustice persists as an open, painful wound for survivors and their descendants, and it is an
illusion of the victors that time alone will do all the healing.

    I had a second impression on that occasion. The audience
was composed mainly of affluent Armenians of moderate political persuasions, the organizers being particularly eager to
differentiate their concern from that of Armenian terrorist
groups that had been engaged for several years in a systematic,
highly publicized campaign to assassinate Turkish diplomats
all over the world. Quite spontaneously, I added the following
remark to my prepared statement: "While we can deplore this

upsurge of political violence, is it not true that this meeting today would not be taking place but for the added salience given to Turkish crimes against the Armenian people by terrorist incidents in recent years?" From prior contact with moderate Armenian groups engaged in public information campaigns, I had been struck by the extent to which their own expansion of involvement seemed to coincide with the eruption of Armenian terrorist activity from 1975 onward.

Of course, the causal connections are complex. Yet it seems evident that the outbreak of terrorism and the expansion of moderate forms of concern were connected. Whether the moderates wished to provide the young Armenians with a sense of their history or to assure them that moderates shared with terrorists a commitment to remember and, if possible, rectify the crimes of the past, was difficult to assess. Moderates and extremists were in a clear rivalry over tactics and effectiveness. Some moderate elements believe that the weakness of the Armenian community and its geographical dispersion make it no match for the concentrated power, wealth, and influence of the Turkish state except with respect to the moral debate. Yet, to win the moral debate requires Armenians to renounce political violence; otherwise their moral claims are easily dismissed. The other side argues that only the headline-grabbing terrorist attacks may induce Turkish authorities to adopt a more satisfactory response to Armenian grievances. Because this debate on the political impact of terrorism cannot be resolved by convincing evidence, each side feels confirmed in its convictions.

Further complicating tensions among the Armenians was a middle-class anxiety of a small minority to display their law-abiding decency by distancing themselves from the terrorists without repudiating their Armenian heritage. The media attention given the terrorist incidents had seemed to some to form a collective image of "the Armenian" as an unbalanced extremist, almost as menacing as "the Arab," and this worked against assimilationist impulses always strong in "melting-pot" America.

Afterward, while having dinner with a friend, I noticed a long table of young Armenians from the conference who were by coincidence eating in the same restaurant. They invited me to join them for coffee. When I did, the only thing they wanted to discuss was my chance remark about the consciousness-raising worth of the terrorist campaign. These gracious, intense young people were all convinced that their elders would never have bothered to devote attention to these wounds from the past had not the terrorists—also, mainly young people—acted. Obviously, though they did not affirm as much to me explicitly, these affluent, young, educated Californians of Armenian descent regarded the terrorists as heroes. I had a sense that these acts of violence were themselves redemptive of Armenian honor, possibly satisfying these young people's admiration for action, as well as their stereotypic American identification of action with violence and bloodshed. This confusion, unhappily, is widely shared in different settings with all age groups and ethnic backgrounds. Consider, for instance, the general approval given to governmental uses of violence, provided losses are inflicted on the enemy and the events can be construed as American victories.

Thinking back on this incident I realize that my experiences on that day contained the seed of my subsequent work on terrorism. The misunderstandings and disputes about both the propriety and effectiveness of political violence directed by Armenian militants at Turkish diplomats posed many of the issues that make terrorism such a problematic topic. Of course, in the Armenian setting terrorism raises very specific, even exotic concerns, and yet broader implications are present. A vast spectrum of terrorist causes exists, and an equally wide array of effects flowing from terrorist activities makes each context very distinct.

As a Jew, I was particularly struck by two elements of my contact with Armenians, and that was the degree to which a tormented people feel their wounds fester over time and the persistence of their inborn fear of vulnerability to injustice no matter how secure they may seem to be. Auden's line

"Those to whom evil is done do evil in return" is suggestive here of the terrorist cycle of action and reaction that permits each side to regard itself as the wronged party. To overcome the haunted recollection of past victimization and break the cycle of violence require acknowledgment of the cycle. In this regard, overcoming terrorism does have something to do with remembering the past as it was, no matter how painful. In this regard, the differences between the Armenian and the Jewish experiences are striking.

The analogue to the Holocaust is suggestive in several ways. It has remained vitally important for Jews and other victimized groups to remember the horrors of the past and that impulse to remember has, if anything, grown in intensity rather than faded with the passage of time. Recalling and adequately acknowledging past horrors seem to be abiding emotions that touch the core of human identity. Respect for the Holocaust by the wider community seems like a coded message to survivors that such a fate will not befall them again. The incredible intensity of these feelings was manifested in the outbursts among Jews who were provoked by President Reagan's announced plans to lay a wreath at the Bitburg Cemetery in Germany where SS officers were buried. What was for the White House an innocent expression of forgiveness to *all* Germans for the experience of World War II was interpreted by the Jewish community as a terribly threatening betrayal of the legacy of the Holocaust. A similar worldwide reaction among Jews occurred when Kurt Waldheim was elected president of Austria despite the disclosure of Nazi activities during his period of military service.

The quality of remembrance is very closely connected to the presence or absence of remorse by the group associated with the perpetrators. Thus, it was of great significance to the Jewish people that Richard von Weizsäcker, then president of the German Federal Republic, delivered a major address to the Bundestag on the fortieth anniversary of the ending of World War II acknowledging the full extent of the evil inflicted on the Jewish people by the crimes of state committed during the Nazi years. It was ironic that the German leader was so much more attentive to the still festering wounds than was the American leader, yet it was not surprising. For non-Jewish American conservatives, the abstractness of the Nazi past made the Bitburg gesture a plausible way of cementing current German-American ties, long a priority given the primacy of cold war considerations, whereas the events of the past continue to press concretely upon the consciousness of the German leadership. The German choice is to accept the responsibility for the past or to turn away defiantly, issuing denials, claiming exaggeration, and questioning the veracity of accusations, as the Turks have done.

It is notable that Turkey to this day devotes vast resources to a public relations campaign designed to discredit Armenian allegations and suppress the historical record of the systematic massacres of 1915, bloody occasions that were part of a wider design to destroy the Armenian people as a people and, as such, the first instance of genocide in this century.

The pain of that suppression is, I think, important for an understanding of the human dynamic that can result in the bloody rituals of terrorist forms of political violence. The Armenian instance is exemplary in that there is no credible political project to reestablish the Armenian nation as a part of modern Turkey, much less as a distinct state. Yet individuals risk their own death and involve themselves in the self-brutalizing undertaking of seeking to kill off essentially innocent Turkish diplomats, individuals doing their job and having no connection to or even presumed sympathy for or knowledge of events that occurred mainly before their birth. My impression from Turkish friends is a sincere ignorance of the character and circumstances surrounding Armenian grievances; they are generally vague about the events and, if informed at all, discount the genocidal accusations, explaining the occurrences as possibly excessive reactions during wartime conditions when Turkish nationalism was making its historic bid to control the political future in the wake of the collapse of the Ottoman Empire.

5

One notices that the torch of dignity is kept lit among suppressed and mutilated nationalist causes by terrorist practices. Whether among the Irish, Croatians, Basques, Moluccans, Ukrainians, Sikhs, Palestinians, Puerto Ricans, or others, the common impulse seems to be an incredibly deep urge to keep faith with the past and with one's specific identity. The mode of doing this is to make the victors or their representatives share some of the pain. Such recourse to terrorism is not mainly instrumental (a means to a political end), but rather symbolic or expressive (seeking to register a statement of grievance as powerfully as possible, by inducing shock, even trauma). In some settings, the main terrorist purpose is to mobilize the victims, challenging their indifference and ignorance. Recovering a sense of cultural identity need not require such violence: witness efforts to revive cultural identity by encouraging language study, music and art, and observance of folk rituals. Powerful experiences of national recovery have taken place among various indigenous peoples throughout the world. Among these peoples there is no project to dispossess the settler civilization, nor does such a capability exist, but there is a sense that cultural vitality can overcome the humiliations of the historical past. Some indigenous peoples, such as the Maoris in New Zealand, have made impressive progress despite the great difficulty of reestablishing cultural identity in opposition to the whole weight of modern industrial civilization.

But there is another distinctive source of terrorism in the modern world. It is the general suspension of limits with respect to political undertakings by, for, or against the state. The state claims for itself an unconditional security rationale, a rationale that culminates in making preparations to wage nuclear war and in envisioning a nuclear winter or other forms of catastrophic collapse. Many leading states have established intelligence agencies that engage in covert operations against foreign enemies without respect to the limits of law or morality. Analogously, those who aspire to statehood regard their nationalist aspirations as unconditional, therefore not subject to limits on their tactics.

But it is not only extremists who reject limits on their tactics, including recourse to violence. The pervasiveness of the terrorist phenomenon reflects a generalized breakdown of moral and legal inhibition to violence throughout society. To the extent that terrorism is perceived by the players to be "useful" it will be authorized even by liberal democracies that proclaim their *raison d'être* to be human dignity and the worth of the individual. In a quasi-official publication of the RAND Corporation, Brian Michael Jenkins (a prominent specialist on terrorism) summarizes his belief that the United States government must use terrorism to fight terrorism, as part of its need to engage in what he calls "indirect forms of warfare":

> Indirect forms of warfare include clandestine and covert military operations carried out by other than the regular armed forces of a nation, providing asylum and support for guerrillas in an adjacent country, *providing support—and sometimes operational direction—to terrorist groups opposing a rival or enemy regime, and governmental use of terrorist tactics, such as assassinating foreign foes or troublesome exiles.* [emphasis added][2]

Only ignorance could excuse the view that the United States or other major governments renounce terrorist practices even when they serve accepted foreign policy goals. All that is unusual about the Jenkins formulation is its candor. Any examination of official practices would disclose the adoption of a wide series of terrorist undertakings, veiled in secrecy and disguised by the antiseptic semantics of covert operations, low-intensity warfare, and indirect modes of conflict.

So it is misleading in the extreme to characterize a few Arab states as international pariahs because they alone sponsor terrorist activities. It is equally misleading to construct an elaborate conspiracy theory that links instances of terrorism with a network masterminded and financed in Moscow.[3] Opportunistic support of terrorist activity is an ingredient of geopolitical rivalry. No one would deny that the Soviet government has lent support to groups using political violence in a manner that qualifies it as terrorism under most accepted definitions, and that these groups have transnational links. But it is equally undeniable that the United States is similarly engaged. Indeed, given the relative openness of the American political system, it is impossible to mount a denial. The attempt is rather to provide a justification, in the form of either promoting democracy or resisting the expansion of Soviet interests. The debate over the Nicaraguan Contras has not yet seriously drawn into question the reality of U.S. official support for political violence against civilians that could generally be identified as terrorism. The attempt is rather to provide an abstract justification for support by reference to democracy and strategic interests.

This second source of terrorism is the absolutism of secular politics, whether statist or antistatist. Terrorism is deployed (more or less intelligently and successfully) as a rational instrument by policymakers on *all sides* of the political equation.

This kind of idolatry finds its theoretical validation in a tradition of Western realist thought, especially that of Machiavelli, Hobbes, and Clausewitz. The terrorist sensibility is only one manifestation of the Machiavellian mind-set that proclaims the absolute primacy of state interests. We condemn the political adversary who engages in indiscriminate violence as a barbarian and outlaw and reward our own officials with accolades for their "statecraft," even conferring a Nobel Peace Prize from time to time on those who oversee this second type of terrorism.

I believe that it has become as essential to eliminate terrorism from our world as it is to eliminate nuclear weapons, and that it is possibly more difficult. To overcome terrorism we must respond to both of its sources: the unrelieved pain of groups who are victims of severe abuse and the unconditional pretension that political goals associated with state power can be pursued without respect for the limits of law or morality. In the foreground of this undertaking is a new consideration of the place of political violence in human affairs.

Admittedly, there are additional types of terrorism that

do not flow from the two sources discussed, as well as depraved behavior that exerts a terrorist impact on the community even if it is derived from purely personal motives. There is the kind of nihilistic violence that is directed at modern societies by alienated intellectuals who feel betrayed on all sides, not least of all by the collapse of a viable Left project for the seizure of state power. The Baader-Meinhof Red Army Faction, Red Brigades, the Symbionese Liberation Army are illustrative, expressing as much rage against the accommodationist politics of nationalist Communist parties as against the established order.

There is also the kind of pseudo-political private pathology that is associated with drug-induced, antisocial random violence that was frighteningly displayed by "the Manson family" in the Sharon Tate murders. This is not terrorism, but it spreads fear and acute anxiety throughout the society and may also be self-aggrandizing in the sense of seeking personal notoriety, even leadership among those sharing the same antisocial ethos.

Although pain and abuse seem to lie in the background of the terrorist personality in both these instances, the problems these individuals pose can usually be dealt with locally by standard law enforcement techniques. True, this kind of normative breakout is not nearly so likely to occur in societies that aspire actively to social justice and that sustain the social fabric of child development and community, but neither can complex societies tolerate expressive and symbolic violence, nor are such activities likely to put down deep roots. Unlike the two sources of terrorism, these variants cannot acquire potency from the notion of a sacred struggle, mutilated or thwarted by oppressive political arrangements that may currently have ascendancy, but not in the hearts and minds of those vanquished.

In any event, my emphasis will be upon those forms of political violence that are tied to the existence of states and to the vitality of nationalist strivings. Hence the two critical terrorist types for my purpose are revolutionaries (who act to oppose the state or to gain control over the state) and functionaries (who act on behalf of the state). There is a period of overlapping identity that occurs in the time after revolutionaries acquire control of the state and functionaries lose control. Some of the worst orgies of political violence occur in the aftermath of revolution when the fear of counterrevolution is both a pretext and explanation for bloody terror.

TWO

The Cult of
Counterterrorism

*Three things about the border are
known: It's real, it doesn't exist,
it's on all the black maps.*

JAMES GALVIN, "Cartography"

*They said: The more terror,
the more security.*

GÜNTER GRASS, *The Rat*

The American understanding of terrorism has been dominated
by recent governmental efforts to associate terrorists with Third
World revolutionaries, especially those from the Arab countries, and counterterrorist literature has been largely an echo
of this narrow, self-serving conception. The media have generally carried on their inquiries within this framework of selective perception. As a result, our political imagination is
imprisoned, with a variety of ugly and unfortunate consequences.

To begin with, this partisan way of perceiving reinforces a disposition in Washington to use military force under the banner of counterterrorism, and with wide public backing. The United States attack on Libya in April 1986 is illustrative of the pattern. The rationale for the attack was based on the view that crazy leaders in Arab countries are exporting a virulent brand of terrorism aimed particularly at American civilians and overseas servicemen. And to counter such provocation, something must be done whether or not the response helps or harms the proclaimed goal of discouraging terrorism.

This counterterrorist outlook admires Israel's image of consistency and toughness in meeting terrorist challenges. Israel's daring rescue of hijacked hostages at Entebbe, Uganda, in 1976 is regarded as a model of an effective counterterrorist action. Whether this admiration is justified by a record of effectiveness is difficult to assess, but it certainly has not discouraged Palestinian extremist forces from terrorist activity against Israeli targets.

American mainstream opinion displays a kind of scorn for more compliant European attitudes toward the terrorist threat. The main European governments, with the exception of Thatcher's Britain, withheld their support from the 1986 air attack on Libya and refused even to involve themselves in a passive, cooperative way. Similarly, Japan has tried to distance itself from American counterterrorist militancy. The attack was an American operation, defiantly undertaken in the face of allied ambivalence and applauded in conservative circles by a sense that the United States as a mature superpower must be prepared to act alone.

As might be expected, mainstream counterterrorist thinking in the United States is rather contemptuous of European efforts to combat terrorist activity, regarding it as essentially cowardice. Most European countries have taken steps to avoid arousing the vindictive passions of revolutionary groups in their region, being reluctant to extradite or prosecute those charged with terrorist activities and, when they do prosecute, hesitant to impose heavy punishments. Again, as with Israel's harsh alternative, it is virtually impossible to assess the consequences of the European approach.

There is another factor here. European governments seem to follow a much tougher counterterrorist approach when their own government is under attack. Italy's response to the Red Brigades, Germany's response to Baader-Meinhof, France's response to Action Directe resemble Israel's response to Palestinian violence. In this regard, there is a certain consistency among Western governments with regard to counterterrorist policy, and it is based on drawing a distinction between terrorism directed at one's own political arrangements and that focused on the political arrangements of others. In the latter instance, avoiding attention often seems more significant than joining a counterterrorist crusade.

Such considerations help us understand the tensions between Israel and the United States on the one side and the Europeans and Japan on the other. Because Israel's enemies are largely dispersed beyond its borders, and in various relations of allegiance to its international opponents, there is a strong counterterrorist need to act extraterritorially and to gain as much cooperation as possible from likeminded governments: hence the disappointment in the European attitude that the brunt of their terrorist challenge is territorial.

Similarly, the United States has become the symbol of support for those political forces that oppose revolutionary movements. Its citizens, and especially its soldiers and leaders, have become prime targets for terrorist groups. The close tie with Israel and NATO makes this true particularly in the European-Mediterranean region. The extraterritorial character of the United States military presence and geopolitical commitments makes the terrorist challenge seem almost exclusively a nonterritorial issue, a problem that is posed overseas. This perception is strengthened in the American case by the virtual absence of a domestic terrorist threat. As a result, to be effective, counterterrorism depends on the cooperation, or at least the indulgence, of friends. But this expectation of cooperation runs against the American interest in confining terrorist challenges to territorial adversaries.

On this basis, the tension between an international and a domestic approach to counterterrorism is inevitable and understandable, although as yet apparently not well understood by policymakers on either side of the Atlantic. Both sides, adhering to mainstream counterterrorist thinking, are trying to uphold their particular national interests by minimizing threats to their citizens.

As will become clear later on, in my view, there are many weaknesses in the underpinnings of mainstream counterterrorism. At the same time, I am disturbed by many efforts on the Left to explain away or ignore the terrorist phenomenon. I agree with progressive critics of counterterrorist practice that governments, including those who most vigorously denounce terrorism, are themselves practitioners of comparable forms of violence, generally on a larger scale, with greater devastation and bloodshed as a consequence. Yet I don't think it adequate simply to shift the burden of effort to opposing such state-sponsored anti–Third World political violence. The gravity of revolutionary terrorism cannot be disregarded because of the small number of casualties. It is true, but largely irrelevant, that more people are hit by lightning than by terrorist bullets and bombs, and that homicide and automobile lethality rates produce far more American deaths per capita. Body counts are not the point. The terrorist is generally seeking to use violence symbolically to reach an audience of millions. An estimated 800 million were watching the Munich Olympics in 1972 when twelve Israeli athletes were gunned down. The violence was directed at and inflicted upon all those who watched, as well as upon those who died. It was intended as a form of blackmail—notice us or we will ruin even your sporting events and idealistic diversions. The main purpose of most forms of modern revolutionary terror is to instill fear in the general population by striking at random victims in a shockingly grotesque manner or to expose the vulnerability of the state by seizing or killing members of its elite, or even its leaders. A government in a democratic society must prevent or punish such terror or else suffer a decline in prestige; and if the challenge persists, its legitimacy as the guardian of security for civil society will be eroded.

A government can choose from a range of responses, but it is not possible to ignore the challenge, and to do so would be to invite vigilante justice and fascist-style politics. Indeed, the ineffectual responses of liberal governments to revolutionary terrorism in such countries as Brazil, Argentina, and Uruguay during the 1950s and 1960s provided a powerful impetus for the onslaught of right-wing paramilitary torture and violence in the mid-1960s and early 1970s. These fascist forms of counterterrorism destroyed not only the revolutionary movements, but a lot more.

Certain other factors help account for the particular U.S. focus on international terrorism as a challenge warranting popular enthusiasm for overseas military responses. In the aftermath of the Vietnam War it has been difficult for the political leadership in Washington to build support for military intervention. Particularly since Ronald Reagan's election the White House has sought a foreign policy of resolve that would reverse the impressions of decline emanating from the Vietnam years, Watergate, the fall of the Shah, Soviet gains in Africa, and the frustrating months of American diplomats held hostage in Tehran while angry mobs chanted anti–United States slogans outside the embassy walls and the Khomeini government threatened to conduct spy trials. The Reagan forces interpreted their 1980 victory as a mandate to stand tall, that is, to protect Central America, especially El Salvador, where a friendly government was threatened by a spreading revolutionary movement believed to be Marxist in inspiration and a beneficiary of Sandinista support. But it turned out to be difficult to do more than hold the line. Orchestrating a shift in emphasis to an anti-Sandinista destabilization program proved difficult and never became popular at home. A second option was to stabilize the pro-Western government in Lebanon that had been established after the 1982 war. Here, too, the undertaking involving deploying marines and using naval forces did not succeed, making the American military presence a stimulus for anti–United States terrorism, climaxing in the October 1983 suicide truck attack on the marine barracks that killed 241 American marines and prompted the U.S. withdrawal from Lebanon.

Perhaps coincidentally, perhaps not, the United States invaded Grenada later in October and succeeded in delivering "a success" for the tactics of resolve. But it was clear that there were not many Grenadas—tiny, isolated, virtually unarmed islands governed by hard-line leftists who had lost popular support—in the world.

To demonstrate resolve, something more general was required, and overseas terrorism seemed made to order for analysts in search of an assertive foreign policy. Besides, there was a generalized American distress heightened by the extent to which Americans, even businessmen and tourists, were being singled out as quality targets by terrorists, especially in the Middle East, where the most publicized and extreme incidents were taking place. Opposition to terrorism of this variety was also an appealing basis on which to reconstruct bipartisan support for foreign policy. Even liberal Democrats generally opposed to interventionary diplomacy were ardent antiterrorists, and there seemed to be a tacit connection between being out front on the terrorism issue and sustaining political credentials as pro-Israel.

As will be discussed later, the crux of this antiterrorism foreign policy was combating radicalism in the Middle East. Terrorism was perceived and presented as a mixture of revolutionary and fundamentalist groups and sponsoring governments, with the Soviet Union standing in the shadows, but providing guidance and resources as necessary. Fighting terrorism, then, was a way to pursue the cold war without risking a dangerous breakdown in international relations.

Of course, the delineation of terrorism was confined to anti-Western political activity and violence. It did not include violence directed by the West at radical and fundamentalist groups or their state sponsors. It did not even include military strikes against civilian targets if these actions were undertaken by friendly governments. This selective sense of terrorism made the term an expression of a given sense of international conflict (we versus them) and sought to mobilize support for destroying "them" by affixing the label "terrorism."

Progressive critics of this sort of counterterrorism must do better than shift the debate to governmental violence or keep silent because they feel a kind of tacit sympathy with revolutionary goals, even as they genuinely deplore the cruel and violent means. It cannot be denied that sympathy for goals of national self-determination exists, especially in most Third World settings, and is reinforced by the politics and militarist approach of the United States. Many progressives believe that terrorists have good causes, and that a sincere counterterrorism would center on this acknowledgment, satisfy grievances, not mount a public relations drive to vindicate militarist responses. The issues here are complicated, and their assessment varies with the circumstances. No one can say that all terrorist grievances rest on the same footing, nor are there practical solutions for many grievances, especially if the victimized group is dispersed or dissipated. The standard critique of mainstream counterterrorism is insufficient because it is mainly, if not exclusively, antistatist and antiestablishment in content, thereby creating an unavoidable impression of tacit acquiescence. A more constructive response is appropriate, one that takes account of grievances, makes specific recommendations for peaceful settlement, but also supports efforts to achieve societal security against all forms of impermissible political violence. Minimizing political violence has to become the core of a progressive outlook, replacing a leftist tendency to promise deliverance from evil if only the old order is replaced. My own goal is to make a contribution to progressive thought on the subject of terrorism. I prefer the characterization *progressive* to *Left* because the orientation of the argument presented here is an attempt to define new political space free from traditional Left/Right debates.

It isn't paranoid to notice that the right wing takes delight in the Left's dilemma. Rightist promoters of the cult of counterterrorism push and strain to establish a Kremlin-directed terrorist network and, by so doing, link the phenomenon of transnational revolutionary terrorism to the maintenance of a cold war posture toward East-West relations.[1] Also, neoconservatives use terrorism for a variety of secondary projects, including support for Israel (as prime target of revolutionary terror and as the acknowledged master of a militarist style of response) and for interventionary diplomacy. Every Left or Marxist-oriented government is presented as a vital arena in the overall spread of international terrorism under Soviet auspices. For instance, despite the absence of any evidence, a rightist formula connects the survival of the Sandinistas with the spread of revolutionary terrorism in the Western Hemisphere and condemns support for sanctions and the African National Congress (ANC) in the antiapartheid struggle going on in South Africa because such stands abet terrorism. Finally, the Right is dogmatically one-sided when it comes to delimiting the scope of "terrorism." What the Contras do to Nicaraguan civilians is blandly characterized as part of "the Nicaraguan resistance," despite the abundant documentation that Contra violence has mainly been directed against Nicaraguan peasants and village authorities in exposed areas of the countryside.

As well, governmental forms of terrorism are not taken into account. If functionaries plan "covert operations," they are respectable servants of the citizenry playing the game of nations, not displaying themselves as barbarians or as outlaw states. The double standards here are so pronounced that no sense of incoherence is encountered when mainstream politicians or journalists decry "state-sponsored terrorism" but confine the terminology to those that promote the cause of anti-Western political violence or, more narrowly, to revolutionary nationalism.

Underneath this rightist politics is the effort to associate revolutionary terrorism with evil incarnate, thereby validating an exterminist style of uncompromising counterterrorism. Consider, for instance, the inflaming rhetoric of the noted British author Paul Johnson:

> Terrorism is the cancer of the modern world. No state is immune to it. It is a dynamic organism which attacks the healthy flesh of the surrounding society. It has the essential hallmark of malignant cancer: unless treated, and treated drastically, its growth is inexorable, until it poisons and engulfs the society on which it feeds and drags it down to destruction.[2]

It follows that political violence used against "terrorism" is associated with protecting the well-being of the body politic. In this regard, partisanship and antirevolutionary ideology are used to make counterterrorism a noble cause that must be advanced in the most drastic manner.

This most influential discussion of what to do about terrorism ignores altogether whether patterns of grievances explain recourse to political violence, whether reasonable peaceful solutions exist, and goes so far as to repudiate such concern as tantamount to an expression of sympathy for terrorist methods. There is a risk, of course, that interpreting the sources of terrorism will be dismissed as a kind of tacit expression of sympathy, no matter how strenuous the protestations to the contrary. Such unwarranted dismissals have been directed at scholars who have explored the wellsprings of Nazi patterns of persecution.[3] In my view, for both normative and pragmatic reasons it is essential to look inside the phenomenon of violence—and not just in terms of geopolitical alignment—to grasp the root causes of the recent terrorist upsurge among oppressed groups.

Comprehending terrorism as a form of political violence, lacking moral and legal foundation, extends the scope of inquiry. It leads to an emphasis on the interaction between state and society, and the fate of dispossessed peoples as pawns of wider conflicts in the world. Above all, it produces an appreciation that there is violence on many sides, that terrorism begets terrorism, and that describing a policy as counterterrorist does not necessarily change its character as an intensification of terrorism, but by other means. For instance, if a bus is terrorized by a revolutionary group and then a refugee camp is bombed or shelled, a rocket is fired against a village, a large-scale military response follows, and so forth, it becomes evident that the basic process is violent, and where the terrorist component begins and ends is largely a matter of political outlook.

To seek a fuller understanding involves shifting the semantic axes of terrorism confined to antistate revolutionary and insurrectionary violence to an enlarged conception of terrorism that embraces all impermissible political violence and is properly associated mainly with the statist and antistatist conflict. This enlarged terrorism does not only include all dimensions of the conflict waged between the state and civil society in a variety of national and cultural settings: It involves transnational intervention and sponsorship on both sides of the internal struggle of factions aiming at the stabilization or destabilization of a particular political arrangement. In this regard, the United States government program of destabilization during the period of Allende's leadership in Chile (1970– 1973) was an instance of "terrorism" to the extent it deliberately facilitated political violence against the constitutional order by antigovernment rightist factions that lacked a clear legal and moral foundation. Whether such United States accountability for terrorism should be extended to include the crimes of the Pinochet regime that followed its takeover is another matter, but certainly to some extent such a responsibility exists. To encourage and finance insurrectionary violence by alienated rightist elements, and then to back off from exerting any influence once their plan to gain power has succeeded, seems an endorsement of their violent practices. In a bureaucracy as complex and diverse as that in Washington there is no single line on such issues. At the same time, there is a certain coherence of response that is measured by the character of policy as supportive or resistant. In this instance, American policy was generally interventionary during the

Allende period, noninterventionary during the Pinochet years. An overall assessment based on such gross patterns is possible, especially if consistent with behavior elsewhere (for example, the United States helped overthrow the constitutional order in Iran back in 1953 and then helped the Shah restore stable control by organizing a secret police that committed many crimes of state against real and imagined opponents of dynastic rule). The patterns of covert operations undertaken mainly by the CIA disclose this general disregard of the sovereign rights of other peoples, a disregard justified as being part of a wider struggle with the Soviet Union.[4]

The cult of counterterrorism emphasizes violence as the means of response to the challenge of terrorism. It regards terrorism as caused by others and as a prime example of impermissible violence. The cult seeks to control the process by which terrorists are identified and to reserve the term for enemies. Counterterrorism then becomes a species of warfare by the legitimate state against its illegitimate enemies.

Such an understanding of the terrorist challenge is self-serving for those in power within target states. By its very nature its own actions are exempted from moral and legal scrutiny even if innocent lives are wrongfully taken or threatened. If terrorism, in its essence, is violence against innocence, then various claims associated with counterterrorism are more properly appreciated as a form of terrorism.

THREE

A Step Toward
Constructive
Counterterrorism

If the cult of counterterrorism is ineffectual, tends to generate violence, and fails to protect the innocent, then it does not meet the challenge of terrorism. But a critique of this cult as antirevolutionary is insufficient, as well; the terrorist menace is genuine, although it cannot be confined to the revolutionary side of the political ledger. This chapter begins the task of depicting an alternative approach, what is being called here, somewhat optimistically, *constructive counterterrorism.*

In my judgment, no response has any hope of succeeding unless it is premised on a coherent view of terrorism that is applied in a consistent and nonideological manner. A framework of interpretation that relates terrorism and counterterrorism to the overall place of violence, especially random violence directed at the innocent, in political culture is required. To the extent there is a unifying thread to my argument it is this: a beneficial counterterrorist approach seeks to discourage indiscriminate and other forms of impermissible violence and to identify as terrorism indiscriminate and impermissible violence that can either be carried on independently of warfare as generally understood or featured as an incident of warfare. The work of discouragement is mainly a matter of substituting ethics, persuasion, and nonviolent conflict resolution for reliance on unconditional violence. Reliance on military and paramilitary responses to control a political challenge is generally a sign that the counterterrorist policy is somehow stuck or acting mainly as a pretext for an unacknowledged agenda of suppression.

There is at this stage no quick, satisfactory approach to the dual character of the terrorist threat. Political democracy is seriously damaged to the extent that the citizenry find themselves caught in a lethal cross fire between revolutionaries and functionaries, each deploying indiscriminate and otherwise impermissible violence as the medium of exchange by which to resolve deep-seated conflict; such a discourse depreciates the value of peace and the search for equity and justice in human relations. Even free discussion is jeopardized to the extent that the other side can be portrayed as "terrorist," and hatred mobilized to validate a hypermilitarist attitude that aspires to extermination. Despite their differences in political style, revolutionaries and functionaries both endanger political democracy by their adoption and dissemination of exterminist attitudes, policies, and practices. "Final solutions" are never acceptable, no matter how the category of victims is delimited and no matter what line of justification is proposed. Reliance on nuclear deterrence is very problematic in relation to any coherent societal stand against terrorism. If a threat of indiscriminate violence of essentially unlimited magnitude is made to coerce or deter a potential adversary, then there is endorsed at the highest counsels of government a willingness to protect the national interest by resort to extreme forms of terrorism.[1] The terrorist prohibition or taboo is weakened decisively and applied only to weaker adversaries.

One of the most respected and influential interpreters of

the armed conflict is Thomas Schelling, trained as an economist, but renowned for his creative contributions to strategic thought. For Schelling political conflict is about winning, and terrorist methods may be more or less helpful (even, arguably, more or less humane) as a tactic to achieve diplomatic goals. Significantly, given my argument, Schelling never shrinks from calling coercive tactics aimed at frightening an audience wider than the target or violence directed at the civilian population terrorism. It is all part of war, or even diplomacy, and can neither be praised nor condemned, except instrumentally, that is, as useful or not useful to reach a given end. Such an instrumental view of violence is so "normal" in strategic discourse that, as far as I know, no policymakers or political leaders have ever tried to distance themselves from Schelling's outlook, or that of others who wrote from a similar, reigning "realist" perspective.

Let me illustrate briefly, but not atypically, by quoting Schelling's own words. Writing evaluatively about tactics in World Wars I and II, Schelling writes, "But as terrorism—as violence intended to coerce the enemy rather than to weaken him militarily—blockade and strategic bombing by themselves were not quite up to the job in either world war in Europe." Terrorism is used matter-of-factly and assessed by whether it can be credited with achieving victory. Such a use of the word *terrorism* is similar to that in this book, except that it extends to antistate as well as state violence and is viewed as alarming, rather than as a normal incident of conflict.

Schelling even evaluates the atomic attacks on Hiroshima and Nagasaki as unquestionably terrorist in conception: "The political target of the bomb was not the dead of Hiroshima or the factories they worked in, but the survivors in Tokyo." Schelling ties the atomic attacks to earlier military tactics of outright terror and then refrains from assessment, providing only a chilling kind of agnostic view of how difficult it is to know what works in violent conflict. Again, it seems worth quoting:

The two bombs were in the tradition of Sheridan against the Comanches and Sherman in Georgia. Whether in the end those two bombs saved lives or wasted them, Japanese lives or American lives; whether punitive coercive violence is uglier than straightforward military force or more civilized; whether terror is more or less humane than military destruction; we can at least perceive that the bombs on Hiroshima and Nagasaki represented violence against the country itself and not mainly an attack on Japan's material strength.[2]

If Harry Truman, Henry Stimson, and the other American leaders could think as they did in 1945, why not Abu Nidal or Qadaffi in the 1980s? Can we ever really hope to confine the terrorist option to those in power already, and, at the same time, stigmatize its use by those seeking to challenge the status quo?

We are caught up in the throes of incoherent discourse. In other postures we are not prepared to treat terrorism as a legitimate form of war. All governments accept the laws of war as a framework for armed conflict, and these laws repudiate terrorism and criminalize its practice. It is not merely, either, a matter of hypocrisy, double standards, and victors' justice, although each is a complicating factor. In the end, we are a political being with two heads, one terrorist, the other antiterrorist, both coexisting, but not graciously or even tenably.

The nuclear issue is a severe test of our civilizational capacity and willingness to disentangle official policy ("national security") from an avowal of terrorism. Some influential voices argue that deterrence is the least worst option, that now that the weapons exist, the most effective way to discourage their use is to threaten credibly—to deter and to be deterred.[3] In effect, the security of human society is tragically caught up in an unbreakable circle of terrorism. Unless we can devise ways to break this circle, a posture of counterterrorism will lack credibility and appear to be a double standard administered to serve the priorities of superpowers. Later chapters explore the case for renouncing nuclearism as part of a societal commitment to repudiate terrorism on an unconditional basis.

In the end, our response to terrorism is a challenge to our spirit as a people and as an organized society. The roots of terrorism are deeply embedded in the soil of deprivation *and* depravity that are both part of our social fabric. Terrorists, as practitioners of indiscriminate and impermissible violence, are prominent among both those who are ultimate outsiders and those who are our biggest winners, among those who are desperate and those who are respected and rational upholders of existing arrangements of privilege and power. Terrorism in its variability feeds upon the low-technology ingenuity of the weak and the high-technology innovativeness of the strong. Terrorism is associated with revolutionary challenges to the status quo and with an absolutist insistence that present arrangements of distinct sovereign states be preserved even if the survival of the entire species is put at risk. These connections between terrorism and politics, and terrorism and culture, are expressions of the deep structure of the terrorist phenomenon, and help explain its contemporary prominence.

The menace of terrorism cannot be isolated and associated with a particular group or political tendency. It has been absorbed into the bosom of culture, and is as associated with being secure as it is with being revolutionary or nihilistic. To be rid of terrorism will require, above all, an affirmation of the sacred and immune character of innocence. Rejecting terrorism does not imply an unconditional affirmation of all life. Violence in situations of genuine self-defense—whether for individuals, groups, or states—is permissible provided only that it is proportional to the provocation and deeply serious about limiting responses to non-targets. A first step away from an implicit endorsement of terrorism is to define the phenomenon in a manner that reflects this understanding.

The array of definitions of terrorism generally expresses the selective emphasis of the interpreter. Those who seek to focus on antistate violence emphasize recourse to unauthorized violence as a means to achieve social change. Some authors deepen the ideological content by confining the scope of terrorism to such acts of unauthorized violence to coerce change in a democratic society. There is an implication that recourse to violence in repressive political circumstances may be illegal, but it does not deserve the opprobrium associated with terrorism, and possibly does not deserve opprobrium at all. Often those who endorse the goals of violence suspend moral judgment with regard to the specific means, and merely celebrate the revolutionary character of the undertaking. This is typical of the rhetoric of freedom fighters and of wars of national liberation, of resistance. Carlos Marighela in his *For the Liberation of Brazil* expresses this defense of what he elsewhere calls "revolutionary terrorism": "The police accuse us of terrorism and banditry, but we are revolutionaries engaged in armed combat against the Brazilian dictatorship and North American imperialism."[4] Although Marighela offers some reassurances to the civilian population, the moral and political claim being made is that the revolutionary commitment is of such consequence that any recourse to violence on its behalf is automatically exonerated. Implicit here is the image of "the good terrorist," a claim explored in a later chapter.

The resonance of the word *terrorist* makes it an often valuable tool in political conflict. If the tactics and organizational entity of rival political forces can be described as terrorist and that label can be made to stick, two consequences follow: no pressure for concessions on political grievances and acceptability of the use of ruthless means and suspension of normal constitutional limitations to inflict pain and death. The high ground for battle depends significantly on this sophisticated campaign waged in the media and bureaucratic trenches for control over the standard operating language. Imagine, for instance, how valuable it would be to the Palestinian or Irish nationalist causes if their main movements could successfully shake the label of terrorist or how disabling it would be for the CIA to be routinely degraded by being described as a terrorist organization. Note that evidence of nonviolent undertakings by the PLO or Provisional IRA cannot save these organizations from being perceived as essentially terrorist undertakings. Similarly, consider how apologists for the CIA are quick to claim that its principal identity arises from its information-gathering functions and that its involvement in covert operations is quite incidental to its basic character as an intelligence organization.

When the emphasis shifts to the means, then there is a tendency by some revolutionaries to avoid randomness and not target innocent civilians. Here again the premodern terrorist is held in esteem because he aimed only at legitimate targets, either oppressive figures (the merciless landlord or cruel tax collector) or at tyrants and their representatives.[5] Premodern antistate terrorism was essentially associated with the practice of political assassination.[6] The classical terrorist manifested an appropriate moral inhibition by refusing to kill civilians, taking personal risks of capture or even death to uphold this commitment to innocence. Such restraint is admirable, and its rehabilitation on all sides of political conflict is certainly at the center of the struggle against terrorism. But to point to the revolutionary or anarchist terrorist in isolation is to express a biased judgment as to the decline of ethical sensitivity of political radicals. The antistate side of political struggle cannot be detached from the wider setting of modern conflict without causing serious distortion. In reality, the abandonment of constraints has been "pioneered" by the military and paramilitary strategies of the main states, especially through the mobilization for war of the entire population and economy and the targeting of society in the course of war. The terrorist is as much the well-groomed bureaucrat reading *The Wall Street Journal* as the Arab in desert dress looking through the gunsites of a Kalashnikov rifle.

In contrast to the imagery of the terrorist as revolutionary savior is the effort to cast the terrorist in the role of subhuman or nonhuman, fair game for exterminist tactics and rhetoric. Commenting on the substantial loss of civilian lives in a counterterrorist operation carried out in Malta to rescue a hijacked plane in November 1985, Secretary of State George Shultz defended the action as follows: "Terrorists deserve no quarter. Terrorists should have no place to hide. We must stamp out this terrorist activity." And when pressed on the topic during a TV news program, Mr. Shultz revealed his underlying attitude: "These people [the terrorists] are not worth the time of day . . . they're not even people, doing what they're doing."[7] The practical effect of such language is to cordon off those persons called "terrorists" and to bar no means in taking action to destroy them. Such a broad brush also validates uses of force in the name of counterterrorism such as the Malta raid even if they result in little damage to the alleged terrorists and loss of a far greater number of nonterrorist lives. It also justifies suspending the civil liberties of those suspected to have links, or even sympathies, with groups alleged to be carrying on terrorist activities, especially in behalf of the Palestinian nationalist cause. In February 1987 a group of Arabs was arrested in Los Angeles and threatened with deportation because of their supposed links with the Popular Front for the Liberation of Palestine.[8] The protections of political democracy are swept aside by associating targets of arbitrary governmental action with terrorist imagery, despite the indications that those apprehended were normal students with some evidence of political sympathies for revolutionary Palestinian groups. No one would think of apprehending others from different backgrounds who were adhering to solutions at odds with American values. It is a new and especially vicious form of guilt by association. The government claims more power to the extent that the threat of revolutionary terrorism can be lifted onto the front rank of public concern. There is a seldom noticed convergence of interest between the terrorist group seeking to have a chilling impact on public opinion so as to get its message across and governments seeking a mandate to set aside constitutional restraints.

The relative territorial locus of terrorism is important in relation to issues of constitutional erosion. For a country like India or Italy, the domestic character of the terrorist challenge puts a premium on internal security, reaching its epitome by establishing a condition of martial law. In contrast, the United States and Israel are more worried by what occurs outside territorial boundaries and are, therefore, disposed to claim retaliatory prerogatives as an instrument of foreign policy, relying on high-technology weaponry to attack those associated with assailants in sanctuary (Lebanon, Tunisia) or sponsoring (Libya) countries. The result is to weaken greatly the efforts of international law to restrict claims of self-defense to situations of prior armed attack. As a result, many weak states have become vulnerable to the loss of their sovereignty to the extent that they have become identified with revolutionary causes or cannot prevent their territory from being used as a base for operation.

Perhaps the worst consequence of branding terrorists as nonhuman is that it confuses our perception of how the phenomenon arises, particularly insofar as it obscures the broader connections of terrorism with the overall social fabric. The issue of responsibility is completely dissolved in a facile orgy of condemnation. Careful psychological studies have disclosed that most revolutionary and nihilist terrorists are in Richard Rubenstein's phrasing "the guy next door."[9] In posing the question, Who is the terrorist?, Rubenstein argues that it is "someone more like us than we ordinarily care to admit."[10] In essence, the terrorist is someone who is responding to deprivation and perceived injustice, sometimes using political means to reach a desired personal goal, sometimes acting in a desperate spirit of revenge and retaliation, making those who have caused the suffering pay. The apparent causation can be more prosaic, even routine: a sensitive child insufficiently loved by parents or a young adult without the capacity to attract love. In *The Good Terrorist* Doris Lessing writes perceptively about a group of young British middle-class youths drawn by a blend of personal alienation, boredom, and shallow idealism to embrace the cause of Irish nationalism, and with it, the ethos and life-style of urban terrorism. The political rationale is quixotic, a mask of sorts, and the quest for personal meaning and excitement in restless, empty lives is the pre-

dominant motivation.[11] Rubenstein finds that "the urban guerrilla is likely to be a young adult of more than average education,
fervently committed to a political cause, and driven by a com-
bination of hope and desperation to commit acts of violence
in its service."[12] His cruelty is not of a different order than
that of others brutalized by the ordeals of "battle," including
those honored as heroes by the very same government for
their valor in war. Additionally, in the phrase of Hannah Arendt,
the "banality of evil" permits those who sit behind desks to
authorize, without feeling any remorse, various tactics of low-
intensity war or covert operations that produce acute suffering
for noncombatant victims. George Shultz is fully capable of
condemning the terrorist as subhuman and on the same day
pleading to Congress for additional funds to train and equip
Contras to attack Nicaraguan civilians living at peace in the
countryside.

There is another element here. States frequently justify
cruel military tactics by claiming that they will end the war
sooner or save lives by convincing the other side that persisting is not worth the pain. The most celebrated instance is
the justification given for bombing Hiroshima and Nagasaki
in 1945. It was overwhelmingly (and successfully) justified as
"saving lives" by its intended and actual effect of inducing a
Japanese surrender without the need for an invasion, estimated at the time to put at risk as many as one million Allied
lives. Leaving aside the results of recent research that show
fairly convincingly that Japan could have been induced to
surrender without an invasion, the logic that exonerates cruelty on the magnitude of the atomic attacks encompasses the
cruelty of the most vicious terrorist attacks. It can be argued
that such attacks were acceptable because the United States
held the cards of victory in its hands, and thus a gigantic
display of indiscriminate and punitive violence was somehow
instrumental. It was not, at least, violence without political
purpose.

But neither are most forms of revolutionary terrorism
"senseless" in ways that distinguish them from forms of po-

litical violence chosen by governments. Terrorist undertakings are often the outcome of intelligent individuals' assessing their range of options in the pursuit of a variety of goals, including the dignity of sustaining struggle and resistance to provide some hope to society of an alternative future. During World War II, French resistance against the Nazi occupation was celebrated even if its prospects for success at the time seemed nil. It was a symbolic expression of political will that was credited with an inspirational impact, helping thereby to sustain the morale of the wider war effort. The character of the violence or its degree of disruptive effect was hardly noticed. In our rush to brand terrorism as "cancer" or terrorists as "subhuman" we repudiate terrorism in such an extreme and partisan manner as to preclude the sorts of understanding that are needed to fashion curative, constructive responses to any and all forms of unacceptable political violence. Even the most shocking forms of violence need to be understood, in part, as generated by the particular history and conditioning of a given place. The long and heralded German film *Our Hitler: A Film from Germany* made the same argument in relation to Hitler—he was nurtured by specific features of German political culture, including the confused romantic quest for national greatness. To show these connections to the overall background of German society is not to excuse Nazis, or to make them less responsible for their deeds. It does imply that Nazism flourished in a certain political setting present in post-1918 Germany, but not elsewhere. Every society has a latent disposition toward terrorist behavior in the name of this or that cause. This latent tendency can be activated on a broad scale in the name of counterterrorism.

These official denunciations of terrorism are extended to encompass state-sponsored terrorism in a special, polemical way, to establish a cult of counterterrorism. American leaders in recent years have only identified governments that favor and support Third World revolutionary movements as sponsors of state terrorism. The list has been generally restricted to Libya, Iran, Syria, Iraq, and Cuba.[13] The use of political violence by governments to destroy these terrorists, to engage in "covert operations" of a retaliatory character, and to destabilize regimes deemed illegitimate are thus excluded from the purview of terrorism. Indeed, these options are favorably described as "strategic assets" despite their potentially terrorist quality.

In opposition to this style of specifying terrorism are those who are sympathetic with revolutionary nationalist movements, who associate violence against these movements as being directed essentially against "the people" and, hence, as the most objectionable and serious form of terrorism on the current scene. State sponsorship of terrorism is viewed then as being essentially an extension of Western, and especially United States, intervention in the Third World and as the repressive rule of dictatorial leaders. The "real terrorism" on the international scene is centered on the activities of the superpowers. For instance, the influential political commentator Eqbal Ahmad asserts that the ratio of losses of life "by illegitimate state and state-sanctioned terror, when compared with revolutionary terror or non-official terror, is probably half a million to one."[14] Condemning state action as terrorism makes the advanced Western states responsible for almost all of the dying associated with indiscriminate violence. From this perspective, to pin the label *terrorist* only on revolutionaries is a hoax, a gigantic dosage of brainwashing. In general, this assessment of the comparative loss of life is accurate and revealing, if possibly somewhat exaggerated, except to the extent that it tends to understate the seriousness of revolutionary and nihilistic terrorism as a threat to civic order and human well-being. Part of the explanation of the greater loss of life as a result of state terror is that it seeks to eliminate its enemies by force, whereas revolutionary and nihilistic adversaries, lacking the state's weaponry, proceed by way of fear and intimidation, but with an overall impact on public rectitude that can be massive.

The U.S. State Department definition of terrorism claims to stake out a middle position: "Terrorism is premeditated, politically motivated violence perpetrated against noncombatant targets by subnational groups or clandestine state agents, usually intended to influence an audience."[15] By stressing the intention to influence an audience this definition seems to stress revolutionary violence, yet the language is somewhat vague. It is certainly reasonable to extend the notion of "clandestine state agents" to include the covert operations of the CIA and kindred operations under direct or indirect government control, including death squads made up of "off-duty" police. This definition of terrorism does not seem to embrace bombing raids carried out by naval and air units of a state even if the target is a refugee camp or civilians living in a big city. As such, the nature of the target and the damage are subordinated to the identity of the perpetrator. The state, as such, when it uses military force, can never be properly charged with terrorism according to this official appropriation of language, except possibly to the extent that it acts covertly and indirectly.

The definition also seems to limit the reach of terrorism to violence directed at noncombatants, that is, morally and legally impermissible targets. But this surely is not the intended result. The government routinely identifies as terrorism any use of violence against military personnel, diplomats, or business leaders. And, in fact, the State Department report singles out the attack on the U.S. Marine detachment in Lebanon as such a notable instance of terrorism as to distort the statistical account of terrorist incidents: "The year 1983 was anomalous, however, because of the extraordinarily high death toll of 241 in the bombing of the marine barracks in Lebanon."[16] But how can this act of violence be classified as "terrorism" given the State Department definition? Surely, the marines could not be viewed as noncombatants. U.S. Marines were deployed in Lebanon as the main expression of an American presence intended to stabilize the Gemayel government and were removed by President Reagan in response to the incident. It is arguable that this attack on the marines was one of the most successful uses of military force in the history of recent international relations, leading a very strong power to accede to the demands of a very weak opponent. It could only be terrorism because the violence could be attributed to terrorists, that is, to a group with no legal authority to use violence, and because the means used, a suicide truck filled with dynamite, is not an expression of normal military combat.

Why was such an act treated as terrorism? Only because it was violence directed at United States soldiers by a sub-national group with a revolutionary outlook. More objectively viewed, this kind of violence was selective as to target and hence, if it was terrorism, it has the quality of premodern terrorism, resembling an act of war. As such, this definition breaches the boundaries between terrorism and war, or more selective types of political violence. And, then, the harsh denial of "personhood" for terrorists becomes obviously very arbitrary.

Even if the revolutionary violence is not selective and abhorrent, it seems cruel and misleading to deny the humanity of the perpetrator. Similarly, those who act on behalf of the state should never be deprived of their status as individual human beings entitled to some sort of presumption of innocence before being judged guilty. One of the most shocking recent incidents of revolutionary terror was the attacks in the Rome and Vienna airports on December 28, 1985, that killed 17 and wounded an additional 121. Among those killed was Natasha Simpson, the twelve-year-old daughter of an Associated Press correspondent in Rome who was returning home after a Christmas visit. Shooting this young girl in cold blood is a horrifying crime that cannot be condemned too strongly, and it was made even more horrifying by a report that the gunman fired a second burst of bullets at her head. And yet these operations were alleged to have been undertaken in retaliation for an Israeli air attack a few months earlier, on October 1, on PLO headquarters in Tunis that had caused at least sixty deaths, including those of many women and children. Israel, in turn, promised "revenge" for the December airport attacks and was not dissuaded from such a course. The

35

important perception to be derived from these events is the two-sided cycle of violence, each side receiving ample nourishment for its self-righteous recourse to punitive violence that inflicts terrible suffering on innocent civilians by its interpretation of what the other side has done.

One of the Arabs who participated in the Rome attack was apprehended at the time. His name was Mohammed Sarham. He was nineteen years old and carried a note written in Arabic: "As you have violated our land, our honor, our people, we in exchange will violate everything, even your children to make you feel the sadness of our children. The tears we have shed will be exchanged for blood. The war has started from this moment. . . ." The words here speak out of a deep human suffering. Anyone who has visited the Palestinian camps in Lebanon where so many of the terrorist gunmen have grown up knows that Mohammed Sarham's note expresses a part of the truth of the Palestinian experience, even if the literal circumstances in his instance could somehow be discredited or interpreted as a cheap propagandistic gesture. Also, the mind of the terrorist is not so far removed from the mind of the warrior, that we should view combat by men in uniform as honorable and action on behalf of a revolutionary cause as reprehensible. A related circumstance is the overall blurring of the civilian/combatant distinction in a variety of guerrilla warfare situations, including patterns of infiltration into villages and even governing structures. There is, as well, the disorienting notion that the way a combatant is dressed determines the propriety of killing him: the crazy claim that it is okay to shoot "a soldier" in uniform but not if he is wearing a jogging suit.

The film *Platoon* makes it vividly evident, if it wasn't already, that soldiers in war can be barbaric to undefended civilians, as expressed in the scene when an American platoon destroys a Vietnamese village and wantonly brutalizes its innocent inhabitants. Similarly, both soldiers and revolutionaries can act in heroic and compassionate ways toward civilians caught up in the maelstrom of war.

I believe that my interpretation of the terrorist threat provides the best hope of minimizing and overcoming random, indiscriminate political violence, and that its vantage point is one that affirms the sacredness of human life and the criminality of all deliberate killing, except that which is done within the reasonable purview of self-defense. My condemnation of terrorism does not depend on the adoption of a pacifist ethos, but it is influenced by the expanding practical role for pacifist tactics and the diminishing role for justifiable violence.

To be counterterrorist in my sense is to oppose all forms of political violence directed at innocent persons as well as to oppose any reliance on tactics of potential or actual warfare that rely on indiscriminate violence or that deliberately target civilians. To appreciate the setting, it is crucial to realize that the major wars of this century have all been conducted as if terror were a normal and appropriate incident of combat, and legitimate to the extent that it contributed to military victory or was perceived to do so by policymakers. Politicians and citizens alike have accepted the idea that their government and its military establishment were limited in their tactics only by criteria of efficiency. True, innocent civilians could not be the legitimate objective of gratuitous cruelty, but if the violence against them could be presented as part of the war effort, then it was treated as acceptable. Since revolutionary violence generally focuses on fear and intimidation as the essence of its "war effort," horrendous undertakings against civilian targets can appear efficient and effective, precisely because of their shock value. Thus, so long as belligerent antagonists are constrained only by considerations of effectiveness, and not by limitations imposed by law and morality, we must expect terrorism to be a central feature of political conflict that assumes a violent form.

Constructive counterterrorism is concerned, then, only with opposition to all types of political violence that rejects moral and political constraints. It is not restricted by the identity of the actor or by whether the violence occurs within the framework of war or of some other mode of conflict. As such, terrorism can be identified by its indiscriminate, generally secretive character and by its intention to incite fear. All violence against innocent targets falls within our conception of terrorism. Both private groups and governments are capable of terrorism and of political activity. Michel Foucault and others have shown that coercive practices of everyday life, especially the treatment of deviants in prisons and patients in mental institutions, are intensely political in implication, modeling order, authority, and propriety for the society as a whole. To the extent that indiscriminate and deliberate violence is embedded in these practices terrorism is present, and it contributes to a climate supportive of political terrorism. Constructive counterterrorism seeks the removal of terrorism from all levels of social discourse, including those between parents and children and between men and women. Our focus in this book is not upon the coercive aspects of everyday relations, but upon those violent struggles involving governments and private groups that are conventionally treated as "political."

The position argued here is not against violence as such. If oppressive political violence is used in a setting that precludes reasonable recourse to nonviolent methods of resistance and struggle, then reactive violence of a proportionate and discriminatory character is a legitimate exercise of popular rights (inherent in popular sovereignty) of self-defense. As with certain interpretations of the nuclear predicament, there are political situations that are tragic in their tendency to give victims no option but submission or violent resistance. If we can neither eliminate nuclear weapons reliably nor trust adversaries not to use them at a time of crisis, then *arguably* some posture of minimum deterrence may be the least unacceptable policy. Such a posture is tragic because it is unacceptable, threatening indiscriminate violence against innocence, but it may reduce this threat to the greatest extent presently possible and therefore be preferred to other options, even total renunciation.

As some political movements of opposition, notably Solidarity in Poland, have shown, an imaginative politics of resistance may discover potent nonviolent opportunities for action that are more capable of challenging regimes of oppression than are violent forms of resistance.[17] Part of constructive counterterrorism is a challenge to the political imagination to search for and explore nonviolent alternatives, and if violence is deemed unavoidable, then to restrict it rigidly to morally and legally permissible limits. That is, counterterrorism as advocated in this book is biased against violence but not unqualifiedly, whereas it does oppose unrestricted terrorism. Put differently, the Gandhian ethos of nonviolence is inspirational, but not necessarily controlling. What is controlling, however, is an absolute deference to the sacred quality of innocent life.

FOUR

The Routinization of Terrorism

So they sought relief in extermination.

GÜNTER GRASS, *The Rat*

To respond to the terrorist menace requires us to acknowledge how pervasive terrorism has become in our culture. This is a painful acknowledgment, but such self-knowledge seems to be necessary for change in any kind of addictive activity, whether it be use of alcohol, drugs, or violence. Not only those who act violently but those who endorse the necessity of such violence are caught up in the terrorist swirl.[1]

It is not my claim that every instance of violence is terrorism, but only those instances of political violence that ignore the injunction to protect the innocent. This chapter examines some of the factors at work in terrorist activity, whether carried on against or for the state.

ANTECEDENTS

This is no time to abandon the rhetoric of terrorism. To refer to political violence as terrorism is to reject behavior that is abhorrent. Almost everyone agrees that "terrorism" is to be discouraged, avoided, repudiated. The avoidance of terrorism is related to self-esteem, security, survival, and a more hopeful sense of human possibilities, of the future.

At the same time restricting the term *terrorism* to the enemies of the state, or worse, to the enemies of our state, compounds dangers. It enlists the energies of fear and hatred on behalf of forms of violence that resemble that which is opposed except in name. As such, we enter the dark chambers of Orwellian distortion, giving our souls and minds over to the abstractions of propaganda, and thus relinquish our most precious human qualities of judgment and conscience. We must not allow ourselves to be drawn in and down by such an enterprise of manipulation. As citizens in a democratic polity we must hold ourselves aloof from any and every attempt to break the bonds of trust between state and society by mobilizing the people for a violence that is not genuinely defensive and selective.

For that reason it is necessary to get a better feeling for both the complexity and the ambiguity of terrorism as a phenomenon. We grasp the present by considering the past. We can obtain a better understanding of the core meaning of terrorism by considering a range of usages and contexts.

The kind of violence we now call terrorism has been practiced since the beginning of societies. In Western civilization it finds paradigmatic expression in the massacres of the Old Testament, as when Yahweh instructs the people of Israel to defeat their enemies by killing every man, woman, and child. Giving religious blessings to indiscriminate killing of civilians also has found religious sanction in the Holy War traditions in Christian practice as in the Crusades, as well as in the Islamic notion of *Jihad* that continues in the world of today to animate Middle Eastern political passions. This kind of religious absolutism and partisanship is at the root of the terrorist impulse, even, or especially, when it masquerades in the disguise of counterterrorism. Such highly charged divisions between the sacred and the profane tend to legitimize deliberate killing and abuse and are not far removed from contemporary patterns of rationalization. Such self-justifying categories emerge from Shultz's reference to terrorists as nonpersons or Paul Johnson's proposed treatment of terrorism as a form of cancer.

There is, then, the premodern interplay between concentrated physical power, the mandate of beliefs held holy, and recourse to violence from below or from above. The crime of assassination often proceeded in the premodern world from such a chain of associations, especially when the target was the ruler or a representative of the ruler.

Here, too, religious conviction played a central part. Those in power regarded their mission to include the guardianship of tradition and truth. Heretics, nonbelievers were subverters of societal well-being, dangerous to the public good. To prevent such a challenge produced rituals of repudiation, public displays of the consequences of embracing falsehoods. The Romans fed Christians to the lions, and the Christians some centuries later organized their own inquisitions as means to safeguard the faith.

And against those in power were the resisters. Throughout history there have been those who refused to submit, who stripped away the lordly robes of priest and emperor and struck back at the ruler with violent fury. At times, resistance was directed at foreign or alien rule, at times at tyrannical oppression, at times at alleged deviations from religious truth. In the background, as Western societies evolved, was the complex balance between politics and religion, neither truly separate nor successfully connected. The royal ruler was invested with "divine right" and used such a heavenly tie to validate leadership, claiming that the king could do no wrong. Yet when a ruler was perceived to usurp divine functions by becoming cruel and arbitrary, religious and political thought tended to confer a right of resistance. As early as Aristotle, a right of the people to kill a tyrant has been confirmed. No bond of obedience is absolute, and even those commentators most concerned with the conservation of order recognize outer limits of obedience beyond which a right of resistance exists.

The centrality of assassination to resistance in the premodern period is not surprising. If the king or queen or pharaoh was so powerfully invested with unconditional authority, then the elimination of that particular individual would seem to shatter the illusion that the prevailing order was all-powerful. The very concentration of authority, the mystical extension of this authority by such imagery as that of "the great chain of being," made the uppermost leader a prime target. And for those outside the administrative and military systems of government such a conception of transformative politics had an enormous appeal: It did not depend on mobilizing resources or people. All that was needed was a means to kill a single individual.

Even in modern times, with the most elaborate and sophisticated forms of protection, we have experienced the vulnerability of leaders and the political significance of removing them from the scene. Surely, America became a different country as a consequence of the assassinations of John F. Kennedy, Robert Kennedy, and Martin Luther King. Even though these individuals were constrained by bureaucracies and movements, and by a constitutional order, they proved to be irreplaceable, and part of their vision died with them, decisively altering the path taken by those left behind. We cannot say that these assassinations were political failures.

As with so much else in the modern world we know, the French Revolution was a decisive moment in the evolution of terrorism. Of course, the very word *terrorism* then came into use, describing the reign of Robespierre and the bloody process by which a successful revolution toward the end of the eighteenth century began devouring its children in a series of trials and purges. Here was the first occasion when symbolic

43

trials, supposedly preserving the purity of the revolution, were used to eliminate enemies, but more, to frighten the general population, especially in the city of Paris, into a condition of crazed submission. And as we know, subsequent revolutions have more often than not imitated the French experience, terrorizing adherents and comrades as well as the residue and suspected loyalists of the old order.

What is significant in this French seminal experience is the explicit association of terror with the possession of state power and with the unconditional claim to separate truth from falsehood, purity from corruption, and to rely on these distinctions as the basis of deliberate violence unto death. It does stretch the imagination to notice the linkage between the terror of the French Revolution and of the Islamic revolution in Khomeini's Iran. The distinguishing feature of clerical leadership only underscores the most striking shared feature: a fundamentalist claim to identify truth. Nothing is more characteristic of the terrorist mind-set than the literalism of assuredly being able to identify evildoers and act upon this knowledge. In this regard, every terrorist is a fanatic, that is, someone whose sense of having a correct perception of reality exceeds what is actually possible for the normally functioning human mind.

Appropriately, the other influential antecedent of modern terrorism arose in czarist Russia, with the founding in 1878 of a group called *Narodnaya Volya* (People's Will). This group of radical, alienated young intellectuals foreshadows the media image of modern terrorists and was immortalized, if somewhat distorted, in Dostoyevski's great fictional work, *The Possessed*. Their basic aim was to destroy and disrupt, to enact in symbolic violent terms a defiant posture to prevailing authority, especially by attempting assassinations of preeminent figures of the state. In nineteenth-century Russia this meant that the czar and the royal family, as well as principal ministers and high officials, became prime targets. These Russian terrorists, with their spectacular nihilistic exploits and world view, are the ancestors of contemporary urban terrorists in advanced countries. They lacked any plausible political project and were cut off from movement politics and their own people. They were regarded with contempt by the people of Russia, the supposed beneficiary of their extremist politics. And later on such individual revolutionaries, cut off from the Russian masses, were viewed as an obstacle to revolutionary prospects by the Marxist-Leninist Left. Indeed, the main effect of this kind of terrorism from below is to erode whatever degree of political democracy exists, to impair the civil liberties of the citizenry, and to strengthen the hand of the state in relation to domestic dissent.

An odd connection between the terrorist as functionary and the terrorist as revolutionary emerged in premodern times. To discredit domestic street politics there is a steady tradition among states to infiltrate police agents, who act as provocateurs, to encourage revolutionaries to adopt ultraviolent tactics. In effect, the government relies upon a sort of nihilistic violence from below as a pretext for discrediting peaceful mass movements or of causing divisions within their ranks. A recently documented instance reports that French student protests during 1968 were heavily infiltrated by agents of the police, who then engaged in provocative violence, weakening morale among the protesters, creating a pretext for arrests, and portraying to the public the student opposition as violent.[2]

These antecedent expressions of terrorism continue to resonate in modern settings. Terrorism from above seems especially associated with postrevolutionary politics of consolidation, as prefigured in the bloody purges of revolutionary France.[3] Terrorism from below continues to be associated with individuals and groups that are on their own, uttering radical slogans, fanatical and yet lacking either a general following or a viable political project. The presence of such terrorist challenges from within is especially threatening in a democratic state, seeming to challenge the government claim to maintain a monopoly over legitimate violence and to provide citizens with adequate means to promote social change and political reform.

Unfolding against this background is a modern conception of terrorism as developed by United States politicians and a variety of academic specialists and journalists. As an instrument of official propaganda, terrorism is conceived of almost exclusively as antistate violence by revolutionary elements, though sometimes enlarged to embrace statist violence by hostile Communist and Third World regimes. Many of those who dwell on the terrorist menace are seeking mainly to justify countermeasures and to discredit radical political claims. They do not perceive their own conduct as subject to censure as terrorism and view themselves as genuine antiterrorists. As I have argued, impermissible violence for political ends is the essence of terrorism, and it occurs in many forms. To gain clarity it is helpful to consider the overlap between terrorism (in this sense) and some closely associated concerns: political radicalism, conspiracy, crime, and violence.

POLITICAL RADICALISM

There is a perverse tendency for those entrusted with the status quo to label their opponents as terrorists regardless of their tactics, even if their method involves constitutional process and exclusively nonviolent tactics.

I remember a discussion with some prominent Americans shortly after Salvador Allende was elected in Chile. One participant, a business executive, observed that a big problem for American foreign policy was being caused by "the terrorism" of the Allende government in Chile during the early 1970s. I asked this man, then head of Ford Motor Company's operations in Latin America, why he described Allende's government in such a provocative way. He replied, with great assurance, that Allende was engaged in terrorism because he had announced plans "to confiscate" foreign investment and private property. In fact, Allende was carrying out nationalization plans that had been long in the works in Chile and

46

were approved by virtually the whole spectrum of Chilean politics, excluding the radical right. It was striking that in this roomful of notables in American society no one else was troubled by this linking of nationalist economic policies with terrorism. At the time, in other rooms policymakers in Washington were approving and financing plans to destabilize Allende's constitutionally elected government, thereby contributing to the bloody coup that eventuated in the torture and execution of many Chilean citizens and the establishment of the harsh military dictatorship of Auguste Pinochet. The repressive terrorism of a hard-core and extensive character during the Pinochet years has elicited only the most nominal objections from the anti-Allende notables and policymakers.

In mid-1987 several senior military officers were making a presentation of their views on international issues at Princeton University. One of them said quite casually that he was interested in international terrorism, and that although he had had no direct contact with terrorists, he had been in charge of a Pershing II deployment site in West Germany, where he had "dealt with demonstrators." When asked whether he regarded those demonstrating against deployment of these missiles as terrorists, he replied, "Yes, they cut the wire fence and approached the area where the weapons were. From my point of view as battalion commander these individuals were terrorists." He did not retreat from this position even when informed that the majority of the German people opposed the missile deployment and that the demonstrators were unarmed and had no record of violence. The disturbing point here is that advocates of change in official policies of a society, especially if they engage in symbolic acts of civil disobedience, are perceived as radicals, and hence as terrorists even though they unconditionally repudiate violence. Such a confusion is carried to perverse extremes in South Africa, where so-called antiterrorism legislation is used to apprehend and punish criminally those who peacefully demonstrate against apartheid and racial discrimination.

Keeping clear this distinction between radical politics and

the embrace of unconditional and indiscriminate violence is crucial. A radical political project from the viewpoint of existing arrangements may amount to nothing more than opposition to repression. On the other side, the attempt to crush claimants for change by violent means on behalf of reactionary politics may well qualify as terrorism. Unless such manipulative uses of language can be avoided, any discourse on terrorism becomes a sterile polemic or, worse, is itself a mandate for terroristic forms of violence.

There is, as well, an understandable confusion between political radicalism and terrorism. Nonstate terrorism, whether part of a political project or nihilistic, is necessarily radical, repudiating lawful forms of political participation. Under circumstances of foreign occupation or tyrannical rule violent forms of resistance may be animated by moderate political goals (for instance, restoration of constitutional rule), as when conservatives or moderates organize the assassination of a tyrant or act to oppose Caesarism, as in Shakespeare's *Julius Caesar*. Nevertheless, from the viewpoint of the state such violent undertakings always appear to be "radical."

We need, then, to distinguish between violent acts of resistance in a political setting where the governing arrangements are illegitimate by generally accepted criteria of human rights.[4] These acts would be nonradical if the violent undertakings were selective and minimized, and if the goals were the restoration of a governing arrangement viewed as legitimate by a consensus within the society. In this sense, Hannah Arendt's distinction between the American Revolution and the French and Russian revolutions is pertinent.[5] She stresses the moderateness of the American revolutionary process and attributes it to the avoidance of "the social question" involving property rights, distributive justice, and class relations. The French and Russian experiences were "radical" in a comprehensive sense of means and ends, culminating in a reproduction and expansion of terror from the presiding bureaucratic heights of state power. The Iranian revolution suggests that radicalism in this full sense can be connected with "the cultural or religious question" as well. Of course the various aspects of a revolutionary process are interconnected, but in Iran the constitutionalist strivings of the secular elements of the anti-Shah movement (heirs of the Mossadegh era) were nonradical in the Arendt sense as they did not propose an internal restructuring of Iranian society, but only the removal of a hated and corrupt leader who had lost legitimacy, and possibly the scrapping of dynastic principles of governance. These goals were within Arendt's conception of moderateness as they did not overstep the bounds of "the political question."

More complicated is the movement that led to the removal of Marcos from power in the Philippines in early 1986. As in Iran, the anti-Marcos coalition, including its dynamic leader Corazon Aquino, focused on the deposing of a corrupt and cruel dictator who had allowed the economy to deteriorate and the people to suffer. But Ms. Aquino's mandate is so closely associated with social justice that it is difficult to imagine her sustaining a moderate course, especially with enemies on the two radical extremes of Left and Right and with an unresolved issue of sovereign rights arising from the continued existence of major United States military bases at Clark Air Force Base and Subic Bay. As anticipated, discontent in the Philippines has erupted in a surge of violence and extra-legal politics on both the revolutionary side and from the ranks of the army. The tensions have caused deep fissures in President Acquino's governing coalition, but so far she has managed to sustain her leadership. The prospects, however, for the persistence of her leadership are increasingly dubious. One source of public disillusionment is the reliance on improper use of violence by the police and army, especially in the countryside.

It is, of course, a misunderstanding to associate radicalism of the Marxist-Leninist variety with the adoption of terrorist tactics. The main theoretical writings of Marx, and especially of Lenin and Trotsky, are extremely clear about their repudiation of terrorism in its nineteenth-century Russian sense as a tactic of revolutionary strategy. Their strategy rests on armed struggle and mass action by the people along class lines.

49

Terrorist exploits by small, isolated conspiratorial groups on the model of *Narodnaya Volya* are denounced in Marxist-Leninist literature as "counterrevolutionary" and as expressions of "Left infantilism." Such political activity even in a society where the government is unpopular is generally frightening to the masses and helpful to the state, justifying official claims to use exceptional force.

Again, the perspective and circumstances are relevant. In some Third World settings where revolutionary nationalism confronted a foreign adversary with great technological advantages, recourse to terrorist tactics has proved effective in either raising the political and military costs of sustaining the status quo or putting pressure on the population to take sides in the struggle. Wars of independence in Algeria and Indochina disclosed a coupling of terrorist tactics with revolutionary nationalist goals that seemed to contribute to a successful outcome. An ironic example is the reliance by the Zionist movement on terrorist factions to hasten the departure of Britain from Palestine in the years after World War II. The Irgun Zva'i and the Stern Gang were responsible for the murder of British officials, including Lord Moyne, and for the famous explosion of a bomb in the King David Hotel.[6] As with Palestinian political violence in recent years, the mainline Zionist organization formally disavowed terrorism but privately acknowledged its role in terminating the British mandate and thereafter in "emptying" the territory of Arabs during the 1948 war. Unfortunately, it is not persuasive to claim that terroristic tactics never achieve political results. The most that can be claimed is that reliance on terrorism has corrupting consequences that reverberate for decades after their occurrence.

It is this selective reliance on terrorism in several Third World settings that leads some commentators to move away from an interpretation of terrorism as expressive or symbolic violence to an understanding of terrorism as basically *instrumental* violence. For instance, Adeed Dawisha, a specialist on the Middle East, discusses terrorism as an instrument of radical politics, but not an indispensable ingredient:

Whereas terrorism constitutes one of various instruments of policy, albeit a very potent one, radicalism embodies the very essence of the policy itself, as well as the values, goals and concerns of those who formulate and implement policies. For example, the PLO may disclaim terrorism in certain circumstances, preferring instead the diplomatic path. But it cannot disclaim radicalism, for to do so would be to relinquish the Palestinian's aim to overturn the status quo and establish, by any means deemed necessary, a Palestinian state of some kind. And it is the radicalism of those aims, rather than the terrorism per se, of the PLO which the Israelis fear most.[7]

This is an important passage. It suggests, correctly, I believe, that even an armed struggle movement will subordinate terrorist tactics to the pursuit of its political project. An interesting example of a pragmatic terrorist is that of Abu Hassan Salameh, a PLO fighter whose father had been killed by an Israeli bomb in the course of the 1948 war. Salameh planned the 1972 Munich seizure of Israeli athletes that led ten to their death and then later, when the PLO achieved greater diplomatic standing, abandoned terrorism and became a skillful negotiator.[8] The point here is that terrorism may be adopted and abandoned as a tactic of conflict, and further, that the "terrorist" should not be stereotyped as compulsively addicted to violence. But at the same time accountability attaches to any undertaking of impermissible violence, and an individual's abandoning terrorist tactics does not, of course, exonerate him for the earlier commission of terrorist acts. As such, it provides a constructive counterterrorist outlook with a powerful incentive to make terrorism an unnecessary and unattractive option. More important, Dawisha differentiates the political essence from the instrumental manifestations of an organization such as the PLO. This distinction makes it all the more inexcusable (or at least polemical) to characterize the PLO as a terrorist organization per se. At the same time, it explains why such a characterization is itself instrumental from the viewpoint of the Israeli status quo. Just as the radical project is the acquisition of a Palestinian state, so the conservative project is its prevention. Instrumental to that end is the claim that the

PLO leopard cannot change its terrorist spots, and that therefore the political agenda need not be entertained because the PLO as claimant is illegitimate at its terrorist essence.

To be sure, Dawisha's use of the word *disclaim* is ambiguous. The empirical question remains as to whether the PLO has, in fact, renounced terrorism, and if it has not, whether despite its instrumental rhetoric, it may not be obsessed by or captive to a kind of terrorist ethos. At minimum, it seems clear that since the Rabat meetings of 1974 the PLO leadership has distanced itself, at least overtly, from terrorist tactics and has been itself seriously victimized by terrorist activities, carried on in the name of the Palestinian cause, especially by the Abu Nidal faction working out of Syria.[9] Despite this lethal antagonism between factions of the Palestinian movement, Israel deliberately holds the PLO responsible for all acts of terrorism. It was known, for instance, that the Abu Nidal organization gravely wounded Israel's ambassador in London in a terrorist incident. The Israeli government relied on the April 1982 incident as its principal justification for invading Lebanon a few weeks later, an attack aimed at destroying the PLO. Such an opportunistic manipulation of terrorist imagery is a cynical effort to manipulate public emotion, including a general community inhibition against recourse to violence across an international boundary.

At the same time, this distancing by the PLO may itself be an opportunistic ploy, quite consistent with its covert use of terror. The *Achille Lauro* incident seemed to reveal some disguised PLO involvement. Yet, occasional *covert* reliance on terrorism, although reprehensible, is not enough to qualify the PLO as a terrorist organization. (The United States government does not, after all, lose its legitimacy because it covertly authorizes terrorist tactics, as, for instance, by sponsoring and financing Contra activities in Nicaragua or by giving its tacit support to South Africa's cross-border raids in Mozambique and Angola designed to spread fear of the most extreme sort.)

Closely related to this instrumental view of terrorism is

the profile of the terrorist, and of the leadership on whose behalf political violence is undertaken. To quote Dawisha, "it is important to understand that notwithstanding the sadistic few who perpetrate violence for the sake of violence, terrorism is ultimately used to achieve political and/or ideological ends."[10] This is a far cry from Dostoyevski's powerful evocation of terrorism as the preserve of depraved fanatics. At the same time, to the extent that instrumental violence is loosened from moral constraints or assumes an unconditional character, the human costs can be appalling. But the point here is that when violence is the focus, then it is no monopoly of radicals. Those holding the reins of state power often find it instrumental to unleash indiscriminate violence, to break the will of radical adversaries by attacking refugee camps or even cities. And yet we tend to focus our anger upon the radical claimant and to restrict our sense of the problem of terrorism to the one side of the equation. That is, the labeling of radicals as terrorists is politically useful, and the presentation of terrorists as sadistic fanatics makes it seem reasonable to ignore any claims and even to pursue an exterminist counterterrorist approach.

The fate of the African National Congress (ANC) is instructive in this regard. For many years, the ANC insisted that its followers adhere to nonviolent practice in the course of mounting a radical movement of struggle against apartheid in South Africa. Such restraint did not induce reciprocal restraint on the South African side. Subsequent to the Sharpesville massacre of unarmed African demonstrators, mainly shot in the back while running from the South African police, the ANC did endorse armed struggle, but of a limited character. Despite the vulnerability of the white population in South Africa, the ANC has until now confined its violence to impersonal targets or to those directly connected with policies of repression. Yet the organization has been branded as a terrorist organization by the Pretoria regime, and this label has inhibited support for the ANC by the United States and Great Britain. Nevertheless, if fairly considered, the ANC is

53

an excellent example of an organization that is radical, is dedicated to national liberation, and yet, despite the greatest provocations, has generally resisted the terrorist temptation.

Entertaining the view that a given group of revolutionary nationalists are not terrorists at all, or at least are not terrorists per se, raises the important possibility of compromise and accommodation. At the same time, those with a stake in the status quo have an added incentive to portray such moderating claimants as terrorists or to take steps to destroy their movement physically so as to eliminate its bargaining power. In today's world, it becomes important for Israel to convince the United States government to adhere to the position that a given movement or regime is terrorist, not to be negotiated with under any circumstances. The Palestinian issue presents these pressures and cross-pressures in a complex yet vivid form.

CONSPIRACY

Terrorism is almost necessarily the outcome of conspiracy. Of course, it is possible to conceive of a lone assassin or solitary perpetrator of antisocial violence, but such an undertaking is perceived generally as an expression of political pathology, not as a political project of the sort we associate with terrorism. The conspiratorial nature of terrorism entails utmost secrecy and loss of contact with the outside world.

As a friend of the family visiting a recently arrested member of the Weather Underground in her prison cell, I was struck, above all, by this young woman's obsessive need for reassurance from someone like me about the plausibility of the revolutionary vision that had motivated her and her friends for more than a decade. There is often a self-enclosed reality that shuts out doubt, nuance, or discouraging information. Sustaining an underground commitment presupposes the organizational rigor and outlook of a conspiratorial sect.

The requirements of secrecy are closely associated with the issue of trust. It is, of course, in the nature of such political activity that counterintelligence efforts concentrate on penetrating subversive political groups. Guarding against such penetration requires extreme precautions, almost a total withdrawal, except as a cover, from all activities and relationships outside the circle of conspirators. The extreme assessment that prompts recourse to violence in the first instance leads also to a strong impulse to sustain the initial clarity of resolve. Any expressions of doubt weaken morale, raise the specter of potential defection, and place the group in dire jeopardy. The pressure for group think is overwhelming in a violent conspiracy that is being hunted down by the authorities of the state.

James DeNardo analyzes terrorism from this point of departure, using *Narodnaya Volya* as his principal case. For DeNardo what differentiates terrorism from other forms of political violence "is that terror emanates from the underground, while rioting, looting, trashing, and pillaging rage in the streets for all to see (including the police)."[11] Such a view of terrorism exempts secret political violence organized by or within the state. "Covert operations" undertaken by the state, or by some bureaucratic unit or subunit, share many characteristics with *Narodnaya Volya* and Weather Underground. Secrecy and conspiracy are of the essence. There exists no proper mandate, and often the operations are planned and carried out without knowledge by the visible leaders of the state or in such a way as to allow what is called "plausible deniability," that is, to make possible a persuasive denial or lie by responsible leaders in the event of disclosure. Especially during the Irangate hearings a principal focus has been on the intimate interplay between official lying and covert operations. One of the most vivid aspects of Lieutenant Colonel Oliver North's testimony was his willingness to tell lies to protect the integrity of various covert undertakings.

A conspiracy to carry out political violence is not necessarily condemned as terrorism even by those who adopt the most conventional imagery. Perhaps the most celebrated exemption was the failed plot by Count Stauffenberg and others to kill Hitler in 1944. The participants were widely regarded as heroic, and the moral acceptability of killing Hitler has rarely been questioned, although the issue was much reflected upon by Dietrich Boenhoffer, the Christian martyr who took part in the plot and was subsequently executed by the Nazis. The now-disclosed official conspiracies in the United States to kill such foreign heads of state as Patrice Lumumba and Fidel Castro during the period of the cold war are not treated as terrorist activities.[12] Recently, the allegation that the April 1986 raid on Tripoli had as its principal object the physical assassination of Muammar El-Qadaffi and his immediate family has generated controversy and denials, but no allegation, even, that such a plot, if it existed, might qualify as terrorism.[13] A perverse twist on this logic occurred when Robert Gates, Reagan's initial nominee (later withdrawn under pressure) to be the new director of the CIA, testified under oath at his own confirmation hearing that the agency *deliberately avoided* knowledge of the diversion of funds to the Contras from arms sale to Iran. The notion of an intelligence agency, supported by billions of taxpayer dollars, avoiding ultrasensitive information to circumvent the dilemma of lying to elected officials or disclosure to the citizenry in the event of subsequent investigations reveals some of the tensions between covert operations and political democracy. The pressures for secrecy can confer a special value on ignorance! In the service of the state, ignorance becomes intelligence! Yet even this bizarre claim might itself have been a lie to insulate the CIA from a growing scandal of governmental ineptitude.

Not every secret, conspiratorial undertaking is properly associated with terrorism. If the target is specific, as in political assassination, then the label *terrorism* may or may not fit. Other considerations enter. The removal of someone who has repeatedly engaged in acts of cruelty and indiscriminate violence, under color of authority, may contribute to overall political serenity. And yet the process of assessment available to conspiracies is, by their nature, suspect. There is a tendency to oversimplify reality and to exclude any information that renders perceptions ambiguous. This seems true whether the conspiracy emanates from underground or from government. It is one strong practical reason to avoid the creation of a bureaucratic niche with a mandate (and resources) to decide upon and carry out covert operations as a matter of general practice without any firm duty to respect the rule of law and to accept accountability. It is one thing to respond spontaneously with a conspiracy to an unprecedented assault upon peace and decency mounted by a totalitarian regime, as did the Stauffenberg group in Hitler's Germany. As in that instance, it is reassuring if the perpetrators share a distaste for violence and a general acceptance of personal responsibility for their once-in-a-lifetime undertaking. It is quite another matter to retreat from scrutiny over time, whether underground or aboveground, and accept the propriety and claim the necessity of unmandated violent undertakings, whether for or against the state.

A revealing instance is the destruction by French intelligence agents of the Greenpeace ship, the *Rainbow Warrior*, while it was at port in Auckland, New Zealand, in 1985. It will be recalled that the *Rainbow Warrior* was engaged in an effort to monitor and interfere peacefully with the conduct of French nuclear testing in the Pacific region.[14] True, the French government issued an apology, eventually agreed to a mediation procedure over which the secretary general of the United Nations presided, and accepted some financial responsibility for the death of a member of the *Rainbow Warrior* crew. At the same time, the French official position included the imposition of economic sanctions on New Zealand meat exports as a way of gaining leverage to obtain the release of two of its agents held by the New Zealand authorities in custody awaiting a possible criminal trial. In no sense was the French government prepared to regard the agents as terrorists, or even as criminals, nor was the character of the operation itself repudiated. As it often does in these instances of disclosure involving a covert operation, the main scandal concerned mismanagement and accountability of French officials for cover-up activities and for their loss of credibility. The recourse to political violence was not scrutinized, nor was there any serious indication of a willingness to repudiate the conspiratorial option to engage in violent covert operations without the cover of law or the comfort of morality.

It is easy to understand how a counterterrorist role for an intelligence agency leads to a deterioration of judgment and an absence of accountability as aspects of an unavoidably conspiratorial process. Unlike a mass movement that relies on mobilization or a war that requires some degree of public support, conspiracy, by virtue of its insularity, disposes its practitioners to extreme behavior that often incorporates a one-sided worldview. As already noted, a persuasive justification can be made for conspiracies to kill in exceptional circumstances of tyrannicide, but even here the routinizing of such an option is dangerous. Experience has shown that secret police and paramilitary operations are corrosive of constitutional order.

It is often argued that the realities of the nuclear age require such a conspiratorial option. Suppose a leader or faction contemplates recourse to nuclear weaponry or plans to explode a reactor to produce a meltdown. To postulate a dependence on mainstream counterterrorism is to underscore the unacceptability of prolonged reliance on nuclear technology in either its military or civilian form. In effect, political democracy based on the essential premise of popular sovereignty cannot tolerate a condition of permanent national emergency such as is a consequence of nuclear weaponry and nuclear power plants. The situation is permanent in the sense that a nuclear power plant is like a bomb waiting to be exploded by attack or accident. It is a matter of emergency because a prospective danger must be identified early enough to enable a response, and this requires the mobilization of energy and resources in a manner that in many respects resembles actual warfare. The state must be mobilized to intervene in civilian society at any moment and to engage in warfare of the utmost magnitude. These capacities, even prior to nuclear weapons,

could not be efficiently developed without special prerogatives of an antidemocratic character. We are all aware that
basic civil liberties have been abridged during wartime, when
even dissent is treated as treason. Not only is counterterrorism
unreliable as a guardian of our future, but those with such a
mission cannot be trusted over time to adhere to the limits
of their role. There is a built-in tendency to encroach upon
citizens' rights.

Conspiracy, then, is a menacing feature of political activity whether in its underground or governmental form. There
is no reason to restrict our association of conspiracy and terrorism to the underground stereotype. As we have seen, the
same dynamics of secrecy and distortion are likely to enter
the domain of covert operations if such an option is institutionalized in government.

WAR

The connections between terrorism and war are exceedingly
complicated and confusing. Among those who seek to stigmatize terrorism as an isolated category of reprehensible political violence there is a definite tendency to compare it
unfavorably to war. At the basis of this comparison is the
notion that war proceeds within a framework of agreed rules,
whereas terrorism is a domain of antistate, antisocietal violence beyond all restraint.

For instance, Walter Laqueur, an influential writer in
the conventional mold who has long studied terrorism, begins
his book in this manner: "War, even civil war, is predictable
in many ways; it occurs in the light of day and there is no
mystery about the identity of the participants. Even in civil
war there are certain rules, whereas the characteristic features
of terrorism are anonymity and the violation of established
norms."[15] Reinforcing this imagery, Michael Walzer emphasizes that "randomness is the crucial feature of the terrorist
activity . . . terrorism in the strict sense" is "the random murder of innocent people."[16]

There are two points combined in these perceptions. The first is to record the decline in ethical consciousness evident in much of modern revolutionary terrorism. In this regard, Laqueur and Walzer associate premodern terrorism with selective violence, making assassination attempts on specific political figures perceived as tyrants or wrongdoers. Such a terrorist acknowledged a responsibility to protect the innocent and often refused to carry out an assassination plan if it involved a substantial risk of killing others, including even the immediate family of the target person. Famous instances of this premodern outlook include Kalyayev's last-minute unwillingness to throw a bomb at Grand Duke Sergei Alexandrovich because the intended victim was unexpectedly accompanied by his family, including young children, as was also the case with an Italian anarchist, Angiolio, who relinquished an opportunity to shoot his target, Canovas, the Spanish prime minister.[17]

The argument of those adhering to a counterterrorist consensus is that modern terrorism, in sharp contrast, has renounced these earlier self-imposed varieties of normative restraint. As such, it has become an indefensible mode of armed struggle, and retaliatory action tends to be unconditionally validated.

The second general observation is that those who plan and conduct wars acknowledge the "just" war tradition that protects the innocent and prohibits recourse to random and indiscriminate combat tactics. Such an assertion accurately invokes the traditional law of war, as well as the more religious traditions of thought associated with such thinking, to substantiate the claim that only proportionate, selective violence directed at military targets is legally and morally permissible.

There are several problems with these ways of assessing modern terrorism. To begin with, governments themselves have a poor record of adhering to the laws of war, especially in recent decades those governments that most loudly and self-righteously proclaim their adherence to a doctrine of counterterrorism.[18] This practice by governments has displayed the same trend toward the adoption of indiscriminate tactics, often intended to focus on civilian morale, inducing fear and suffering as ends in themselves. It is a merit of Walzer's inquiry that suggests to a degree that patterns of modern terrorism are derivative from and a sequel to patterns of modern warfare; they also do not support the view that revolutionary morality has independently declined. He writes that terrorism of this unrestricted character "emerged as a strategy of revolutionary struggle only in the period after World War II, that is, only after it became a feature of conventional war."[19]

Nevertheless, counterterrorist hard-liners seek to deny this connection as often as possible. It is a type of ideological posturing for the state to contend that extending humanitarian protection to its adversaries amounts to awarding a bonus to revolutionaries. Captured personnel can always be prosecuted under military law for terrorist tactics, that is, for violence directed at civilians or for random violence and acts of cruelty.

A further difficulty with this effort at distancing war from terrorism is related to the prevailing doctrines and attitudes pertaining to war. Associated with the rise of the sovereign state have been attitudes of unconditional security concerns. Machiavelli, Hobbes, and Clausewitz are the most influential realist thinkers who emphasize that victory in war is a paramount political goal that dictates the shape and character of "military necessity." If bombing cities or blockading a food supply achieves positive military results, or is believed by commanders and leaders to do so, then the policy tends to be accepted as a legitimate tactic, at least by those on our side. The assessment of violations of the laws of war has often deteriorated into "victors' justice," if it has been undertaken at all. There are exceptions, especially in unpopular wars. Prosecutions of Lieutenant Calley and others were initiated after disclosures of the 1968 My Lai massacres during the Vietnam War, although the inquiry was cut off at such a low level of responsibility that it was widely regarded by Americans at the time as scapegoating military personnel who were doing their duty in a war carried on without respect for civilian life.

If it is acceptable to use political violence indiscriminately and cruelly because it will contribute to attaining military goals, then a premium is placed on grotesque and shocking forms of violence (that is, the greatest psychological effect on the enemy for the smallest loss of life). Note that the Hiroshima apologia for saving American lives did not even claim, except very incidentally and much after the fact, that Japanese lives were saved as well. If revolutionary nationalists were to be allowed this same freedom to vindicate their violence by the economizing of their own deaths, then there could be no condemnation of even the most extreme acts of indiscriminate violence. As elsewhere, following the counterterrorist reasoning back to its source reveals a corrosive double standard. To differentiate terrorism from war in any rigid fashion is to mistake the character of both activities.

A further point: The development of a capability for "covert operations" behind enemy lines has always been an incident of general war and has seemed legitimate, indeed heroic, even if as a consequence it subjected innocent civilians to death and destruction on occasion. It was the effectiveness of these tactics during World War II that led directly to the formation of a covert operations arm of the CIA as an element of peacetime international diplomacy. As is now abundantly documented, the CIA has used secret violence to "neutralize"—that is, to kill—persons perceived as hostile to United States interests.[20] Such activities are not reliably scrutinized and seem uninhibited by just war or laws of war restraints. What knowledge we have of such CIA abuses is largely accidental, following upon an unpopular war or accidental disclosure. There is no inherent deference to legal and moral constraints. On the contrary, the prevailing pressure is to get the job done, with effectiveness the only driving force. State practice, in other words, has institutionalized and normalized a capability to engage in "terrorism" quite apart from its activities designed as a response to terrorist challenges. It is striking that during the congressional hearings on arms sales to Iran even the most intense opponents of the disregard of the rule of law and of public policy stands by the Reagan administration made a point of accepting the necessity for a covert operations capability under the authority of the president. Such a necessity seems vaguely connected with the idea that international society is a jungle and that, in any event, the Soviet Union engages in covert operations, and what they do, we must do. Such reasoning prevails without benefit of argument or reflection. Despite a dubious track record, the retention of a covert operations option for the U.S. government is blindly accepted by all sides in mainstream politics.

There is, finally, the connection with war perceived by revolutionary groups. Here it is necessary to distinguish terrorism by isolated groups lacking mass support and terrorism by revolutionary nationalist movements eager to gain or possessing the backing of their people and intent on achieving recognition and support in international circles. In this latter setting, revolutionary groups voluntarily describe their armed struggle movement as a species of "just war," that is, as justified violence, and often insist that this description is reinforced by their adherence to humanitarian standards of warfare, including the minimization of damage to civilians, as well as by their commitment to the principle of national self-determination, which is accepted widely as a legitimate goal of political struggle. Each instance must be assessed on the basis of the available evidence as to whether claims are reasonable.

There are many modern examples of revolutionary terrorists' acting to avoid civilian casualties. In very few hijackings were threats to kill passengers carried out, and in none so far was there an attempt to maximize casualties. The use of fear and the taking of hostages are themselves terrorist practices, but they are not nearly so extreme as they might be or as some combat practices by state military forces (such as policies of taking no prisoners) are. Even the 1979–1980 seizure of the U.S. Embassy by Iranian revolutionaries did not produce fatalities. The striking feature about revolutionary terrorism is that it exerts such an influence on the imagination despite the small number of casualties as compared to the statistics of crime or war.

My impressions from discussions over the years with many

revolutionary nationalists is that they mostly retain a strong ethical attitude toward political violence. They generally regard themselves as victimized by the criminal and cruel tactics of their adversary, including the use of crude violence against suspected civilian sympathizers. They present their own violence as much more limited, selective, and reactive and less productive of civilian suffering. I am not prepared to accept such self-serving assessments at face value, but neither would I reject such presentations altogether. They often display a moral sensitivity, reinforced by this reality of fighting on behalf of "the people" and living among the people. The search for legitimacy is also a much more prominent aspect of struggle for those who take on the established order.

However one reacts to these more controversial claims, it seems at a minimum unreasonable to regard revolutionary violence as more indiscriminate and random, less respectful of innocence than the kind of tactics relied upon by respected states. The connection between war and terrorism in those circumstances is genuine. The armed conflict associated with sustained revolutionary violence, especially in the Third World, definitely deserves to be treated as a subspecies of modern warfare. Furthermore, there is no convincing grounds on which to deny these groups the protection of humanitarian law, and by most understandings of contemporary international law, this protection has been formally established.

CRIME

As with war, there is a disposition by the counterterrorist mainstream to compare even the most violent criminals favorably to the generality of terrorists. Laqueur writes, typically "criminals have frequently shown greater humanity than terrorists; they are out for profit, not for psychological satisfaction. They don't normally torment their victims. Terrorists are fanatics and fanaticism frequently makes for cruelty and sadism."[21] Here, also, the encoded message is that terrorists in the narrow, polemical revolutionary sense are the most depraved of all elements in society, including hardened criminals. Of course, generalizations will not hold across the spectrum of antistate revolutionary violence, and there have been notable instances of cruel and shocking violence.

Yet, the sadism of violent crime is a much pervasive element of our daily life. It is a rare day that tabloids don't feature an array of crimes that create fear and disgust by their sadistic character. True, professional criminals engaged in "business" operations are reluctant to jeopardize their economic returns by violent action of a nonfunctional sort. To the extent that selective violence, whatever its goals, is relied upon for narrowly instrumental purposes it will tend to avoid sadism. It is false to suppose that revolutionary violence is not generally disciplined in these respects, being influenced by Maoist precepts on the need for revolutionaries to live as fish in the sea of society if they are to achieve success as a movement.

Of course, if terrorism is defined still more narrowly as revolutionary violence without links to the general population, then sadistic elements are more likely to be present. The urban revolutionary groups of Europe, Japan, and North America, alienated children of the middle class, have often acted out of rage and hatred, scorning society for its failure to rise up in revolutionary ferment. As Bommi Baumann, the former German urban terrorist, expressed his commitment: "For me, K-1 [a West German revolutionary commune] was the right connection of politics and counterculture. Today I can see that—for myself—it was only the fear of love, from which one flees into absolute violence."[22] Under these circumstances, there is a disposition to adopt a life-style and worldview that results in fanatical behavior and blurs the distinction between criminality and politics. This distinction is further blurred by the tendency of revolutionary groups to rob banks to secure their financial needs or to enter coalitions with drug dealers and others either to earn profits or to acquire weapons. One example is that of the insurgent group M-19 in Colombia, in which both revolutionary politics and drug traffic have forged a mutually reinforcing coalition that has greatly strengthened their hand in relation to forces of order.

But such depravity can also result from a simple criminal mentality, as expressed by the latter violent stages of action associated with the Manson family, especially the Sharon Tate murders. Although portrayed as an instance of political violence, the action in essence was an amateurish attempt to throw police off the scent of a drug-related homicide without any political content whatsoever (except an insistence on living by a set of rules that defied social norms). Charles Manson's self-characterization: "a person who was dealt a hand that couldn't be played by the rules and values of your society."[23] Or more tellingly, "so goes the feeling of power when coupled with hatred."[24] Manson evolved extreme in-group loyalty to "his family" and seemed insensible to the fate of all others. But there was no political motivation beyond the vague view that drug immersion and the 1960s countercultural ethos would subvert and supersede a dying, cruel civilization. When it came to the Vietnam War, civil rights, or political causes, the Manson family was notably apolitical, unmoved, and inert, as compared to such revolutionary outlooks as those adopted by the Black Panthers, Symbionese Liberation Army, and Weather Underground.

At times, revolutionary groups engage in crime to carry out political goals or to sustain their own efforts. Bank robberies to put resources at the disposal of the poor or to enable the group to buy weapons and operate are illustrative. But crime, whether to make a profit, to inflict pain, to satisfy needs and desire, or to express hatred and mental disorder, is not by itself political violence, although the two modes can become closely entwined, given the pressures and realities of an insulated life-style and a spirit of unconditional self-justification.

Yet, as elsewhere in our discussions, these same features pertain as well to bureaucratic undertakings. Such ventures often involve a disregard for law and for the rights of innocent people. When Colonel North acts, with at least the tacit endorsement of the highest levels of political leadership, a deliberate and large-scale transfer of weaponry to those engaged in indiscriminate and shocking forms of violence occurs. And yet North has achieved the stature of national hero by invoking his own very coherent imagery of patriotism and anti-Communist struggle, as well as by demonstrating his dedication to what he believes regardless of risk.

There is something formidable about recent terrorist violence that sets it apart from criminality. It induces more intense fear in the general population, despite low risks and small casualties, than does the much more pervasive phenomenon of criminal violence. Partly, this potency arises because the state shapes our perceptions, and the state feels far more threatened by terrorists than by criminals. Terrorists in some degree have an alternative vision of the future that includes the burning of the state, and their activity encroaches upon the prime function of the state to sustain a monopoly over political violence.

At another level, the state seeks to stigmatize its revolutionary opponents as criminals, denying them the dignity of their claims to be engaged in a political process. The issue arises sharply in legal settings, as when governments withhold asylum or sanctuary from revolutionary groups or extradite their personnel for prosecution as criminals. This approach proposed by some governments is to define prohibited acts of violence that governments will punish as crimes and to cooperate in devising ways to facilitate enforcement, including exchanges of evidence and transfers of suspects. By the nature of this process only antistate or revolutionary forms of political violence are considered, accepting implicitly the narrower conception of terrorism that excludes bureaucrats. If understood as a limited effort to achieve better control over political violence, but linked to a broader repudiation of all forms of such violence, then this kind of legal initiative could qualify as constructive counterterrorism.[25]

The various controversies about the character of the Provisional Irish Republican Army are illuminating.[26] There is a push now to enable the U.S. government to hand over "revolutionaries" accused of violent acts through their association with political groups that rely upon armed struggle tactics.

Militants in the IRA have consistently protested against their imprisonment as ordinary criminals by the British government. In 1981 the hunger strikes of imprisoned IRA members leading to starvation and death expressed the degree to which some of these prisoners rejected Margaret Thatcher's insistence that "a crime is a crime is a crime." As Richard Rubenstein notes, "the IRA hunger strikers' suicide by starvation represented their ultimate rejection of criminal status and the legal system that confirmed it."[27]

The recognition of impermissible violence by agencies of the state is obscured by white-collar credentials. Practitioners dress well, exhibit the kind of refinement associated with respect, and are often good citizens. Such individuals often possess credentials of loyalty to the status quo and are likely to seem sincerely motivated by a sense of professionalism and patriotic duty. Such, of course, is the problem of the "banality of evil," as applicable to Adolph Eichmann as to a practitioner of covert operations under the color of law. It is easy to strip away the veil of respectability from a dutiful bureaucrat if we agree that he is serving a reprehensible cause or hostile state. It is far more difficult if he is one of our own, and yet unless we become able to repudiate all impermissible political violence we will never free ourselves from cycles of action and reaction.

In one regard, my argument is that state-sponsored terrorism (whether to promote its own projects, to strike at revolutionary activity, or to serve some mixture of ends) is an insidious form of white-collar crime. In another regard, it represents political violence without normative boundaries and qualifies as terrorism under the more appropriate extensive definition.

CONCLUSION

All forms of impermissible political violence are terrorism. Only when this orientation is applied consistently and rigorously will it be possible to mount an effective campaign against terrorism. To fight fire with fire is to succumb to terrorism. To extinguish fire with water is what constructive counter-terrorism proposes.

As long as political violence claims an exemption from moral and legal constraints because of what the other side does, terrorism will beget terrorism in an endless cycle. The challenge to our moral and political imagination is to break the cycle not by avoiding violence altogether but by respecting innocence and legal and moral limits that have evolved to identify and protect innocence.

FIVE

The Terrorist Mind-Set:
The Moral Universe
of Revolutionaries
and Functionaries

This moral superiority is what
sustains the urban guerrilla.

CARLOS MARIGHELA, *Handbook of*
Urban Guerrilla Warfare

. . . the realization that wild beasts
prowl our airways and waterways.

BENJAMIN NETANYAHU,
Terrorism: How the West Can Win

Crucial to this inquiry is a capacity for consistent identification:
Who is a terrorist? Who is not? Is it possible to depict a mind-
set that is applicable to both revolutionaries and functionaries?
The prospects for constructive counterterrorism depend upon
conceptual clarity and a high degree of emotional detachment
from motivations and goals. That is, no matter how laudable
the motivations or goals and no matter how detestable the
other side may seem, a common renunciation of impermissible
violence must take precedence in our thinking.

Objectivity is important. We cannot suspend judgment when the label "terrorist" is attached by media or officialdom. It is necessary to insist that the label be extended to state conduct that comes within the purview of impermissible political violence.

In this book we define terrorism as the characteristic type of political antagonism in the world of today: political extremism that resorts to indiscriminate violence or to violence against innocent persons in the service of either revolutionary or governmental causes. The controversial element is the inclusion in the terrorist domain of the functionary and of friendly state actors, including the government of the United States.

Political violence as an instrument of government policy whether at home or abroad often establishes the character of a regime as legitimate or not. Yet, basic as is this political rendering of reality, its specific form is often shaped by a particular experience of history and culture. For instance, in examining contemporary Soviet or Chinese political behavior it is essential to take into account such antecedent influences as czarism and Confucianism. In this regard, politics is itself derivative, and it is culture that underlies and shapes politics. What is disturbing about the phenomenon of terrorism is its normality within our culture. From this perspective, we are virtually all terrorists, at least in the passive sense of endorsing or at least acquiescing in indiscriminate violence against enemies, especially if such tactics seem likely to work in either a means/ends understanding of politics or as a symbolic moment. The congressional debate about aid to the Contras is carried on almost exclusively within a framework of accepted terrorism; criticism of the Contras, to the extent offered, relates to their prospects for victory or of inducing Managua to compromise.

Such a debate has a terrorist character because it refrains from unconditionally renouncing as a political option reliance on violence against the innocent and because it even fails to criticize its occurrence. Without such a renunciation, terrorism becomes an acceptable, at least a rational, instrument of

71

political conflict. Such a mentality is easily led to the strategic bombing of cities with a rationale based on provoking civilian fear, as was extensively done during World War II. It forms the core rationale of coercive diplomacy, which seeks to inflict pain on an adversary as a way of gaining political goals. At best, the choice rests upon allegations of military necessity or revolutionary necessity. A frequent claim of those who rely on state terrorism is that inducing societal fear and panic, hastening surrender or victory, will eventually produce a lessening of casualties or that our side is using no more reprehensible tactics than the enemy. Any terrorist can sincerely adopt this "moral" logic. So much depends on the appreciation of the facts, and this process is hopelessly subjective whenever political passions are engaged. The mainstream has no difficulty repudiating these lines of reasoning if they are advanced in support of a revolutionary cause, but they tend to accept or even applaud equivalent behavior by their state in the spirit of a misguided patriotism reinforced by selective moralizing.

This patriotic and ethical suspension of disbelief reaches its climax during a war. Virtually any atrocity, especially if carried out at a distance by high-technology weaponry, is accepted on the assumption that it grows out of a military strategy that is rarely questioned.

"Military necessity" is mechanically equated with degrees of destructiveness, measured by numbers of casualties caused and scope of destruction: the more destructive, the more necessary. Hence, once the capability to destroy more efficiently is in hand, the step to weapons development and eventual use is taken almost automatically. Technological innovation has done its part to make terrorist conduct seem a routine and natural part of war. Even a great technological leap, such as the use of the atomic bombs, is taken with almost no consideration of the long-term effects of relying on indiscriminate weaponry that causes deferred, acute suffering and fear among civilians, even those only remotely exposed. The persistence of the arms race numbs our moral sensibilities and supports the routinization of terrorism.

At issue is the absence of moral outrage when indiscriminate and cruel forms of violence are used by the state, so long as the perpetrator has an overall positive identity and the target is an enemy associated with evil. There was virtually no protest mounted by public opinion in Allied countries against indiscriminate tactics of warfare during World War II, although the war effort itself was validated as a struggle against the evil of fascism. Instead people blandly accepted the necessity rationale, as well as the claim that lives would be saved by such attacks. At the same time, German and Japanese leaders who relied upon indiscriminate tactics, violating the laws of war, were punished as war criminals by the victorious powers, and the crimes of Nazi rule were widely publicized to establish the justness of the outcome in the war.

It is not even possible to argue that a condition of general war suspends normal societal scruples. When it was alleged on the basis of investigative reporting that the U.S. air attack of April 1986 on Libya deliberately targeted Muammar El-Qaddafi and his family, the story was given prominence, but not a murmur of criticism or official retraction or even denial followed.[1] Even the executive order of the president prohibiting assassination plans by the U.S. government was not invoked in Congress or elsewhere as a basis for questioning executive policy. It is a generally undesirable precedent to make foreign leaders a legitimate target of transnational violence even if we believe them guilty of crimes of state. In a world of sovereign states such assessments are partisan; they are not likely to be accepted as authoritative, and acting upon them is likely to intensify conflict. Without central political institutions of government in the world to implement common standards, reciprocal respect for sovereign rights is an important means to moderate international conflict even if one government deeply disapproves of the actions of a leader of another country. One can imagine certain extreme instances of abuse and danger that could justify even an assassination attempt, but only if undertaken in a clearly defensive spirit or with the support of the international community as a whole.

This culture of terrorism has deep roots in the historical experience of what we call "civilization." Building prosperity and dominance on the legitimacy of the slave trade and on the willingness to displace, if not directly exterminate, indigenous peoples has been one part of the civilizing process over the last several centuries. Often extreme deceit and annihilating weaponry have been employed against defenseless and innocent peoples. We read many verified accounts of contaminated blankets given by white settlers to the American Indians or of battles with hundreds of casualties on the native side and none, or a handful, on the settler side. And yet we successfully romanticize our terrorist past so as to convert the Indians into savage terrorists and their tormentors into heroic warriors.[2]

Terror begets terror and colors our expectations about what is permissible. We expect our functionaries to prevail, to win over their adversaries, and nothing else, in the end, is held to matter much.

Jimmy Carter has been perceived as a failed president because he lacked "resolve," was associated with "decline" and also "malaise," seemed less a terrorist than the country required or wanted. To preside over a large modern state implies a willingness to act decisively, without scruples, when national interests are at stake. Those with scruples, being indecisive, might prove an impediment at times of crisis. The armed forces weed out from sensitive roles those tested to have strong moral standards—they are deemed "unreliable." We the citizenry demand of our leaders that they put efficiency ahead of moral restraint. In effect, we demand that "national interests" be promoted by terrorism, if necessary.

So the issue of responsibility leads back to us. We would like to hold adversaries and enemies responsible for wrongs that we have committed ourselves and for which we claim justification as a matter of rational calculation. We describe the same types of violence as if one were horrifying and the other appropriate. And so the functionary is as much a creature of a culture of terrorism as are those who act, invoking revolutionary prerogatives.

What ensues is terrorist dialogue between the state and its revolutionary enemies, with many citizens drawn in on the side of the functionary, a few on the side of the revolutionary, and many more caught in the cross fire. Violence is an instrument of this political melodrama, appropriate when used by the good side, criminal when used by the evil side.[3] In such circumstances the dynamics of melodrama completely overshadows supposed general prohibitions on terrorist methods. Those who call for an end to all terrorism remain lonely voices in the wilderness.

Astonishingly, and despite contrasting life-styles and dress codes, revolutionaries and functionaries live in the same world, not in distinct worlds. Of course, there are many variations of sensibility and outlook, but there are deep-seated shared attitudes, assumptions, and practices that make meaningful the assertion that there exists an overarching "terrorist mind-set."

At its core this mind-set validates violence by diminishing the status of the target, often by falsifying the true character of the victims. I remember a very determined attempt in 1967–1968 by Robert McNamara, then secretary of defense, to present the heavy U.S. bombing of North Vietnam as consisting of "surgical strikes" directed exclusively at military targets. It took a series of long investigative articles in *The New York Times* by Harrison Salisbury, written beneath a Hanoi dateline, to explode this myth and to portray unmistakably the extensiveness of the civilian damage done on a daily basis by the bombing campaign commenced in the mid-1960s and continuing through Lyndon Johnson's announced intention in 1968 not to seek a second term as president. I visited North Vietnam a few weeks after the Salisbury articles and found the scale and character of the bombing attacks far beyond what even his assessments had led me to expect. Entire cities were devastated, turned into twisted wreckage by repeated, and presumably deliberate, attacks. Daniel Ellsberg, a prominent Pentagon consultant during most of the pre-1968 period of United States involvement, spoke of "the need not to know" among policymakers as an explanation of why his many recommendations that civilian side effects of military policies be assessed were persistently ignored and scorned. No matter how insistently he urged these humanitarian concerns upon policymakers, nothing was done. This need not to know readily complements the attitude, also prevalent during the Vietnam War, of destroying a village in order to save it.

Generally, such a refusal to consider civilian side effects of military tactics does not reflect a cruel or depraved state of mind on the part of a policymaker or commander. It expresses a mentality of "total war" in which destroying the enemy is contributing to the overall war effort. Victory is the ultimate objective, but short of that, the war is about doing damage, and human suffering for the other side is a form of damage, especially in guerrilla warfare where the combat relationship cannot be resolved by encounters between armed forces arrayed on a battlefield. Inflicting pain becomes in a very real sense what the war is about. But considered objectively, this lapse into total war erodes the distinction between war and terrorism. When revolutionaries inflict pain on civilians in an isolated incident of violence it is labeled immediately as terrorism, but when antagonists in war inflict pain routinely on the civilian population it is assessed, if at all, by reference to measurements of battlefield effectiveness. Of course, perceptions are further complicated by wartime propaganda that tends to present what one's own side does by reference to its success in inflicting pain while castigating the other side for its callous and brutal behavior.

The argument here is that revolutionaries and functionaries occupy symmetrical and equivalent roles in relation to political violence even if their motivations and goals are fundamentally dissimilar. There is no intention here to belittle struggles against injustice or for democracy and human rights, or to deny their historical role as liberating. Each context carries with it a relationship to historical circumstances and to the promotion or inhibition of world order values. The position taken in this book is that regardless of historical role or normative vision, recourse to political violence of a terrorist character can never be excused or justified. Neither statist nor emancipation logic can release participants in struggle from their absolute duty to protect innocent civilian life and to avoid indiscriminate violence, including efforts to generate widespread fear.

Political conflict often is carried on between unequal adversaries. The functionary is by the nature of his role an officer of the state, with generally superior access to and control over symbols of legitimacy and more advanced and abundant weaponry of destruction. The Soviet purges, the Cambodian genocide, the Indonesian massacres of the West Irian people, and the paramilitary operations of the 1960s in the Southern Cone countries each resulted in massive death totals exceeding by far the casualties from terrorist incidents staged by revolutionary groups. The numbers killed by any major outbreak of state terror by far exceed the totals of victims arising from incidents of revolutionary terrorism, unless the level of struggle assumes the character of guerrilla warfare or even combat between opposing armed forces, in which cases casualty figures can be large on both sides. To offset this paucity of numbers, the revolutionary side seeks to register its impact through shock effects or through an expressive dramaturgy that relies on the media to transmit intimidating messages. Terrorism on the revolutionary side is more likely to be mainly symbolic, whereas on the functionary side the emphasis is substantive. In the former case, the spectacle of violence is paramount, whereas in the latter the objective is to decimate the ranks of the revolutionary group. And yet the two types of terrorist logic are often intertwined. If a revolutionary can execute a key figure in the state, an instrumental goal is served, and similarly, if a government uses violence in a frightening manner (as with death squads), then the results may not only eliminate the particular enemies but produce a general intimidation of all oppositional tendencies.

The revolutionary has generally rejected usual patterns

of participation offered by civil society and cannot achieve self-esteem by having a successful career or making money. Counterterrorist ideologues assert that a revolutionary terrorist "parts company with humanity. *He declares a total war on the society he attacks.*"⁴ But if the essence of terrorism is related to the unbridled character of violent practices, then the functionary is equally, if not more, culpable, although harder to detect and condemn, his activities being hidden behind walls of secrecy or vindicated by the fiery rhetoric of patriotism.

Compare, for instance, the reverential attitude of the media toward Lieutenant Colonel Oliver North with its extreme disdain for someone from a revolutionary movement associated with the promotion of terrorist activities, say the Palestinian nationalist Abu Abbas, apparently the mastermind of the *Achille Lauro* hijacking. Even those who disagree with the substantive and ethical rationale of North's undertakings are careful to refer to him respectfully, by his proper military rank, and to take due note of the loyalty and affection displayed toward him by his confederates, attitudes that would be overlooked if the target of investigation were on the revolutionary side of the ledger.

Another aspect of this asymmetry relates to the portrayal of victims. The media lavishes attention and compassion on the victims of revolutionary terror. Many recall the name and horrifying experience of Leon Klinghoffer, the crippled man shot to death and thrown overboard by the *Achille Lauro* assailants, but we know virtually nothing about the human tragedies caused by counterterrorist attacks such as the 1985 Israeli bombing of Tunis that caused sixty-three civilian deaths or the April 1986 U.S. bombing of Tripoli that produced upward of one hundred civilian casualties. In many accounts, civilian casualties caused by counterterrorist attacks are not mentioned at all or are treated as mere allegations. Almost never is there any focus on the tragedy inflicted upon particular individuals. Again, the victims of revolutionary terror are humanized in harrowing fashion, whereas the victims of functionary terror are generally reduced to a cold statistic (if reported at all) or their death is swept beneath a geopolitical or statist rug, called "retaliation."[5] Of course, if functionary terror is the work of a geopolitical adversary, its character will be featured, as it should be, in agonizing detail. Solzhenitsyn is honored by the White House for his graphic depiction of the *gulag* dimension of the Soviet experience in the Stalinist years, but Noam Chomsky found his name on Nixon's "enemies list," presumably because he told the other half of the story about functionary terror, mainly through specifying the crimes against humanity and gross violations of human rights attributable to the U.S. government and some of its friends in the Third World. To be genuinely antiterrorist in our sentiments and behavioral patterns would be to want both stories fully disclosed and to honor both individuals for their dedication to the antiterrorist cause that is claimed to lie at the core of civilization. As matters stand, most citizens are not antiterrorist at all, although they can be mobilized to express outrage or to feel fear about the "terrorism" of the adversary, while willingly accepting the terrorism of their government as *raison d'état*. Behind the closed doors of official secrecy, or the obscuring protection of a language game in which the same thing is called by two names that evoke contradictory reactions, deep moral confusion persists.

A revolutionary or functionary with a terrorist mind-set will adopt a series of strategies that appear to reconcile his indiscriminate violence against innocent civilians with his seemingly sincere claim to be the representative of humane values against the cruel corruption of opponents. In social situations over the years with both revolutionaries and functionaries engaged in terrorist activities, I have rarely discerned manifest cruelty, depravity, or other normative deficiencies. Partly these are hidden from the perpetrators themselves who really do seem to regard themselves as either doing their job ("professionalism") or as agents of a validating, even ennobling, moral purpose. A number of distancing strategies conceal the terrorist taint from the terrorist.

LANGUAGE

The terrorist avoids in most instances associating his recourse to violence with practices stigmatized as "terrorism." Abstractions and technical jargon are used by functionaries; more romantic words about participation in the struggle and carrying the battle courageously to the enemy are relied upon by revolutionaries. Functionaries tell of "free-fire zones," "crop-destruction programs," "pacification," not about the human costs associated with carrying such policies out in a heavily populated countryside in which the real combatants fade into the forests. Abstractions help to achieve distance between policy and pain, and high-technology warfare with its reliance on remote electronic controls, computer information flow, and quantitative assessment is far removed from its flesh-and-blood effects. Revolutionaries rely on the engaged language of liberation to lift the tactics of revolutionary struggle beyond moral and legal scrutiny.

The same holds true in the shadowy domains of covert operations. Those who join the CIA often never discern the degree to which terrorism constitutes the essence of their "intelligence work." A few who finally became harsh critics report how difficult it was to face the reality of impermissible political violence carried out under the banner of national security, covert operations, and counterterrorism. One major justification for terrorism by functionaries arises from according primacy to geopolitics. The CIA attempted assassinations of Fidel Castro on several occasions because his leftist political identity was perceived as a threat to the hemispheric interests of the United States; plans to eliminate him were discussed, even in secret, in relation to geopolitical stakes rather than his personal culpability.

A revealing instance of how the conventions of language split our sense of reality in a manner that overlooks one variety of terrorism while condemning its twin is present in the literature on "nuclear terrorism."[6] An untutored interpretation of such a phrase would undoubtedly call to mind nuclear threats or uses of the weapons amounting to gross violation of the prohibition upon impermissible political violence. Yet in actuality the published literature on nuclear terrorism is concerned about the threat posed by revolutionaries, anarchists, and criminals to nuclear facilities or the prospect that such groups might acquire the weapons or the means to produce them. In other words, language habits lead us to separate our distaste for terrorism from our attitude toward the weaponry itself. True, some popular discussion uses the phrase "balance of terror" to describe the nuclear standoff, implying that it is a generally positive or at least ambiguous phenomenon, as the word *terror* with its negative connotations is here linked with the word *balance*, which has generally positive connotations.

DOUBLING

The bloody side of terrorism is repellent to our moral sensibility. Most of us need to gain distance, preserving intact the illusion of our decency. Extreme political orders, like those maintained by Hitler and Stalin, are illuminating and pose questions about the psychological survival of the self under the stress of daily terrorist practice.

The high functionary has available language and layers of protective bureaucracy as a means of gaining distance. Albert Speer, a convicted war criminal and Nazi administrator, associated state terror with the blend between "unrestricted rule" and "the power of technology" that produced a depersonalization of politics enabling the state to do anything, and its chief policy architects to feel no sense of responsibility.[7] At the same time, middle- and lower-level functionaries gained distance by rigid deference to their duties of obedience to the orders of their superiors.

On a personal level, Speer explains his adjustment to Nazi atrocities by the claim, "I was trying to compartmentalize my mind."[8] In effect, he was struggling to avoid acknowledging the terrorizing implications of his role, of the system he was serving. He accepts, in retrospect, that he was responsible for all that was done and so assumes responsibility (an anti-terrorist attitude): "But in the final analysis I myself determined the degree of my isolation, the extremity of my evasion, and the extent of my ignorance. . . . Those who ask me [about the extent of my knowledge] are fundamentally expecting me to offer justifications. But I have none. No apologies are possible."[9]

Robert Jay Lifton, in his important study of Nazi doctors serving in concentration camps, relies on the concept of "doubling," a splitting of personality that allows the bloody work to be done by a second self that is assigned the performance of evil.[10] Hence, a figure like Mengele is able to do the most unspeakable kinds of things in the course of his "work" and yet in other settings act as a considerate, even compassionate, family member or friend. This doubling phenomenon can be activated by extreme situations that place stress on the conventional domain of good and evil. Lifton portrays doubling as a type of Faustian bargain "likely to mean a choice for evil" even if "much doubling takes place outside of awareness."[11] The essence of doubling is to validate the destruction of innocence by eliminating ethical, even professional inhibitions and thereby losing any sense of responsibility or even of guilt. The Auschwitz self, in Lifton's phrasing, develops "its own criteria for good (duty, loyalty to the group, 'improving' Auschwitz conditions, etc.), thereby freeing the original self from responsibility for actions there."[12] The bargain is peace of mind in exchange for allegiance to evil. Every contented terrorist has struck such a bargain, if only unconsciously.

FUNDAMENTALISM

A terrorist in some way subscribes to revealed truth, that is, to a set of understandings that justify recourse to killing and maiming human beings. The fundamentalism may be quite overt as in the case of convinced followers of Khomeini's Islamic revolution or adherents of a very literal reading of Marx-ist-Leninist revolutionary doctrine. For such individuals, the truth is often clear enough to justify death sentences for their opponents. In a modern secular state fundamentalist faiths are less respectable yet they survive, making their presence felt indirectly, often hiding out in highly rational doctrines of "national security" and "nuclear deterrence." Geopolitics can provide fundamentalist justifications for terrorist undertakings to disrupt a foreign society or kill its leaders. But the result is the same. A mandate to kill indiscriminately is presupposed, even if a particular action produces suffering out of all pro-portion to the interests and values being defended and lacks a moral and legal foundation. Political murders—of a leader, a union organizer, a progressive military officer, or even a religious leader—may also be justified by reference to some unconditional mandate. Each such figure has been targeted by terrorists working in an official capacity on behalf of en-lightened states.

Justifications for nuclear deterrence, implying an ac-ceptance of the risks of human extinction and nuclear winter, are extreme endorsements of terrorist practice, what E. P. Thompson has aptly termed "exterminism."[13] For a country or group of countries to base its security on a nuclear option (especially when opportunities for nuclear disengagement seem present but are generally ignored) is to incorporate terrorism into the very center of the governing process. This is the case even if the reasoning is based on a lesser of evils argument.[14] No one would hesitate to label as terrorism any threat by a revolutionary group that it would poison the water supplies of the entire world if its vital interests were jeopardized. This form of deterrence by revolutionaries is unquestionably ter-rorist even if kept at the threat level, and if the revolutionary group moved toward making its threat credible it would be (appropriately) castigated in the most vilifying language avail-able even if the whole purpose were to avoid carrying out the threat.

DEMONIZATION

The other side is demonized by the state and its allies as a justification for resort to violence that is not conditioned by normal legal and moral limits. Revolutionaries are castigated as monsters, beasts, as subhuman in an effort to generate hatred, to demonize the opposition. Castro and Qaddafi can be executed because they are themselves demonized as "misfits," "criminals," and "terrorists." Responsibility for conspiring to assassinate exists even if it is indirect, giving encouragement to a military coup in which the prospects of political murder are high. Other targets, more obscure, are treated as lieutenants in a terrorist cause or merged into their organizational identity as members of the Red Brigades, the Baader-Meinhof Gang, the PLO. These "lieutenants" can be more quietly murdered or maimed, the line of responsibility being cut off by the notion of "plausible denial." Robin Erica Wagner-Pacifici brilliantly depicts the role of demonization in her presentation of the way the Red Brigades were treated by the various protagonists in the drama that unfolded in the days and weeks after Aldo Moro's startling capture on March 16, 1978, during which all five of his bodyguards were slain, and throughout his prolonged detention in a hiding place, his ordeal of being sentenced to death by "a peoples' trial," and his execution some fifty-five days later. As Wagner-Pacifici expresses the effect: "The Red Brigades were depersonalized to the point that their very membership in humanity, let along Italian humanity, was challenged. They were monsters and beasts."[15] She notes also that it came as a shock to this kind of stereotype imprinted in the popular mind to be confronted by even the most prosaic details of ordinary human identity, such as the fact that the leaders of the Red Brigades (those on trial in Torino at the same time as the Moro kidnapping) wore homemade sweaters or even "that they had families (as did other Italians) and that they were loved (and thus human)."[16] On both sides of the terrorist divide it is easier to do the killing if there is a simple line separating antagonists into heroes and villains. Yet the rigid divide introduces a serious false note. The disturbing reality is that terrorist practice is embedded in the human experience and terrorists, like others, exhibit a range of qualities, some of which may be admirable, even endearing. A part of this terrorist practice is to demonize the other. Demonization took many forms during the Moro affair. Perhaps the most notable example was a written appeal by Pope Paul VI to the Red Brigades, published a week after the kidnapping, that appears to end with an emphasis on shared humanity: "Men of the Red Brigades, give me, the interpreter of many of your co-citizens, the hope that a victorious sentiment of humanity still resides in your soul. I wait, praying, and always loving you, for the proof."[17] Yet this appeal coexisted with strong Vatican support for a no-negotiations stand, which by its purity expresses a refusal to acknowledge the humanity of "the other."

On the revolutionary side, the rhetoric of demonization is also used to override moral categories of restraint. The functionary is condemned as an infidel, corrupt and decadent, fascist, capitalist, whatever. Ulrike Meinhof, writing about the killing of functionaries (judges, business executives, police), put it this way:

> We say the guy in uniform is a pig, not a human being, and we have to tackle him from this point of view.[18]

Demonization is a death sentence imposed on the adversary. It also implies the issuance of a hunting license, a deprivation of rights, a declaration of total war.

The terrorist mind-set demonizes its adversary and releases its adherents from moral/legal restraints. Demonization follows from fundamentalist claims to knowledge of the truth.

Not all terrorists necessarily demonize their opponents. Some are more cold and professionalized, regarding the other side as an enemy to be eliminated, but not unconditionally evil. As argued, the fundamentalist stance can be expressed rationally, being presented as a bureaucratic calculation or as an expression of political desperation, but it discloses its character by making an absolute claim to engage in violence beyond the limits of moral and legal accountability.

THE MELODRAMATIC IDIOM

Nothing reveals the terrorist mind-set better than the interaction between the act of violence and the broad societal background. The media, the leaders of the state, and the main figures of moral and political authority all perceive and present terrorist events within a melodramatic idiom.[19] The dramatization process occurs as an incident unfolds in public over a period of time, creating a sense of anguished uncertainty as to the eventual outcome and pitting the resources of the established order against those of its most virulent enemies. The Moro kidnapping (1978), the Iranian hostage crisis (1979–1981), and the hijacking of the TWA 747 (1985) are prominent instances.

To convert an encounter over time into public melodrama is to drain reality of its ambiguity. Such an encounter between forces of good and evil allows no space for responsible dissent or middle positions. The citizenry, as audience, is mobilized around a unified response, with an overall attitude of deference to the state as guardian of an antiterrorist social order. As such, the citizen is simultaneously mobilized (for the sake of enlisting his/her outrage) and demobilized (to assure the absence of any challenge to the legitimacy of the state as upholder of public order). The tragic idiom, in contrast, emphasizes ambiguities of action and reaction and uncovers a need for change on *all* sides if an eventual reconciliation at a higher level of public consciousness is to be achieved. The audience, along with the dramatis personae, learns and comments and participates. In a melodrama the audience becomes a cheering section for the virtuous side.

This basic theatrical distinction between melodrama and tragedy contributes to political understanding, specifically of terrorism. To the extent that the perception of terrorism is stage-managed, it takes on the character of a melodrama (at most) offering the citizenry a kind of morality play. Such an idiom tends to reproduce itself each time enacted. If terrorism is perceived to be a part of the body politic itself, then all sides in conflict are vulnerable to the terrorist temptation, and the political circumstance is a kind of tragic predicament. The only way out is through transformation and transcendence. Instead of repetition, hope arises from the possibility of growth, or as the Greeks expressed it, wisdom through suffering. So long as terrorism is interpreted melodramatically we will not be able to overcome its presence, but if we regard it as a tragedy, then the possibility of overcoming it exists.

On the revolutionary side of terrorism there is also an absence of tragic sensibility, and hence, an inability to forgive. As a rule, the revolutionary side is in no position to compose a melodramatic script, except as guerrilla theater performed at the underground fringes of society. The Iranian hostage crisis, because of its transnational dimension, provided a rare instance of a melodramatic spectacle in which scripts were being simultaneously enacted by the two chief antagonists. For Iranian society, the embassy seizure was a radicalizing morality play exhibiting the power of the Ayatollah to humiliate "the Great Satan." For many in American society, it was a confirming melodrama that those swarthy and turbaned Third Worlders were indeed barbarians at the gates.

The terrorist mind-set discloses itself by twisting the morally ambiguous material of human torment and conflict into the mobilizing falsehoods of melodramatic clarity. The substance of melodrama is cold killing, an interplay of sentiments devoid of sorrow and pity, and a lack of any evolution of moral and political understanding.

THE REALIST ETHOS

The grounding of the terrorist mind-set has been established over the centuries by a cynical view of human nature and political community. Niccolò Machiavelli, early in the sixteenth century, set forth in *The Prince* a commendably lucid

REVOLUTIONARIES AND FUNCTIONARIES

account of how power should be exercised by a successful ruler. There are several main ideas: human nature is flawed; whatever helps sustain the state is justifiable; a ruler cannot succeed by adherence to norms of decency and good faith.

Machiavelli argues the need to accept reality as essentially darkened: "If men were all good, this precept would not be a good one; but as they are bad, and would not observe their faith with you, so you are not bound to keep faith with them."[20] For these reasons, it may be necessary so as "to maintain the state, to act against faith, against clarity, against humanity, and against religion." To do this requires a ruler with "a mind disposed to adapt itself according to the wind, as the variations of fortune dictate. . . ."[21]

What pertains to the state, pertains to its foes. The consequence of Machiavelli's outlook is to encourage unscrupulous behavior on all sides of political conflict. From such a collision of wills many of the modern torments ensue, including the drift into total war. The upsurge of terrorism is also an expression of this Machiavellian legacy. The brilliant Florentine observed that "in the actions of men, and especially of princes, from which there is no appeal, the end justifies the means. Let a prince aim at conquering and maintaining the state, and the means will always be judged honourable and praised by every one, for the vulgar is always taken by appearances and the issue of the event; and the world consists only of the vulgar, and the few who are not vulgar are isolated when the many have a rallying point in the prince."[22] In effect, any of us would be prudent to do whatever he can to succeed because we inhabit a vulgar world of uninhibited conflict and rivalry. To keep promises and to show respect for law and morality are to be naive and ineffectual.

Machiavelli elsewhere wrote many other wise and prudent things, including an account of his own preference for moderate and republican forms of politics, but it is his cynical, scornful side that has come down through the centuries to shape and limit our political imagination. The supposed realism of this outlook tells us, above all, to do whatever succeeds if we find ourselves in political conflict, including taking recourse to violence in whatever form might help.

Shifting around the root metaphors of political propriety, Machiavelli insists even that the ruler know how to be "a beast," whether lion or fox, as such strength and such wiles are both necessary ingredients of effectiveness in the world. We demonize terrorists as beasts, and yet we choose as our dominant source of worldly political insight and guidance a voice that advises the prince to be a beast.

I would argue that we cannot hope to distance ourselves from terrorism without repudiating this brand of "realism." Virtually all of our leaders are realists accepting dark imagery about human nature and world society, even if they utter pious sentiments on major holidays to satisfy public cravings for peace and justice. Figures such as Kissinger and Brzezinski seem to fit so well in the realms of power because their commitment to realism seems so unqualified and informed. The espousal of realism has been particularly pronounced among American leaders since World War II. It partly expresses the view that the appeasement of Hitler in the 1930s took place because major leaders did not understand power dynamics in the world well enough. As such, it repudiates those "idealist" voices in the American past that thought that law and morality in international life could be strengthened through time. The presence of terrorist tactics and terrorist images of the other side produces a very explosive and unpredictable public mood.

Whatever their inner motivation, "terrorists" of all orientations are realists believing that impermissible violence will help achieve the results they seek, even if these results are no more substantial than inflicting pain and arousing fear. Many realists would argue that only such means as are necessary have been endorsed, but the perception of necessity is highly subjective and uncentered in the modern world, with no way of resolving conflicting interpretations of rights. Many ideas that challenge the legitimacy of rulers and governments and justify disruptive violence at home and abroad have emerged over time. Among the most notable bases for resistance are dictatorial rule, corruption, alien influence, and usurpation of public rights. Both revolutionaries and functionaries posit absolutist ideas of political legitimacy that can lead to violence against "innocent" victims if any should stand in the way of political projects.

For the committed realist, the only virtue in the public arena is prudence; terrorist methods are rejected to the extent they don't work, being perceived as ineffectual or counterproductive. But if terrorism seems the best option or an effective option, it becomes acceptable and even enjoys a certain status as the tough, but necessary, choice for a realist who chooses to be a political actor in a harsh world of struggle.

The realist is less extreme than the fundamentalist, who employs violence to destroy "evil" even if he self-destructs in the process (for example, Iranian suicide squads). At this stage, it is not plausible to suppose that we can be done with terrorism in the near future. To gain time for constructive counterterrorism to succeed it is essential to keep fundamentalism at bay.

TOTAL WAR

One ingredient of the terrorist mind-set is a total war mentality, an extension of the widely held cultural view that because war is hell, anything goes.[23] Such an attitude is deeply rooted in mainstream "realist" thinking and in the conditions of conflict between deeply opposed antagonists, whether states, empires, races, or classes. Class war or racial war, carried on within the boundaries of a state, can be as extreme as war between states. The widespread acceptance of Machiavelli, Hobbes, and Clausewitz as our most helpful guides to political action suggests the legitimacy of a total war posture, which includes within it a terrorist ethos: whatever works, goes. This view of absolute struggle has been reinforced on the revolutionary side by the writings of Lenin, Frantz Fanon, and Sartre, each lauding the redeeming, even therapeutic, quality of revolutionary violence. Both revolutionaries and functionaries declare "war" on each other even if the struggle lacks a military character.

Here is the main point: we have for centuries been taught that what counts in war is winning, and that any effective tactic can be used. International law exists, but mainly to set mutually helpful limits and to avoid superfluous destruction and unnecessary cruelty. In the event of armed conflict, law is generally subordinated to military necessity. Hence, law has never had the potency to enforce its rules in the face of weaponry or tactics that seemed to give an overall advantage to a belligerent, including in relation to civilian morale, that is, by sheer destructive capacity. Wars are won and lost in the society as well as on the battlefield. Technological innovations have extended the domain of warfare throughout modern times, with the tendency to introduce new weaponry becoming more pronounced over time, although arguably reaching an outer limit in recent years. Submarines, aircraft, rockets, strategic bombing, and, of course, atomic bombs undermined earlier conceptions of legal restraint. Conventions governing treatment of prisoners and prohibitions on chemical and biological weapons seem to work generally quite well because neither side gains much from violating them, either because the issue is unconnected with the contest of force or because the specific weaponry cannot be effectively used on the battlefield.

A crucial breakdown of restraint in the character of warfare came at the turn of the nineteenth century with Napoleonic strategic innovations, mobilizing the society as a whole for combat and considering the morale and economic base of military strength as the key to victory and defeat. Once such a mobilization for war occurred on both sides, the whole civilian sector of the other society became a military target, and the distinctions upon which law and morality depend were largely eliminated.

Weapons of mass destruction play out the war game. To the extent a backlash of any sort occurs, it is on prudential grounds and in public attitudes that the process of sorting winners from losers in modern war is too costly even for the winning side.

But such a backlash does not include a repudiation of terrorism. Indeed, the rejection of modern war may be, and has been, accompanied by an expanded scope of terrorist operations, that is, a "total war" but on a smaller scale that does not imperil human survival, with symbolic targets and an economy of force, a new calculus of means/ends. On the revolutionary side, a terrorist assault is designed to provoke the collapse of the state, to arouse mass opposition to it, or to express opposition to authority, even futilely on occasion. On the functionary side, recourse to terrorism involves a range of undertakings by high-technology weaponry against civilian society and a series of efforts to destroy groups at home and abroad associated with revolutionary activities. It is both symbolic warfare par excellence and traditional belligerency, carried on without respect for innocence, and hence terroristic in its essence. This persistence of warfare in the nuclear age represents an attempted reconciliation of realism and the war system.

Only nuclearism itself stands as a partial exception. It represents a form of terrorism that is no longer fully consistent with some variants of political realism even for those who accept total war as inevitable in human affairs. The realist believes that states pursue their own interests by all means at their disposal, and that war is both a natural outcome of international conflict and an absolute contest of wills. Idealists do not disagree, but believe that global reform is feasible as well as desirable. Realists do not often doubt the desirability of reform, but they are skeptical of the willingness of states to diminish their sovereignty. Because nuclear weapons convert this war system into a pervasive threat of mutual suicide, even realists are convinced that general war must now be avoided (mutual deterrence) or the weaponry eliminated (disarmament). Hence, some prominent realists such as George Kennan and Robert McNamara believe that a process of denuclearization is both possible and necessary, not because they reject terrorism or the total war mentality, but because they assume a perspective of rationality. Reliance on nuclear weapons, even when only for deterrence, shatters means/ends relationships and draws into question the overall foundation of international relations.[24]

In contrast, an antiterrorist version of denuclearization would emphasize the religious, moral, and legal repudiation of weaponry that cannot be confined to military targets; that does disproportionate damage to any plausible battlefield end in view; and that inflicts cruel forms of suffering that extend far beyond the time and space dimensions of combat, genetic distortions to subsequent generations.[25]

The terrorist mind-set is dominated by its melodramatic preoccupation with the destruction of evil. It rejects self-doubt, ambiguity, human solidarity, moral and legal inhibition, constitutionalism. It is a law unto itself, and the bearer of some "higher morality" to be established later on. The modern world has nurtured a realist orthodoxy that limits political violence only by criteria of effectiveness and, for some, by the expectation of survival. In certain respects these limits of rational restraint are preferable to the purity of fundamentalists who employ terror for its own sake to enforce their vision against evil forces, no matter how self-destructive the consequences. In other respects, the fundamentalists acting out of conviction are more attractive than the realists as they seek a better world and are prepared to risk everything to realize their vision.

The terrorist mind-set lies latent in every societal setting. It may not be visible if the established order is generally perceived as legitimate. The revolutionary option may be virtually preempted by a totalitarian state that occupies the political space so completely as to preclude sustained opposition, at least for a certain period of time. In effect, functionary terror prevails over revolutionary terror in a stable totalitarian society.

Unfortunately, the cynicism of realism (there are no normative limits on political violence) and the extremism of fundamentalism (truth as perceived by us is alone correct and worth defending unto death) are prevalent in our world. The functionary and the revolutionary mind-sets both consist of a mixture of realist and fundamentalist thinking that leads naturally to the adoption of terrorist methods.

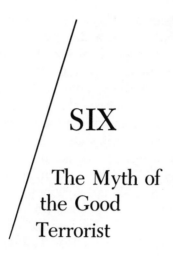

SIX

The Myth of the Good Terrorist

*Still it would be marvelous to terrify
a law clerk with a cut lily.*

PABLO NERUDA, "Walking Around"

Doris Lessing's novel *The Good Terrorist* is about a group of young English adults who put themselves at the service of the IRA and dedicate their lives to serving the cause of revolution and liberation. Or do they? Lessing portrays the characters in her novel as fugitives from society who have drifted, for one reason or another, into a role and posture that express their extreme alienation. The Irish cause to which they dedicate their lives is a pose. Their real animus is to wage war against society, and, more vividly, against their own parents, to avenge real and imagined wrongs of childhood. They adopt an underground life of terrorism haphazardly, to find meaning and excitement, to fulfill cravings for gratification. The quest for a satisfying life-style, amid anger and confusion, is played out in the form of an antifascist, antistate charade, but in the

95

end the excitement and actuality of violence result, producing the death of innocent victims and destruction.

This sense that the personal agenda of frustration and alienation is responsible for the turn toward terrorism underlies Lessing's ironic understanding of "the good terrorist." Yes, there are no selfish motives of a mercenary sort. Yes, a life of poverty and risk is voluntarily adopted. Yes, ideals based on genuine perceptions of injustice in English society and a real distaste for the British role in Northern Ireland are posited. Yet ultimately the reader is meant to be disturbed by the ethos of the terrorists: their search for personal excitement by disruptive, politically meaningless violence; their lack of compassion toward those who are leading ordinary lives; and their tendency to act out unresolved family dramas of dependence and rejection in which a persisting revolt against parental authority is carried on at the expense of society. And all this amid gross hypocrisy; alienated children seeking money and comfort from the old bourgeois parental homestead while waging war against the bourgeois society that sustains them. The personal becomes the political, each embodying the contradictions of the other.

But we mean something else when we endorse a specific variant of political violence that is carried on without deference to norms of legality and morality. There is a sense of identification at a distance with the undertaking or project that includes a refusal to face up to the terrorist quality of the activity. The manipulation of language is relied upon to provide us with an image of the good terrorist. The language of liberation, freedom, and patriotism is currently used by propagandists of various persuasion, whereas earlier patterns of justification were associated with devotion to mystery cults and expressed religious conviction.[1] The imagery of the good terrorist thrives on the distance between the abstractions of apologists and the concreteness of violent deeds.

In a typical document of the mainstream antiterrorist campaign, the Final Report of the Working Group on Terrorism of the North Atlantic Assembly (an organization that links parliamentarians and the NATO leadership) there is a discussion of why "the label 'terrorist' . . . has ethical and legal implications which some are loath to see applied to proponents of a cause they support."[2] The good terrorist is set apart as a freedom fighter; the distinction between terrorist and freedom fighter is validated by reference to an alleged contrast in behavior:

> There are, however, clear differences between freedom fighters and terrorists. Freedom fighters are soldiers, albeit irregular ones, who wage war against regular military forces. They do not attack civilians. Terrorists on the other hand deliberately select the innocent as their target.[3]

Yet, in practice, the terminology of freedom fighter and terrorist seems to follow from patterns of political alignment and does not consistently reflect different styles of armed struggle.

A good contemporary example is the gap between the romantic rhetoric of those who endorse the Contras as "good terrorists" and the treacherous actuality of their deeds and life histories. In Ronald Reagan's words, "the freedom fighters of Nicaragua" are waging a struggle that "promises to give freedom a second chance" after its betrayal by the Sandinistas:

> You see, when the Sandinistas betrayed the revolution, many who had fought the old Somoza dictatorship literally took to the hills and, like the French Resistance that fought the Nazis, began fighting the Soviet-bloc Communists and the Nicaraguan collaborators. These few have now been joined in struggle by thousands of other Nicaraguans.[4]

The language of deception here is quite artful even aside from the issues of the normative quality of the Contra violence. It is not correct that the early cadres of the Contra cause were recruited from those who had earlier fought against Somoza. On the contrary, the mainstays of the recruitment were the remnants of Somoza's National Guard.

Further, for Reagan to associate the Contra cause with the French Resistance against the Nazis is to invoke a revered past that seems without any true relevance to the struggle over the future of Nicaragua. The French Resistance formed as a reaction to a cruel form of foreign occupation that coincided with an international war pitting fascism against a coalition of antifascist forces. By no stretch of even the right-wing imagination is Nicaragua an occupied country. The Sandinistas have, in fact, greatly loosened the hold of foreign countries upon Nicaragua, and the notion of Soviet-bloc subordination is absurd hype. At most, there exists a measure of Soviet and Cuban logistical support, but there is also a strong resolve in Managua to sustain the essentially nationalist character of the Sandinista experience. To describe those serving the government in Managua as "Nicaraguan collaborators" of the Soviet Union is to magnify the distortion.

Without recounting instances, we now have countless reports of Contra atrocities and of tactics that are directed toward spreading fear among the civilian population in the Nicaraguan countryside by violent and cruel acts against peasants and village officials. And there is little indication of Contra capacity or willingness to engage the military forces of the Sandinistas. The United States government, by virtue of the close connection with the Contra cause as a major CIA operation, was fully aware of these patterns of practice and indeed encouraged such patterns.[5] Numerous media accounts and investigative studies establish beyond reasonable doubt the terroristic character of Contra activity.[6]

In the background, of course, are the Washington functionaries at various levels of government that sponsor the Contra cause. Even without the aggravating circumstances of ignoring congressional will, as expressed by the Boland amendment, official undertakings of support cannot be reconciled with the most fundamental standards of international law. The World Court has determined by a decisive majority that most aspects of the United States government support for the Contras violate international law. As a member of the United Nations the United States is obligated to respect such a decision.[7] As these obligations relate to uses of force in a foreign setting they involve potential crimes of state in the

Nuremberg sense.[8] Individuals engaged in such conduct remain obligated, whether or not they acted under color of domestic law and in response to orders from superiors.

And yet, the good terrorist banner is waved by functionaries to validate their dedication to the Contras. In this vein, Lieutenant Colonel North is depicted as a hero and patriot carrying on a noble effort, a characterization that took hold with the American people. Appearing before the congressional hearings on the Iran/Contra matter, Robert W. Owen, "a foot soldier" working to assure delivery of money solicited from various sources to the Contra leadership, requested permission from the committee to conclude his testimony with a poem of undisclosed authorship. A short excerpt reveals the halo of the good terrorist hovering above the head of Lieutenant Colonel North:

> We have held in our arms children no more than four years of age who'd been shot while trying to flee Nicaragua to a safe haven.
> We have a burning desire to strike back at those whose intent is to enslave us and to try and stem the red tide that threatens to overwhelm us. . . .
> Fear, anguish and despair are with us daily.
> Yet in our darkest hours we have three things that help sustain us:
>> Our faith is God Almighty;
>> The love and support of our families
>> The knowledge that on this troubled earth there still walk men like Ollie North. . . .
> For the future, you are giving our children a chance to live as free individuals.
> And for these things we say thank you, Ollie North.[9]

Owen concludes with a final flourish of his own: "And I can only add that I love Ollie North like a brother and I believe when he comes before you and he's allowed to tell the American people his side of the story, that he will do it honestly." It is evident that passion can exist on the functionary side as well as on the revolutionary side—indeed, that the political drama represents the unfolding of a morality play. But does that make Ollie North a genuinely good terrorist (i.e., someone acting within a framework of moral and legal limits) or only one more surrogate of "the good terrorist" (i.e., someone failing to protect innocence under the pretext, possibly sincerely, even fanatically accepted, of a justifying cause), a figure whose delusions and partisanship are unwittingly dedicated to spreading violence directed at the innocent?

The claim to be engaged on behalf of good terrorists, even if sincere, does not remove political violence from the stigma of terrorism unless two tests are satisfied: that one avoid direct targeting of those who are innocent; that one respect prevailing standards of international law and generally accepted notions of morality. The championship of the Contras fails both tests and fails them miserably.

Let's approach the issue differently. One of the witnesses in the Klaus Barbie trial in Lyons, Michel Godot Goldberg, testified about his decision *not* to kill Barbie in revenge for his crimes as a Nazi. Goldberg, whose father had been rounded up on February 9, 1943, by the Gestapo unit in Lyons headed by Barbie and shipped off to his death at Auschwitz, discovered by accident that Barbie was living in Bolivia under an acquired identity. He also discovered that the Bolivian government was unwilling to extradite Barbie to face criminal charges in France.

On this basis, Goldberg went off to Bolivia to kill Barbie. He had identified someone guilty of extreme criminality by both international legal and moral standards. That person was being shielded from criminal prosecution by the Bolivian government. There was no apparent way, at the time, to arrange for the sort of legal process subsequently constituted in France.

Beyond this, there were powerful motivating factors. There was a special quality of suffering associated with the absence of tangible remains of the victims. Goldberg testified, "Our deaths are abstract deaths. We have no coffins, no corpses, no cemeteries. We were deprived even in our grief."[10] And Goldberg himself as a child was only spared by a capricious decision by his mother not to let him go out on the streets of Lyons that particular wintry day because he had no snow boots.

Goldberg pursued Barbie to Bolivia, encountered him, and abandoned his plan: "I met him. I found him contemptible; I found him full of contradictions. . . . I just didn't feel enough hatred inside of me. . . . I decided that we simply belonged to two different races of men."[11]

Such a process of moral reasoning is quite idiosyncratic in an ambiguous situation. Barbie is certainly not "innocent," although in a civil society he is entitled to a presumption of innocence, a day in court, a defense against charges. Yet, here, the prosecution of Barbie was evidently being obstructed by the Bolivian government, creating an impression that only a private initiative could inflict a suitable punishment. The Bolivian "shield" was inappropriate as those substantially accused of crimes against humanity should not be exempted from extradition. Given the enormity of Barbie's crimes and the clear identification of Barbie as perpetrator, the case for private action seems strong.

At the same time, for an individual, acting on his own, to carry out an execution under even these circumstances seems questionable. Many of us believe that capital punishment is *never* appropriate, even if the accused is given the benefit of full and fair legal protection. Besides, Barbie, however horrible his past offenses, was not a menace or engaged in ongoing harmful activity, although evidently he had earlier given several Latin American dictatorships advice on repressive techniques. Goldberg's motivation was to settle scores from the past. Such a motivation is not totally without its social rationale, as the expression of such enmity by an individual such as Goldberg sends a message to others that crimes against humanity, no matter how long past, are not forgiven or even forgivable. Yet in the end Goldberg's claim to be a good terrorist in the event he had gone ahead and killed Barbie must be rejected. We need to confine our acceptance of such political violence to those instances where the targeted individual is doing active harm or actively and plausibly threatening to do harm, and governmental authorities are unwilling or unable to act. Otherwise, the proper role of government to provide individuals with complete protection against violence becomes seriously eroded.[12] Furthermore, as developments in the Barbie case illustrate, a change in the government of Bolivia altered policy on his extradition, which enabled a major trial under positive auspices to take place in Lyons. Now, instead of a debate about whether an individual act of vengeance is justifiable, the full drama and disclosure of a comprehensive trial are presented, providing a vehicle of political education for the whole range of crimes of state committed by Barbie and the Nazis in the World War II period.[13]

The strong case for the good terrorist is, of course, an intervention against an active perpetrator of ongoing or imminent crimes. The argument can be made on either side of the state/society equation in a variety of circumstances, actual and hypothetical. An intelligence service plans a covert operation to kill those who torture or order torture in a foreign country or to assassinate the head of state of a government engaged in persecution or genocide. Even more compelling is action taken to prevent an anticipated recourse to nuclear weaponry. The scenarios for violent action supporting peace and justice can be spun out endlessly. Yet there are grounds for skepticism, as well.

It is possible to approve retrospectively of actual decisions to adopt violent methods for laudable ends because the grounds for such claims are quite easy to evaluate. Perhaps the most famous instance is the failed plot in 1944 to kill Hitler led by Count Stauffenberg. Had Hitler been killed, the perpetrators would have been praised for their courage and for their contributions to humanity. If the assassination had led, as intended, to a complete change in German policy, bringing World War II to an immediate end, then the decision to act would have received the widest possible endorsement.

THE MYTH OF THE GOOD TERRORIST

Such a positive evaluation would be given by most antiterrorists even if the plans that culminated in Hitler's assassination included killing his guards and even if large numbers of "innocent" bystanders perished. Such an assessment would be made whenever a tyrant or dictator was removed from the scene through a deliberate plan of action. If the target is more obscure, say a police official accused of torture, then vengeance becomes more problematic. The Costa-Gavras film *State of Siege* explores these issues in the setting of the seizure and eventual assassination of an American official in a South American country who has been associated with encouraging the government to rely on torture. The film is apparently based on an interpretation of an actual incident that had occurred in Uruguay and is intended to arouse a positive identification with guerrilla tactics, regarding the climactic killing as a justifiable execution of an evil person. The guerrillas are portrayed as genuinely good terrorists—idealistic patriots struggling to bring social and political justice to a country held in militarist thralldom as a result of a coalition between local reactionary forces and Washington.

Is this kind of imagery propaganda by the Left with no objective status? It could be. The real test has as its basis an impartial reconstruction of the facts. For a good terrorist political violence is a last resort, is necessary to prevent even greater evils, and is directed at the source of wrongdoing with as much precision and care as possible. There is, however, a contradiction: implicit in the concept of the good terrorist is the renunciation of terrorism. If conditions that make a violent undertaking acceptable are satisfied, then such violence is not terrorism even if it involves contravention of domestic law; it is norm-constrained violence. Thus, even assassinations are not necessarily terrorism.

At the same time, neither functionaries nor revolutionaries should be entrusted with a blank check. Self-serving interpretations that circumstances warrant violent action are very suspect. From the detached view of social policy, a claim to intervene violently, in light of necessity, and qualify as "good" terrorism, must overcome a strong presumption against claims to engage in political violence. There is no such political animal, in reality, as the good terrorist. Individuals and groups who reasonably conclude there is no effective nonviolent alternative in situations of stress and danger cannot be considered terrorists by my definition if they confine their violence to appropriate targets.

THE ETHICAL NUCLEARIST

An important variant on the theme of the good terrorist is the defense intellectual or government official who sets forth an ethical rationale for the use of nuclear weapons. To classify these weapons of mass destruction as terrorist is to express the considered judgment that threats or uses of nuclear weapons are crimes against humanity, and that their large-scale use involves severe risks to human survival and inflicts catastrophic harm upon societies that are not parties to whatever conflict gives rise to nuclear war. These third countries are placed at ultimate risk despite their status as pure bystanders. Reliance on nuclear threats repudiates the inhibition on violence against the innocent.

Nowhere has the reliance on abstractions been of greater service to the functionary than in the effort over the years to reconcile nuclearism with some affirmation of ethical standards. Strategic discourse, its mystifying language of deterrence, helps disguise the terror from the terrorist, making the issue one of word play, offsetting numbers, and hypothetical responses. Even the prospect of human extinction is assimilated into the abstractions of nuclear theorists and the security obsessions of political and military leaders. A feature of this style of distancing is to avoid the concreteness of Hiroshima: the imagery of total destruction and the anguished voices of survivors. The strategists also evade the issues of medical effects or the apocalyptic scenery of a destroyed planet. Understanding, reasoning, and recommendations are based on cold logic and war games, in their essence technocratic adjustments of the mind to the terrorist undertaking, perhaps combined with such illusions as the assumption that technology cannot be eliminated from use once invented and that state interests as defined by current leaders provide an absolute justification for violence and destruction. It is undeniable, of course, that technological momentum, reinforced by the war mentality, makes it exceedingly difficult to get rid of a weapon once it is developed and deployed. At the same time, technology is subject to societal control and is not an autonomous force, however much it may appear to be. Human freedom entails the responsibility to control that which imperils survival, and this can be done in a variety of ways, including establishing social and political arrangements to eliminate forever the technology in question. As with all arrangements, these would be fallible and might fail, but what is assured is that we are not precluded by the supposed irreversibility of technological momentum from making a heroic effort to do just that—to "disinvent" nuclear weaponry.

It is not uncharacteristic of the calculation of revolutionaries that the deliberate killing of Olympic athletes or airport tourists is justified as a suitable way of gaining an audience for grievances long ignored or shunted aside. The calculating mind is capable of any atrocity selected as a means once the end in view is postulated as a virtual absolute—the sanctity of the revolutionary cause, the security of the sovereign state.

Consider Joseph Nye's attempt at nuclearist reasonableness: "We can give survival of the species a very high priority without giving it the paralyzing status of an absolute value. Some degree of risk is unavoidable if individuals or societies are to avoid paralysis and enhance the quality of life beyond mere survival."[14] The epitome of this style of moral reasoning is its role as a justification for reliance on nuclear deterrence despite the element of risk to future generations:

the acceptance of risk to preserve values other than survival does not do an injustice to future generations. On the principle of equal access to values, and given the fact that there is no harm to identifiable individuals (since they do not yet exist), there is no reason to assume that future generations would make survival an absolute value and not wish to take proportionate risks to ensure their access to culture and political freedoms.[15]

Underneath this kind of enterprise of reassurance is the conviction that nuclear weapons, if properly managed, contribute to peace and stability in the world and can be legitimately relied upon in diplomacy. The ethical nuclearist believes that these threats to survival have prevented World War III, inhibited Soviet challenges, and helped maintain United States interests in the world. These weapons, in any event, can't be disinvented, so the argument runs, and the desirable stance is not nuclear renunciation but learning to live with nuclear weapons.[16]

The good nuclearist goes further, counseling the prince to confine these weapons to military targets, as if such containment were possible. Such reasoning is a kind of response to the argument that the weapons, by attacking indiscriminately, violate moral and legal limitations on the use of force.[17] Another normative attempt is to develop a framework of restraint that acknowledges the special dangers of nuclear weapons while accepting their utility. Normative guidelines, or maxims, are set forth and explained. Once again it is Joseph Nye who seems to perform this task most successfully, setting forth with considerable elaboration what he calls "Five Maxims of Nuclear Ethics":

1. Self-defense is a just but limited cause.
2. Never treat nuclear weapons as normal weapons.
3. Minimize harm to innocent people.
4. Reduce risks of nuclear war in the near term.
5. Reduce reliance on nuclear weapons over time.[18]

Such a nuclearist stance is to be preferred to an outright embrace of nuclear war or first-strike options. At the same time, the maxims impose no fixed inhibitions such as renunciation of first-use options or commitment to enact in good faith and suitable prudence a process of total denuclearization.

Even the vague injunction to "reduce reliance" implies a continued reliance for the indefinite future.

This kind of moderate nuclearism that has been generated in the last several years at Harvard University can be seen as a response to both the nuclear abolitionists who insist upon a world without nuclear weapons and the nuclear-war advocates who seek to drive the Soviet Union into bankruptcy or surrender by stepping up the nuclear arms race. The Harvard identity is expressed by their choice of the owl as a preferred alternative to both dove and hawk, presumably an expression of wisdom and choice in contrast to preset peacemindedness and compulsive belligerence.

The real issue here is whether the nuclear owl is a nuclear terrorist. Perhaps the owl's status as a kind of hawk provides a decisive clue. It is acceptable to argue that getting rid of nuclear weapons is more dangerous than keeping them or to contend that the Soviet Union would have the geopolitical edge in a world without nuclear weapons. Yet this kind of argument avoids the issue of whether reliance on nuclear weapons is not a species of terrorism and must be rejected from the perspective of antiterrorism even if there might result some additional risks for those who renounced the nuclear option. We would not accept from the revolutionary side of the debate on political violence arguments based on the efficacy of terrorist tactics as providing acceptable justifications. Similarly, there is no reason to be persuaded that reliance on nuclear weapons is acceptable because efficacious. What seems most disturbing here is the realization that the state can rely on terrorist methods of the most extreme sort if it seems convenient to do so without generating much public distress. What distress is expressed is not associated with the terrorist properties of nuclear weaponry, but with the realization that their use is likely to be catastrophic for the user and that it might even imperil the survival of the species. Although these arguments are of great consequence, they are not repudiations of terrorism as such.

Reliance on nuclear weapons is terrorism per se. Increasingly, legal and moral assessments of nuclear weapons regard them unconditionally unacceptable as instruments of war for the following reasons: they are indiscriminate; they result in disproportionate damage; they are poisonous; and they produce acute pain and suffering. To retain possession of these weapons as a hedge against threats by others, at least during an interim period of search for a reliable disarming framework, seems more acceptable, although policies surrounding their potential use still violate strictures against terrorism.

These conclusions as to terrorism are based on the properties of the weapons and targeting plans governing their probable use.[19] The scale of destruction, given routine reliance on warheads from five to more than fifty times the magnitude of the Hiroshima bomb, suggests the absurdity of the claim to confine damage to military targets. Besides, dense civilian settlement and military targets that are considerably intermingled in modern societies, especially in and near urbanized sectors make discriminate use virtually impossible. Also, the fallout produces radiation sickness, genetic abnormalities, and food contamination at great distances from the point of impact, causing harm without respect for sovereign rights and political boundaries.

If terror centrally involves causing symbolic and actual fear, then nuclear weapons are terror weapons. The threat of nuclear war and preparations for it induce widespread fear, even if they are not used, although its extent and depth is the subject of controversy. That the complete removal of such fear may be difficult at this stage is a troublesome truism, undoubtedly suggesting "a tragic predicament." But it is not helpful for these ethical nuclearists to reassure politicians and policymakers that this most destructive form of terrorism is somehow all right, if it is only undertaken by governments that accord due seriousness to a series of unspecified efforts to minimize harm to those who are innocent. The wielder of nuclear weapons is a terrorist even if these arguments proceeding from reason and utility can be appreciated as masterpieces of concealment.

In the end, the issue of choice, and of ethics, involves the limits appropriate to reliance on political violence. Nuclear weapons cause even defensive claims to burst necessarily the limits of discrimination and proportionality, leading some astute observers to question whether nuclear weapons should even be conceived of as weapons.[20] Because of the excessiveness of the violence, its lack of normative justification, and the presumption that exposure induces fear and anxiety even if no immediate, direct injury results, the ethical nuclearist cannot avoid the taint of being just one more "good terrorist."

I think that many of those who embrace terrorism are virtuous in many respects—kind, careful, sincere, even sympathetic—and that their outlook is such that the terrorist option seems to them the only practical one. Such tendencies seem to be common at both sides of the political spectrum: those who challenge the state and those who uphold its prerogatives. The attractiveness of terrorism is linked to several facets of technology: its awesome destructive potential, its symbolic status as expressive of power, and its provision of weapons for both the strong and the weak.

Those who choose violence in extremis to engage in armed struggle, to stage a coup, or to kill a tyrant are not terrorists. Their violence is limited and selective, their claims backed up by prevailing moral traditions. By and large, up to this time, the antiapartheid movement is a legitimate armed struggle, even if some of its tactics are terroristic in design and execution (for example, bombs in public meeting places, necklacing or executing suspected informers in African townships by placing a tire over their heads, soaking it with gasoline, and setting it on fire). It is crucial to condemn and reject these practices if the validity of an underlying recourse to armed struggle is to be sustained.

By my understanding, there are no good terrorists. The image is a myth that generates obfuscation whether invoked by revolutionary or functionary. There are, however, good counterterrorists, those who do combat to contain, prevent, and punish terrorism without themselves resorting to terrorism. The good counterterrorist is appalled by the specter of violence directed against those who are innocent and by violence unleashed without respect for the limits of law and morality. The methods of the good counterterrorist range from persuasion and peaceful settlement to restricted and defensive violence designed to protect society against terrorism, whether emanating from revolutionary or functionary sources.

SEVEN

Why Iran?
Why Libya?
Iran/Contra Revelations
and Terror Networks

Cruelty has a human heart, and
Jealousy a human face;
Terror the Human Form Divine;
And Secrecy the Human Dress.

—WILLIAM BLAKE, "A Divine Image"

There is a virtually forgotten side of *Rambo,* the relationship to the bureaucratic expression of government. Most attention has been given to Rambo as demonical war hero shooting up Vietnamese and their Soviet controllers. But Rambo's encounters with Murdoch, the bureaucratic overseer of the rescue operation, are far more revealing. Virtue is associated with the Special Forces leader, a Green Beret, named Colonel Trautmann in the movie. Trautmann is patriotic, clear about the location of evil in the world, and unconditionally loyal to his men and to America. What Rambo discovers is that the covert operations bureaucrat is tied into Washington's abstract concerns in a world of corrupt politics and human indifference, and that these concerns take precedence in the way government policy is carried out even if it means leaving American soldiers to languish on distant battlefields.

Murdoch lies about his war record, is unconcerned about the rescue of Americans allegedly held in cruel captivity by the Vietnamese, and is mainly mindful of how his actions will play back in Washington. The bureaucrat is seen as lacking loyalty, courage, and conviction and yet being in control. Rambo's life is more jeopardized by this dependence on political backup than by his numerous bloody encounters in the Vietnamese jungle. The struggle to liberate American virtue from this bureaucratic stranglehold is both a reenactment of the Vietnam War and the core meaning of the Iran/Contra revelations. Put differently, for a brief, glorious interlude, Rambo and Trautmann managed to get the upper hand, took over the National Security Council, and implemented a foreign policy that enabled support for friends, death for enemies, and no interference from the corrupt, cowardly, and confused politicians and bureaucrats. The acceptance, although grudging, by Reagan of the Tower Commission Report and its congressional sequel represented the reassertion of control by the bureaucrats. Rambo is once more out in the cold, just as his real-life and more talented counterpart, Oliver North, seems destined to be, but not without a hero's farewell.

There is another aspect of *Rambo* that is surprisingly suggestive. Apparently, the original script called for the death of Rambo, expressive of the death of this kind of American myth of heroic individualism. Sylvester Stallone decided he didn't want to die at the end of the movie, nor did he want the myth to be dead. The screenwriter objected, and it was decided to film both endings, and let the reaction of test audiences decide. As audiences overwhelmingly preferred that Rambo walk away alive, available for yet another sequel, the ending sustains rather than quells the myth. As recounted, this anecdote, whether apocryphal or not, contains a tantalizing bit of ambiguity: did Stallone as performer act primarily from mercenary motives—seeking the option of *Rambo III, IV*, ad infinitum—or from ideological, aesthetic, commercial motives pertaining to the structure of *Rambo II*. We will never know, as even a direct response by Stallone would be quite suspect. Again in the Irangate setting, the mixture of mercenary, ideological, and managerial motives is probably impossible to untangle and may vary from performer to performer. Until further notice each applies significantly. All important public occurrences seem, in the end, to be overdetermined. Reducing explanations to the true motive usually reveals more about the outlook of the interpreter than the object being interpreted.

Underneath the Iran disclosures are several very elusive puzzles. In the foreground is the realization that Iran was directly encouraging the most extreme forms of anti-American terrorism, especially the seizure of random hostages in Lebanon. More than this, Iran's public posture was virulently anti-American, portraying the United States quite literally as the Great Satan, and there never was any solid basis for supposing that moderate factions existed in the Khomeini regime or that, if they did, receipt of arms from official representatives of the U.S. government would help their cause rather than discredit them. It seems quite likely that the Iranians were toying with the Americans, perhaps seeking arms, but certainly not risking any genuine endorsement of moderation.[1] And then, of course, to obtain arms, given the Iranian drift of the Iraq/Iran War by 1985, seemed much more likely to strengthen the hand of those in Tehran demanding an Iranian victory than that of those disposed to a negotiated compromise. Such retrospective comments can often be discounted as grandstanding, but here the proclaimed tactics seem so manifestly implausible as to question either their sincerity or the competence of those who advocated the Iranian initiative.

Why, then, seek some kind of influence in Tehran, but forego even the most ardent peace overtures being forwarded by Managua? The Sandinista diplomacy has been remarkably mild, even forthcoming to an astonishing degree. As Carlos Tunnermann, the Nicaraguan ambassador to the United Nations, has expressed matters: "Nicaragua is prepared to sign treaties that would assure compliance with a halt to importation of arms, removal of all foreign military advisers and a prohibition on foreign bases in Central American countries."[2] Nicaragua has consistently offered to shift their conflict with the United States to a diplomatic setting either under the auspices of the Contadora process, by way of a Central American peace process, or through bilateral relations. Why would not the Reagan leadership sign such agreements and point to the outcome as a sign of its diplomatic success in the region? After all, the task of drumming up congressional and public support for the Contras has never been easy nor altogether successful and in the aftermath of the disclosures may turn out to be virtually impossible.[3] The Reagan leadership withdrew quickly and adroitly from Lebanon in 1983, without political repercussions, despite suffering considerable loss of American lives by hostile political forces. Why was it so easy for the White House to shift commitments in Lebanon with great flexibility and yet it was seemingly impossible to do so in Central America? Tentative answers to these questions shed light on the true character of the terrorist menace at this stage.

The unfolding story of the Iran/Contra proceedings revealed shifting patterns of disclosure and suppression. Even after two sets of elaborate governmental inquiries, many observers remain in doubt as to vital elements of the whole story—What exactly was the president's role at various stages both as assessed by actual knowledge and mandate to subordinates? What were the links of the operatives within and without government to organized crime, especially to large-scale drug dealing? The official explanations do help us comprehend the underlying tensions in American foreign policy, especially as these pertain to the role and character of covert operations. At issue is not the willingness to engage in covert action, but the locus of bureaucratic responsibility for its execution and the degree to which the means and ends of a covert operation should conform to American values and to the general drift of overt foreign policy. In the foreground, as well, is a raging debate as the respective roles of the Executive and Congress in relation to the authorization and supervision of covert operations.

The changing character of the United States–Iran relationship, as well as its underlying continuity during the post-1945 period, tells us much about the many-faceted character of terrorism, and the confusing and shifting identity of victim and perpetrator, revolutionary and functionary. Overall, it is an occasion for mixed responses: fascination, empathy, and, finally, bewilderment. Iran is one more instance of a non-Western country in which the United States has sunk deep roots quickly, ignorantly, cynically, and with generally disastrous results for both countries.

My own preoccupation with Iran began in the mid-1970s, following on a decade of opposition to American policies in Indochina. I was disturbed by the repressive character of the Shah's regime, as well as by the enthusiasm in Washington for Iran's mode of modernizing development. As well, it seemed troublesome that a government at odds with its people should also be the scene of deep American military involvement. There were some forty-five thousand Americans in Iran, mainly involved in servicing the Shah's excessive war machine and in producing arms. I was influenced to some extent by lurid accounts of torture told by middle-class Iranian college students in the United States who seemed to agree on little except their hatred of the Shah.

When Carter entered the White House at the beginning of 1977 there were many early signs of a more enlightened United States foreign policy, especially a stress on promoting human rights overseas. Running contrary to this pattern, however, was an announcement that William Sullivan was Carter's choice to be ambassador to Iran. Sullivan symbolized everything I opposed during the Vietnam years. As ambassador to Laos during the late 1960s, Sullivan had reportedly taken a personal daily role in the selection of bombing targets, a program of calculated destruction that wiped out many villages in northeastern Laos. Sullivan deceived Congress about the character of the U.S. military effort in Laos and exemplified a new style of ugly American—the counterinsurgency diplomat. Even General Westmoreland, no bleeding heart, noted in his memoirs that William Sullivan (and Graham Martin) were too militarist for him. As he put it, when referring to Sullivan and his hawkish counterpart in Cambodia, "the power they held turned them into field marshals."[4]

After Laos, and a role in the Vietnam negotiations, Sullivan had been sent to the Philippines in 1972 and there encouraged Marcos to stiffen martial law as a way to achieve the sort of discipline needed to attract overseas capital. Such diplomacy represented, it seemed to me, a kind of cruel and shortsighted anticommunism that relied on violence directed at the citizenry and placed a positive value on repressive order. I volunteered to testify against Sullivan's appointment at confirmation hearings held by the U.S. Senate Foreign Relations Committee. After my appearance, several respected Democratic party members of the committee took me aside and said, "We agree with you, but we can't go against Carter this early. We'll lose our credibility!" In retrospect, my disappointment with these politicians resembles in a way Rambo's discontent with Washington bureaucrats.

In the years that have ensued, Iran has tumbled from one form of terrorist rule to another with the United States doing a bewildered and embarrassing dance in the background. What emerges in the most recent period, however, is a pattern of terror on terror, with little regard for the integrity of U.S. constitutional democracy, human rights, sovereignty, and even common sense.

Intriguingly, the United States' deep involvement in Iran goes back at least as far as 1953, when the CIA helped restore the Shah to the Peacock Throne and, at the same time, replace Britain as the main foreign power. Earlier in 1946–1947, the slowness of Soviet withdrawal from northern Iran and apparent efforts by Soviet agents to foment the formation of a separatist state in the Iranian border province of Azerbaijan contributed to a consensus in Washington that a global rivalry with the Soviet Union was inevitable in the postwar world now that fascism had been defeated in Europe. Iran was early defined as a vital stake in the Central Asian phase of the cold war, mainly because of the presence of oil, but also as the result of an appreciation of Iran as a gateway to the Persian Gulf and a crucial link between the Arab and Indic regions of Asia.

These concerns surfaced in the early 1950s when antimonarchical sentiments in Iran converged with ardent economic nationalism. A secular and nationalist movement led by Muhammed Mossadegh challenged the Shah and British control of Iran's oil wealth. Mossadegh, emotional and dedicated, took a dramatic step in 1951—nationalizing the British-dominated Anglo-Iranian Oil Company—on the grounds that it was depriving Iran of its proper share of the oil wealth. The British retaliated with a naval blockade to prevent Iran from exporting oil and a global propaganda campaign to discredit Mossadegh's competence, drawing into question even his sanity. These efforts, together with Iranian discontent on both the Left and Right, produced considerable economic and political instability in Iran.

In this setting, the United States and Britain agreed to act clandestinely to protect their interests. The United States government may have been influenced by intelligence reports that Mossadegh was paving the way for a Communist takeover in Iran and was planning to turn to Moscow for a loan, as well as contemplating a strategic alliance. At this stage, in 1953, the CIA entrusted Kermit Roosevelt, grandson of Theodore Roosevelt, with management of a covert operation code named *Operation Ajax*. The plan was to encourage a coup d'état by mobilizing anti-Mossadegh forces, especially the religious Right and the army. Spending only about $200,000, Operation Ajax was at the time considered a complete success; the Shah returned from a brief exile; Mossadegh was imprisoned; the oil industry was restored to private Western ownership (a consortium in which the American companies acquired 40 percent, and the British share was reduced from 100 percent to 40 percent); and the structure of an authoritarian state was deliberately created. The CIA took a leading role in the creation and training of the SAVAK, Iran's dreaded secret police that operated overseas and at home, and was deeply implicated in systematic torture on a large scale, supposedly to assure that the Shah could retain power for the indefinite future.

In this process, the United States government deployed a new type of tactic in the struggle for control of the international order emerging out of the ruins of World War II. It was cheap, secret, and effective. Note that the United States not only restored a pro-Western reactionary ruler to his throne but also assured the repression of domestic radical political forces, succeeded in displacing the British from economic primacy, and obtained bases for a military buildup and intelligence operations. Iran became a model country in the central cold war effort to contain Soviet expansion with a ring of staunchly anticommunist governments. From 1953 onward the CIA intervention paid dividends beyond America's wildest dreams. Henry Kissinger in his memoirs singles out the Shah for praise as "that rarest of leaders: an unconditional ally."

Well, what has this tale to do with terrorism? Everything and nothing. The whole chain of events seems to be a matter of geopolitics and state interests. It can be described by those familiar abstractions: containment, stability, responsible rule. Mossadegh was regarded in the West as a hysteric who would lead Iran to economic ruin and, hence, into the Soviet orbit. His overthrow was seen as no loss by informed world opinion at the time and was regarded as a boon for the Iranian people.

Yet here is the rub: To carry out this policy the American embassy became a nerve center for illegal and violent actions against a legal and constitutional government. To assure that the Shah and a Western orientation would not be soon again challenged from below, it was felt necessary to help set up police and paramilitary capabilities to control political opposition in Iran. Also, it was deemed desirable to help the Shah exercise unlimited power. Dynastic absolutism produced widespread corruption and cruelty over time and by the late 1970s generated a revolutionary backlash that swept aside all that stood in its way and produced a tidal wave of virulent anti-Americanism that has yet to recede.

Kermit Roosevelt proudly recounts the Shah's triumphal return to Tehran in 1953 and proudly reports the famous toast the Shah offered at the start of the first royal reception: "I owe my throne to God, my people, my army—and to you!" Roosevelt continues, "He picked up his glass and raised it, as if in a toast, to me. I raised mine in return, and we both drank."[5] This is heady stuff even for a Roosevelt descendent! Perhaps such gloating was exaggerated. No independent source has confirmed this toast, but the sense of acknowledgment claimed by Roosevelt seems plausible and sincere.

The CIA role involved the United States as complicit in overturning the constitutional order of Iranian internal politics, thereby depriving the Iranian people of their sovereign rights of independence and self-determination. It associated the United States prominently with such deprivation. And it associated the United States with the deliberate institutionalization of an apparatus of state terror to secure these gains. Even if the Shah had retained his health and throne, the United States would have achieved and sustained its foreign policy goals in Iran by way of state-sponsored terrorism. And note that United States sponsorship prevailed not just in 1953, to get rid of Mossadegh and put the Shah in control, but as a permanent feature of Iranian governance. Iran was even described in subsequent years by Washington insiders as falling within the diplomatic jurisdiction of the CIA. This linkage was reinforced in 1973, when Richard Helms left his job as director of the CIA (1966–1973) to become ambassador to Iran (1973–1977). And then even liberal Jimmy Carter felt obliged to sustain this orientation by putting a diplomat notable for counterinsurgency credentials, William Sullivan, in the embassy at Tehran. Up until the fall of the Shah in early 1979, the United States did not loosen its terrorist embrace of the Iranian governing process.

Even at the end, the story involved state-sponsored terrorism, but this time of an ineffectual character. The United States government desperately counseled the Shah to take firm steps against unarmed demonstrators. Carter and Brzezinski interrupted the Camp David negotiations on the Middle East to telephone their support for "the bloody Friday" massacre in Jaleh Square, when General Ali Gholam Oveissi ordered troops to turn machine guns onto a crowd of thousands caught in one of Tehran's most enclosed public squares during a demonstration in September 1978. Later on, the White House assigned General Robert E. "Dutch" Huyser, deputy commander of NATO, to search for a way to induce the military to reverse the course of popular revolution by seizing the reins of power, apparently without reference to the human costs to the Iranian people.[6] Only the political abstractions counted!

It is against this background of ferment and agitation that the subsequent phases of terrorism must be seen. Evidently, when the Shah was first admitted to the United States, Khomeini had no objections.[7] Later, when radical students protested in Tehran, the political potential in Iran of anti-Americanism became evident. The embassy seizure on November 4, 1979, holding the diplomatic staff hostage until the day of Ronald Reagan's inauguration, January 21, 1981, was a traumatizing experience for the American people. Carter's confused handling of the incident, according it a prominence that accentuated American helplessness, fanned flames of frustration in the United States. It now seems possible that Carter's problems might have been complicated by a preelection deal between representatives of the Republican party and the Khomeini regime to hold on to hostages until the next presidential inauguration, in exchange for which Iran would be sold arms.[8] The media seized upon the theatrical potential of the human drama, giving nightly accounts, including recurrent footage of virulently anti–United States demonstrations on the street that ran by the embassy. Evidently, the demonstrators would heat up their protests to fever pitch whenever the TV cameras were rolling.

The iconography of these happenings during the hostage crisis shaped the political imagination of the American people at the start of the 1980s. The Third World, especially the Middle East, became a frightening and fanatical new threat to the well-being of Americans. Despite the ethnic inaccuracy and political incoherence of the association, the Iranians and Arabs were lumped together as posing a single, coherent terrorist threat. The United States under Carter was humiliated by the prolonged hostage crisis, feeding the general post-Vietnam impression of "imperial decline" and a loss of geopolitical nerve.

Such an image was sharpened by the failed U.S. rescue mission in April 1980 when three of eight helicopters malfunctioned in the Iranian desert and a fatal plane crash occurred. A midwestern legislator commented that one could no longer describe the Italian military as the worst in the world!

The CIA intervention in 1953 ultimately produced a backlash of its own: the fight-back syndrome of the 1980s as mounted by a neoconservative leadership in Washington. The United States will no longer tolerate being pushed around by Third World barbarians. According to this understanding, if one examines Third World anti-Westernism carefully enough, Soviet fingerprints can be found. In some extreme versions, the Soviet terror network is the real adversary, and the Third World barbarians are merely pawns in the larger chess game for global dominance being waged by the two superpowers. The second cold war, started in the 1980s, has this special texture. Europe is no longer the central stage; instead the focus is on various settings of revolutionary nationalist struggles.

It adds up to this: nuclear weapons have made traditional forms of conquest and expansion unavailable. But the Kremlin has found ways to challenge the peace and security of the West—stir up the resentments of the Third World, aiding and abetting low-intensity political violence against Americans and their interests. The Iranian hostage crisis gave a kind of imprimatur to this view of the world and built the foundation for this era of counterterrorism as espoused by the Reagan administration. But just as Iran ushered in the new counterterrorism, so it has provided the first general public grounds for widespread skepticism in the United States. Americans are finally now asking what's going on beneath the banners of counterterrorism Reagan-style. Whether the result of the Iran/Contra disclosure will be apathy or reform cannot now be foretold. And yet the pattern of revelations raises intriguing basic questions about whether the United States government regards Third World terrorism as the threat it purports, or merely a lurid pretext for lurid undertakings of its own.

In April 1985 William Casey, then director of the CIA, gave the opening address at an elaborate conference on "international linkages of terrorism" held at the Fletcher School of Law and Diplomacy. Mr. Casey focused on what he called "state-sponsored terrorism" as practiced by "Iran, Syria, and Libya." In his words, "Probably more blood has been shed by Iranian-sponsored terrorists during the last few years than by all other terrorists combined."[9] Casey went on to provide more specific information: "In 1983, we identified as many as fifty terrorist attacks with a confirmed or suspected Iranian involvement. Most of these incidents occurred in Lebanon, where radical Shiites of the Hezballah operated with *direct Iranian support* from terrorist bases in Syrian-controlled Bekaa Valley."[10]

Libya's role was explicitly compared by Casey to that of Iran: "Although Libya's Mu'ammar Qadhafi is not in the Ayatollah Khomeini's league, still his reliance on and support for terrorists is well known and must go unchallenged no longer."[11] As other leading officials were doing at the time, Casey emphasized the centrality of terrorism to U.S. foreign policy goals, insisting that it "must be resisted by all legal means."[12] In his conclusion, Casey reminded his invited audience that "terrorism strikes at the very heart of civilization. . . . The aim of terrorists and the ultimate objective of those who sponsor, train, and supply them is to undermine our values, to shatter our self-confidence, and to blunt our response."[13]

At the time Casey was talking it was well established that Islamic Jihad, with close links to Iran, was closely connected with the two main 1983 incidents of terrorism that had occurred in Beirut, the bombing of the embassy and the October 23 attack on the marine barracks that took the lives of 241 U.S. Marines. As two counterterrorist specialists note, the Beirut attack "succeeded beyond the wildest dreams of its perpetrators," as it led to the permanent withdrawal of U.S. military forces from Lebanon.[14] Unlike other terrorist incidents, this one not only changed foreign policy but also took a significant number of American lives as compared to prior military engagements and as compared to overall terrorist casualties. For instance, the number of U.S. servicemen killed in the October 23 incident is about equal to two-thirds of all U.S. casualties during the entire course of the Spanish-American War.[15]

The Iranian puzzle thus presents itself. How can we possibly explain the peculiar incoherence in American counterterrorist policy: Libya, the lesser terrorist sponsor, is provoked repeatedly in the Gulf of Sidra by U.S. naval probes and finally attacked in a manner calculated to cause widespread civilian damage and including a targeting of Colonel Qaddafi and his immediate family? As is generally known, the April 14, 1986, night attack on Tripoli and Bengazi took upward of one hundred lives, including that of the fifteen-month-old adopted daughter of Colonel Qaddafi. The immediate pretext for the attack was an alleged Libyan involvement in the bombing of a West German discotheque frequented by U.S. servicemen. One American was killed; at the time, the U.S. government claimed that it possessed hard evidence of Libya's role in the incident.

Later a Jordanian with Syrian connections was arrested and evidently confessed. The U.S. government has never released its evidence nor done much subsequently to justify the general damage caused by the raids.

Under these circumstances, why arms for Iran, bombs for Libya? And why would Casey, head of the CIA, "mastermind" this undertaking that assigned to the National Security Council (NSC) the main activist role?[16] According to sworn testimony by the deputy director of the CIA (at the time, director-designate, in the aftermath of Casey's disabling stroke), the agency "contributed" to the policy of the Reagan administration by making sure it didn't know about improper diversion of funds to the Contras.[17] This pattern is quite unprecedented given the traditional emphasis on bureaucratic units' fighting to retain and expand their traditional sphere of operations, their turf. It is, after all, rather extreme for an intelligence agency to claim for itself a policy of intentional ignorance.

The issue emerges on two levels: what was the substantive rationale for the contradictory policy on state-sponsored terrorism? And why was it implemented in such an unorthodox manner within the United States government? Underneath these specific questions is the larger issue of whether Iran, North/MacFarlane/Poindexter/Casey, and this pattern of incoherence reveal larger truths about terrorism and state sponsorship that extend beyond these specific factual patterns. The focus in this chapter is on Iran, not the broader reach of United States foreign policy or the wider gambit of governmental structure and bureaucratic practice.

We are given to understand one set of facts by the Tower Commission Report and President Reagan's response to it.[18] The basic interpretation given by the Tower Commission was that "almost from the beginning the initiative became in fact a series of arms-for-hostages deals."[19] In essence, the Reagan administration is portrayed as departing from its antiterrorist policies with respect to Iran because it was so intent upon securing the release of a handful of Americans being held in

Lebanon by groups perceived as susceptible to Iranian influence. In the language of the findings of the panel, as initially formulated by former Secretary of State Edmund S. Muskie and later adopted by the commission as a whole:

> The board found a strong consensus among N.S.C. participants that the President's priority in the Iran initiative was the release of U.S. hostages.[20]

Granting that Reagan was genuinely moved by the intention to gain the release of the hostages, other goals were definitely present, influencing varying actors to different degrees. The Tower Report writes of "three distinct views":

> For some, the principal motivation seemed consistently a strategic opening to Iran. For others, the strategic opening became a rationale for using arms sales to obtain the release of the hostages. For still others, the initiative appeared clearly as an arms-for-hostages deal from first to last.[21]

The report, as reinforced by subsequent hearings, portrays three principal sources of influence, Lieutenant Colonel Oliver North and Vice Admiral John Poindexter of the NSC, but also links to a shadowy network of private sector operatives that appeared to possess the capabilities of a foreign policy beyond the reach of constitutional process and to Israel. The three sources joined together, each with distinct yet overlapping priorities. As a *New York Times* correspondent notes in his introduction to the Tower Report, "a kind of parallel government came into being, operating in secret, paying scant heed to laws, deceiving Congress, and avoiding oversight of any kind."[22] North, Poindexter, and Casey were seen as deploying this private network of Iranians, Israelis, and Americans to work together on the project. At the end, the informality of the arrangements, abetted by President Reagan's loose management style, was held responsible in the report for creating a situation in which "private and foreign sources" obtain "potentially powerful leverage in the form of demands for return favors or even blackmail."[23]

The Israeli relationship was also vital. The motives of

Israel overlapped, but did not coincide, with those prevailing in the shadow land of the National Security Council. As the report observes, "Israel had a long-standing interest in a relationship with Iran and in promoting its arms export industry. Arms sales to Iran could further both objectives." Quite aside from the hostages, the sales of arms to Iran enabled the continuing overseas financing of the Contras, a policy that defied the manifested intention of Congress to deprive the Khomeini government of arms, especially so long as it engaged in terrorist activities.

This tangle of factors led the Tower Commission to worry about secrecy, managerial looseness, and a shift of function from the CIA to the NSC, and then from the NSC to the private sector. President Reagan is portrayed as an innocent above the fray, who can be criticized for his lack of clear control of these unfolding events. Such a narrow focus leaves us in the dark as to why Iran and why not Libya. The easiest answer here is that Iran was in a war with Iraq, badly needed certain weapons, and possessed hard currency; that Israel was eager to boost its export arms sales; and that the private network of arms dealers and former CIA operatives was eager to make money and divert funds for the sake of the Contras and for other undisclosed projects.

Reagan's March 4, 1987, address to the nation reinforced this reading of the Tower Report. The president explained that "what began as a strategic opening to Iran deteriorated in its implementation into trading arms for hostages." Reagan admonished himself: "This runs counter to my own beliefs, to Administration policy and to the original strategy we had in mind."[24] The Reagan speech personalized and bureaucratized the breakdown of policy coherence: it manifested his overemphasis on the hostages, a failure to ride herd on zealous subordinates (North, Poindexter), and a misuse of the NSC to engage in covert operations. In the end, the message Reagan imparted was a simple and not necessarily inappropriate one: "You take your knocks, you learn your lessons, and then you move on." More concretely, it meant carrying out some bureaucratic reforms to assure that the NSC would not soon again play the role of a rogue elephant; that a responsible, moderate management of both NSC and CIA affairs would be achieved, through the appointment of respected and qualified public officials in the persons of Frank Carlucci and William Webster; that the new post of legal adviser to the NSC would be created; that there would be more deference to congressional oversight; and tighter restrictions on covert operations under NSC auspices would begin. The outcome of the congressional inquiries is as yet uncertain, although it definitely reinforces earlier concerns despite the personal popularity attained by Oliver North during his testimony. Also significant has been Reagan's disavowal of Poindexter's decision to withhold from him information about the diversion of funds to the Contras.

The Tower Commission's recommendations, which preceded and largely shaped Reagan's speech, follow a similar course but give a fuller accounting with more detail, especially in relation to the diversion of funds to the Contras, the frustration of congressional will in Central American policy, and the linkage between the NSC initiatives and the shadowy network of ex-CIA operatives, right-wing political groups, and arms dealers. Yet surprisingly, or perhaps not, the bottom lines on both the Tower Report and the congressional hearings were remarkably restrained or, more critically, expectedly innocuous with respect to interference with operating procedures. The more cynical view of the commission process is to appoint prominent and respected Americans with appropriate experience, covering the mainstream spectrum, that will reassure the citizenry, correct the bureaucratic glitches, contribute to an overall perception of legitimate and constitutional government, and give vent to the partisan give-and-take of party politics. The makeup and performance of the Tower Commission—John Tower, conservative southern politician with a record of loyalty to government and a major role over the years in overseeing national security policy; Edmund Muskie, a moderate Democrat from Maine who had been a popular and effective senator and served briefly as secretary of state at the end of the Carter administration during the period of the Iranian hostage crisis; and Brent Scowcroft, a nonpartisan military figure with prior experience as an effective chairperson of a national commission handling the touchy issues of land-based strategic missiles and controversy over whether to deploy the MX and develop the midget missile system—brilliantly achieved these goals.

This trio worked together with diligence and reached a consensus that earned instant respect, being neither too apologetic to be dismissed as a whitewash nor too critical to shake any fundamental foundations of confidence by the citizenry in the capacities and integrity of the governing process. The essence of the Tower assessment and prescription is one of bureaucratic retrenchment with respect to the National Security Council. The situation that produced the Iran/Contra initiatives is attributed mainly to a tolerance of laissez-faire diplomacy within the NSC that extended to encompass the private network and "foreign sources" (mainly Israel) as a means of implementation. The implication is that bureaucratic discipline would have led the president to resist the temptations that in this instance generated arms-for-hostages negotiations with Iran, the principal sponsor of state terrorism, and diverted funds, presumably belonging to the public treasury, to a variety of illicit purposes, but principally to funding the Contras beyond a set of limits very deliberately imposed on the executive branch by congressional action.

Yet even on the level of bureaucratic reform the Tower Report is tepid. It doesn't even go as far as Reagan went in his March 4 speech. In the end, the report recommends "no substantive change be made" in the National Security Act.[25] It only proposes that "as a general matter, the NSC Staff should not engage in the implementation of policy or the conduct of operations." Although agreeing that such practices distort proper constitutional relationships within government, it does not endorse "the inflexibility of a legislative restriction."[26] A similar approach is taken on the issue of secrecy, concluding with nothing more substantive than a recommendation "each administration formulate precise procedures for restricted consideration of covert action, and that, once formulated, those procedures be strictly adhered to."[27]

And even on reliance upon the private network, the Tower Report wobbles toward rationalization of past practices, little more. It admits that "careful and limited use of people outside the U.S. Government may be very helpful in some unique cases" but goes on to point out that such practice "raises substantial questions,"[28] especially the manipulation of official policies by these outside forces with their own quite selfish and possibly contradictory agendas. The concluding recommendation gives aid and comfort to enthusiasts of an imperial presidency: *"We recommend against having implementation and policy oversight dominated by intermediaries. We do not recommend against barring limited use of private individuals to assist in United States diplomatic initiatives or in covert activities. . . ."*[29] The word *dominated* is so permissive that arguably even the Iran/Contra dynamics never was out of NSC control.

Of course, the subsequent congressional hearings have mounted additional pressure for reform, but as matters now stand, there is no reason to think that anything will be changed by the reaction to the apparent incoherence of the Iran/Contra policy. Most striking is the widely held assumption that covert operations are indispensable to foreign policy and compatible with constitutional process. There has been surprisingly little criticism of the Reagan administration for its refusal to abide by the conditions embodied in the congressional mandate to limit U.S. assistance to the Contras. And, finally, there is little discussion at all of the use by this administration (and others) of secrecy as a way to keep controversial, even unacceptable policy initiatives from the American electorate.

Reagan touched on this concern in his March 1987 speech: "I have also directed that any covert activity be in support of clear policy objectives and in compliance with American values. I expect a covert policy that if Americans saw it on the front page of their newspaper, they'd say, 'That makes sense.' "[30] Again, the vagueness of the guideline is striking. The proposed limit is not connected with constitutional or legal constraints, nor with decency and nonviolence. Presumably, the Iran part of the initiative has now been repudiated because it couldn't be reconciled with opposition to state-sponsored terrorism, but diversion of funds to the Contras by Reaganite reasoning remains quite acceptable, as these "resistance fighters" were fulfilling the stated policy of the country as expressed through the Reagan Doctrine, that is, promoting "democracy" in opposition to Marxist-Leninist Sandinista rule in Nicaragua. Or, more pointedly, an attack on the person and family of Qaddafi, despite its dubious status in international law, would continue to pass muster under the Reagan test of secrecy as its disclosure would not conflict with proclaimed policy, nor would undertaking such an attack upset many Americans.

And when it came to the private network, already acknowledged as tantamount to a parallel government, there is no willingness to connect an impulse to privatize with a dubious drift of policy. Otherwise, why would it be necessary to circumvent a normally compliant bureaucracy? To carry out an extremist policy beyond the rule of law depends on mobilizing extremists. By the mid-1980s military support for the Contras had been effectively rejected by public opinion and Congress despite Reagan's ardent commitment and overall popularity. To sustain such a policy under these circumstances meant circumventing constitutionalism in form and substance, a course of action that exceeds the normal bureaucratic capacity to swallow and necessitates recourse to ideological fanatics, right-wing politics, mercenaries, and the underworld of organized crime and arms dealing. Despite the involvement of William Casey, director of the CIA, it was assumed unreliable to depend on the agency for such a controversial set of initiatives. Recourse was made to a deep cover by way of NSC-guided covert operations carried out under the direction of Lieutenant Colonel North. For the CIA to accord this deference to the NSC in an area of its own special competence was quite unprecedented. It is rare for one part of government to yield unilaterally precious bureaucratic turf, a development that can only be explained by Casey's dual role as head of the CIA and mastermind of the Iran arms sales and diversion of funds to the Contras. The Contra diversion, contrary to most conjecture, was the heart and soul of the undertaking, not a secondary afterthought.[31]

But there is also another part of this experience that lurks below the level of official acknowledgment. The question, Why Iran? suggests other possibilities hinted at in the documentary materials. North sends Poindexter a memorandum reporting on a conversation between a foreign diplomat and Dr. Larijani, deputy foreign minister of Iran. Dr. Larijani is reported as calling attention to the fact "Iran and America share similar strategic interests in the region. The danger of pro-Soviet Marxist interests asserting themselves in the region were growing rapidly."[32] This realization was coupled with Larijani's view that "despite Iran's rhetorical invective against USA, Iran wanted [country deleted] to play the role of intermediary in attempting a better understanding with the American government."[33] Running through the documentary materials of U.S. official communications is a theme relating to the primacy of geopolitical factors of the sort referred to by the Iranian official. That is, preventing Soviet influence in Iran—a consistent U.S. geopolitical goal—seems much more important to the policymakers than countering Iran's sponsorship of anti-American terrorism. Thus, the United States, despite admonishing its allies to uphold an arms embargo on Iran, seeks to widen its options and goes ahead with its secret arms negotiations.[34]

But there are further circumstantial elements here. Even Khomeini's Islamic republic, with its intense anti-American stance, is perceived as less of a menace to Washington than was Mossadegh constitutionalism. First of all, Iranian fundamentalism is anti-Left and anti-Soviet to a pronounced degree. Its governmental program is not dramatically dissimilar from other anti-Communist regimes of the Right, with the notable exception of its repudiation of modernization and the culture of the West. The supposition that a moderate faction might gain leverage in Tehran if it could obtain weapons from the United States implies that the basic orientation of the revolution was not a barrier to normal relations with the United States. The ideological static of a secret Iranian connection seems far less severe than what one might have expected if a comparable initiative had been pursued by a liberal Democratic administration with say, Cuba or North Korea. In such an event, the conservative clamor for criminal prosecution and impeachment proceedings would have been overwhelming.

Furthermore, even Khomeini's Iran, despite its fervent anti-Israeli stance, was a useful "partner" for Israel. Here, the partnership was arms for dollars, but with some potential adverse longer-term costs for Israel, especially if Iran prevailed in its war with Iraq and brought the Palestinian struggle back to life closer to Israeli borders. These factors were pushed aside by economic pressures. When the Shah collapsed, Israel lost its major customer for arms export, worth $500 million or more per year in foreign exchange earnings.[35] This customer loss became more serious after Somoza's fall in 1978. Israel had become the primary arms supplier for Nicaragua, accounting for upward of 98 percent of Somoza's weapons imports during his final years. Establishing an Iranian connection, especially given the Iran-Iraq War, meant a bonanza for Israel, with further market possibilities associated with the Contras' receipt of funds that could be used for weapons purchases. Israel became "the foreign source" that promoted the connection mainly to provide profits and export outlets for its arms industry and hard currency for its treasury.

Finally, in the spirit of privatizing the foreign policy, the arms sales provided North with resources that could be thrown in the Contras' direction and could support several other undisclosed "projects." On one occasion, returning from a disappointing trip to Tehran, McFarlane noted in his record of the journey:

North said don't be too downhearted, that the one bright spot is the government is availing itself of part of the money for application to Central America, as I recall, although I took it to be Nicaragua.[36]

In this sense, the locus of the diplomacy was in the private sector, not the government, and North was acting *in* the bureaucracy on behalf of a pro-Contra policy that had the tacit approval of the leadership in the White House, including the president. Even Secretary of State Shultz made it clear that he objected to being back-channeled by activities in Lebanon, but he didn't mind the solicitation of funds from foreign governments or private individuals for dedication to the Contra cause. That is, the imperial presidency of the mid-1980s waged a partial coup against constitutional arrangements by defying congressional will, U.S. neutrality laws, and the general assumption that foreign policy implementation should be exclusively entrusted to the public sector. In this regard the Iran connection, by working to rescue the hostages, was partly designed to achieve good public relations with respect to the hostage families; but more than this, it was an outgrowth of a cold war logic that made every enemy of my enemy a potential friend and that was seeking funds to bankroll an extraconstitutional and unpopular foreign policy.

The counterterrorism motif is definitely pushed into the background no matter how these basic events are construed. Even if the primary motive were assumed to be hostage release, the initiative would reward hostage taking and, over time, encourage such terrorist initiatives, especially by giving the known state sponsor a weapons bequest. Construed geopolitically, the counterterrorist card is seen as a small one compared to the national effort to minimize Soviet penetration in Iran. Those involved in secret American negotiations at the highest levels were quite prepared to overlook the Iranian role in the Lebanese terrorist incidents if some degree of geopolitical leverage could be regained, even at the cost of a military defeat for Iraq, which would mean a further decline in regional security in the Middle East.

This suggests that the public prominence given the antiterrorist campaign mainly involved something other than terrorist challenges. My argument is that the overriding motivation of this campaign was to rebuild post-Vietnam support at home for an interventionary and militarist foreign policy, especially in the Caribbean and Central America. The Grenada invasion was a probe in that direction, a relatively successful one, and the effort to defeat the insurgency in El Salvador was another expression of an assertive foreign policy. The big test, however, has turned out to be the Contra cause in Nicaragua.

In a suggestive recent book, Jonathan Marshall, Peter Dale Scott, and Jane Hunter tie the Reagan commitment here to earlier "deals" struck. Recalling Casey's role as Reagan's campaign manager in the 1980 elections, the Iran/Contra connection contends that back in 1980 some very suspicious solicitation of funds from a variety of rightist constituencies in the hemisphere, implying a deal of unwavering support for the Contras, occurred. There are also complementary speculations that the Iranians were promised arms by representatives of Reagan's presidential campaign if the release of American hostages were postponed until after the presidential elections. The evidence available suggests contacts between the Reagan people and Iranian officials during this period, and some conjecture that Reagan could lose the election to Carter if the hostages were released shortly before November.

The foreground of these various speculations is the consistent search for a mobilizing formula for the 1980s, an approach to foreign policy that would lead most Americans from both political parties to give their leaders enthusiastic support in the event of recourse to force by the government. We return now to the Why Libya? side of our inquiry. The attack of April 1986 on Libya was the culmination of this search for a militarist mandate. And, indeed, the public did support the attack even though at the time they expected it to lead to an increase in anti-American terrorism. Reagan tried to rely on concern over terrorism to regain American control over the Western alliance and to divert attention from the increased tensions associated with economic rivalry and a weakening of Western cohesion. The Libyan attack was a test, and the failure of the European countries other than Great Britain to give direct support strengthened the perception that the United States was a superpower with a unilateralist diplomacy, not an organic leader of an alliance of democratic states. True, subsequently, the main Western governments gave lip service to the Reagan approach by passing a strong antiterrorist resolution at the Tokyo economic summit that explicitly singled out Libya as the most notorious state sponsor of terrorism. As earlier discussed, to pass over Iran and single out Libya can only be understood as a geopolitical tactic by the United States government and can be regarded as a relatively cheap rhetorical concession by the non-American participants at the Tokyo meetings in May 1986.

* * *

At this point I'm not sure who on our side knows what. Help.

Lt. Col. Oliver North to Vice Admiral John Poindexter,
               June 6, 1986[37]

The Tokyo message is inherently self-contradictory: a genuine repudiation of terrorism arising from revolutionaries coexists with a set of policy moves that subordinates counterterrorism to geopolitics. Then, also, there is the intriguing triangle of Iran/Israel/United States. Each is part terrorist, part opportunist, part terrorized.

Beyond this is the structural role of secrecy. The United States has one foreign policy that is public and several more that are secret to varying degrees, and often incompatible with values and stated policies. In this instance even prominent cabinet members, Shultz and Weinberger, were deliberately excluded from knowledge. Counterterrorism is the public stance; arms for hostages, covert arms to the Contras, and geopolitical priorities are the mainspring of the real foreign policy. Secrecy enables policy incoherence to be kept private, but it makes a government vulnerable to and preoccupied with leaks and revelations.

If the gap between the authorized and the actual is too great, then there is a further tendency: the privatization of foreign policy. Since the bureaucracy is quite disposed toward militarist tactics and assertive geopolitics, its resistance suggests that the operative policy is of such an extremist sort that it either won't work or would be too discrediting to defend if made public. To rely on private networks means linking up with fascist elements that are definitely associated to varying extents with organized crime, drug dealing, arms merchants, and covert operations specialists, including former CIA personnel.

The campaign of the Reagan administration against terrorism only partly concerned the challenge of anti-American overseas violence. It was more centrally about the search for a bipartisan consensus that would give back a good name to interventionary diplomacy in the Third World. In effect, it was the search for a post-Vietnam policy fix that would give us back what we "lost" in Vietnam. Similarly aid to the Contras in defiance of congressional will was only partly about Nicaragua. It was a rerun of Vietnam, but this time with enthusiasts for the war in a position to carry on support no matter what the politicians decided or the public wanted.

At the military think tanks and defense colleges the trendy talk of the 1980s is about "low-intensity warfare." The policy attempt is to convert the public anxiety about terrorist violence into a blank check for overseas uses of force. The encounters with Qaddafi have been exploratory. George Shultz, in his widely noticed address on low-intensity warfare, stated the issue as follows: "The ironic fact is, these new and elusive challenges have proliferated, in part, *because* of our success in deterring nuclear and conventional war. So they have done the logical thing: they have turned to other methods. Low-intensity warfare and nuclear strength. . . ."[38] To complete the circle of confusion, Secretary Shultz reduces low-intensity conflict to terrorism: "Terrorism is the newest strategy of the enemies of freedom—and it's all too effective."[39]

To act in response requires "public understanding and congressional support," and this means perceiving the challenge as a species of ongoing war. In Shultz's words, "It must be clearly and unequivocally the policy of the United States to fight back—to resist challenges, to defend our interests, and to support those who put their own lives on the line in a common cause."[40]

Such a line of argument is not new, although the rhetoric is somewhat different. Way back in the 1950s John Foster Dulles delivered a comparable message but organized the argument around the theme of "indirect aggression," and it was the Kennedy administration that brought the focus on counterinsurgency warfare and the training of "special forces" to the fore. The new emphasis on terrorism and low-intensity warfare hearkens back to the cold war and, specifically, to the challenges of revolutionary warfare that eventuated in Vietnam. No one would accuse the current architects of U.S. foreign policy of being "the best and the brightest," but they are nevertheless carrying that same old torch of interventionary diplomacy.

Such an emphasis ignores the real terrorist challenge: the surge of violence, inducing fear, planned and executed in secret, and directed at the sinews of noncombatant society. Ending terrorism depends, above all, on self-knowledge. If the self is exempted, or invoked exclusively as target and victim, then the cycle of violence will be perpetuated in ever more frightening forms.

Inflation is these days a pervasive human phenomenon, and it has afflicted terrorist practice as well. It is not alarmist to posit the nuclear temptation as the surreal culmination of the terrorist mind-set, whether enacted by the revolutionary seeking to produce chaos or by the functionary acting to impose order. Having routinized such apocalyptic outer limits, the functionary and revolutionary become naturally conditioned to rely on terrorist methods in pursuit of their goals, while straining ever harder both to disguise their own behavior and to castigate that of their enemies. On all facets of United States relations with Iran and Libya in the 1980s the imprint of the terrorist mind-set is unmistakable.

EIGHT

On Rescuing Law
from the Lawyers

*. . . and it's upon the law that
terrorists trample.*

RONALD REAGAN, remarks to
American Bar Association,
        July 8, 1985

*. . . the law applicable to terrorism is
not merely flawed, it is perverse.*

ABRAHAM D. SOFAER, legal adviser
to the Department of State,
"Terrorism and the Law," *Foreign
        Affairs,* Summer 1986

Lawyers, of course, facilitate politics and the designs of politicians. If the law pertaining to terrorism is in disarray, that is a good indication of political turmoil and an overall lack of consensus as to what is to be condemned and what to do about it. Diminished moral and legal coherence may also accompany the collapse of a pattern of political domination and the loss of legislative direction provided by the most dominating actors. The process of decolonization, the emergence of the Soviet Union as a superpower, the U.S. defeat in Vietnam, and the rise of the Pacific Basin trading group has since the 1960s splintered the kind of world order structure the United States shaped and then presided over in the decade after World War II. In this more plural world system no one definition of what is desirable can decisively prevail over contending definitions. In the end it is self-defeating to insist that "the law" coincides with *our* conception of terrorism. It weakens law without strengthening the capabilities of international society to deal with terrorism.

So long as political violence is ideologically coded, there will be attempts to make the violence of the other a criminal undertaking and to sanctify the violence of the self. Law never succeeds in domains of double standards. It is demeaned and reinforces the cynical view that the law is on the side of the stronger and more established contestant. The extreme circumstance is illustrated by the repressive function of law in a totalitarian society.

International law is particularly vulnerable to demeaning rituals. As state officials take up the cudgels to do battle against "terrorism," they are busy arming and championing terrorists of their own. This failure of law applies to both revolutionaries and functionaries, although the latter control world information flows to a great extent and have won temporarily the contested semantic battleground. By and large when the public hears the word *terrorist* they think *revolutionary*.

But, truly, it is a pyrrhic victory! The propagandistic appropriation of law is too obvious. To associate terrorists with revolutionaries when functionaries sponsor exile movements that blow up civilian airliners, execute labor leaders and village officials, and seek to displace the constitutional order of a foreign state under the sway of social radicals is to endorse equivalent forms and methods of violence. The common response to propaganda is counterpropaganda.

Thus, the revolutionaries insist that it is the CIA that

produces most of the terrorism in the world, and that the violence used by liberation groups is either exempt or sacred, but certainly not to be condemned as "illegal." The claim to be a liberation group is itself often contested, although the core meaning is the struggle by nationalist elements against colonial or alien rule. For many governments, recourse to political violence to promote liberation objectives is legitimate, an instance of a just war. In the United Nations, especially the General Assembly, the supporters of liberation causes have the votes, and so the law is "perverse" because it reflects this political pressure.

Images and perceptions ensue. The media seems biased because it reflects the viewpoint of Western states, especially that of the United States government. From another, contradictory angle, the United Nations seems biased because it reflects the rhetoric and priorities of the Third World. The efforts to construct a valid and effective legal regime upon such a foundation encounter the frustrations of building once more a tower of Babel.

Let me illustrate this quandary on the basis of some recent professional experience. First, as a critic of the U.S. government orientation toward terrorism and terrorists: as a member of a special committee on terrorism of the American Society of International Law, I have been accused of "hijacking" the group by insisting upon an evenhanded treatment of terrorism as illegitimate political violence (that is, violence that lacks a generally acceptable moral and legal rationale). My accuser, a well-known international lawyer, argues that the only way to make law effective is to promote the policy goals of "like-minded countries," that is, to make use of economic assets, along with media control and scholarly consensus, to stigmatize as "terrorism" the forms of violence doing the West harm, especially attacking and seizing overseas Americans, whether tourists, diplomats, or soldiers.

But the intelligentsia sympathetic to the revolutionary side are little better. At a recent conference on international terrorism held in Geneva under the sponsorship of an Austrian association, International Progress Organization, I found myself once again disappointed. During the conference there were many moving statements from individuals representing Third World points of view, especially those from South Africa. But the arguments were once more one-sided. The delegates insisted that moral and legal censure be reserved exclusively for the enemies of imperial domination and racial emancipation. Necklacing of alleged black informers in South African townships was justified as a necessary tactic for pushing forward the struggle. The expectation of the delegates was that only partisans of revolutionary causes were legitimate participants. This mood of exoneration prevailed at the conference, extending even to the European revolutionary movements, including the German Baader-Meinhof, Japan's Red Army Faction, and the Italian Red Brigades.

How, then, do we rescue law from those lawyers who are adherents of the cult of counterterrorism?

The first step is to acknowledge that law, especially international law, has operated predominantly as a tool of, by, and for functionaries. This fundamental characteristic militates against the law's taking a form that would prohibit either revolutionaries or functionaries from using indiscriminate, fear-inducing violence. It is only because the functionaries are politically and ideologically split, seeking inconsistent results, that international law may be able, with appropriate international backers, to contribute to a more evenhanded counterterrorism. On the other hand, if geopolitical diversity disappears, then "law and order" advocates will be able to compose a coherent law, one that is no longer "perverse" as it will consistently authorize what the functionaries do and condemn what the revolutionaries do. Because international society is deeply divided on the normative status of different "revolutionary" groups, there is some political space within which to negotiate a legal regime that accords protection to revolutionary interests as well as to functionary interests. Because anti-Communist officials want the Contras or the Afghan rebels to be treated well, there is a potential interest in extending mutual legal protection to groups with a radical orientation. The Geneva Protocol I (on the humanitarian law of war), discussed later in the chapter, is an illustration. As the Reagan repudiation also illustrates, an ideologically harsh view of international conflict prefers chaos to according some legitimacy to the existence of the other side. George Shultz, the secretary of state, and Abraham Sofaer, legal adviser to the Department of State, have been most outspoken in the struggle over the legal instrument in the terrorist context. Secretary Shultz's influential address to the National Defense University on "Low-Intensity Warfare: The Challenge of Ambiguity" was a major effort to absorb international law into the Western counterterrorist camp.[1] It is both an affirmation of commitment to law and a partisan insistence that the relevant law is on our side. First, the commitment:

> We believe in the rule of law. This nation has long been a champion of international law, the peaceful settlement of disputes, and the UN Charter as a code of conduct for the world community.[2]

And then, the claim as a sword unsheathed:

> The UN Charter is not a suicide pact. The law is a weapon on our side and it is up to us to use it to its maximum.[3]

In effect, the challenge is to use legal methods to isolate and pursue our political adversaries and their supporters by consigning to them, and to them alone, the label of terrorism. On that basis, then, Shultz and Sofaer call for international cooperation in relation to antihijacking measures, extradition and prosecution of suspects, exchange of evidence and intelligence information, and a tight policy on application so that "revolutionaries" on our side, regardless of their modes of conduct, will not be treated as terrorists.

Typically, one-eyed rhetorical endorsements of counterterrorism are inserted into the formal final statements of the economic summit meetings of the seven leading industrial countries. No criticism of the violence of the counterterrorists is offered, nor is there any effort to assuage the sense of desperate grievance that often leads the oppressed to strike at any target that inflicts some pain on their tormentors.[4] It is an expression of continuing American clout that it can command allegiance to the cult of counterterrorism from its main allies, even though their distinct national policies strike a much less strident posture. Even putting terrorism on the agenda of an economic summit is a reflection of the priority attached to a common stand by Washington, but the failure to push beyond generalities, with the exception of insulating international civil aviation from political violence, suggests that even like-minded governments faced with concrete challenges seek flexibility. And as the Iran/Contra disclosures establish, even the United States severely undermined its proclaimed no-concessions policy and its hard-line counterterrorism when it tried to strike bargains in Tehran with arms for hostages. Under these circumstances, the main role of law becomes exhortatory, summoning public support for uses of force, provided the culprit can be associated with terrorism. That is, international law is useful mainly as part of an appeal to the folks back in Peoria.

But the real effort of counterterrorist ideologues is to make law justify controversial uses of force by the United States as antiterrorist responses. The Shultz/Sofaer approach insists that international law (and constitutional connections between the executive branch and Congress) enable the president to use force legally in two different settings: to bomb targets in countries accused of state sponsorship of anti-American terrorist incidents fairly widely and indiscriminately (the clearest example of this kind of legal claim arose out of the attack on Libya in April 1986, but Israeli cross-border retaliatory strikes by air and naval forces have been establishing precedents for years) and to arm and guide rebel forces that are seeking either to respond to the export of revolution or to overthrow a government supposedly having a Marxist-Leninist orientation (here the best example is in Central America, where the U.S. government has claimed that the

Sandinista government supplied arms to rebels in neighboring El Salvador and that this activity was "an armed attack" entitling the United States to act in "collective self-defense and further that Marxist-Leninist governments are inherently terrorist . . . and are appropriately targets of legitimate armed rebellion on human rights and democracy grounds").

In both instances, the United States claim to invoke international law has been rejected within the United Nations. The Libyan attack was censured by a General Assembly resolution that rejected the factual and legal bases of the United States action.[5] This resolution was only a recommendation, but its position has generally been confirmed by the weight of expert legal opinion outside the United States.

The Central American claims have been rejected more authoritatively by an overwhelming majority (twelve to three) of the members of the World Court in a lengthy, carefully reasoned judicial opinion.[6] Even if Nicaragua is assumed to have helped the rebels in El Salvador—and the evidence is sketchy—such action does not add up to an armed attack entitling the United States to join with El Salvador in counterattacking on the grounds of collective self-defense, nor does adherence by the Nicaraguan government to Marxism-Leninism, even if such a label is granted as accurate, have any inherent implications for human rights unless specific abuses can be shown. And even if they are shown, outside states have no legal right to help rebels. Such help amounts to an illegal intervention in violation of international law.

As might be expected, Shultz is not persuaded. With animistic fury he rejects any legal result contrary to U.S. foreign policy. In a formulation of unmatched arrogance the secretary of state defends the United States' "illegal" repudiation of the World Court judgment:[7]

> As we have shown in response to Nicaragua's hypocritical suit in the World Court, we will not permit our enemies—who despise the rule of law as a "bourgeois" notion—to use *our* devotion to law and morality as a weapon against us.[8]

In actuality, no European judge supported the United States on substantive grounds; the Japanese and British judges based their dissents on jurisdictional and procedural arguments, leaving only Stephen Schwebel, the U.S. judge, to support the self-defense rationale for aiding the Contras. For Shultz/Sofaer, then, the failure of "international law" is really a failure of international society as an organized entity.

Sofaer appropriately criticizes those governmental representatives who argue that if the perpetrator of violence is motivated by an effort to overcome oppression, then whatever tactic is chosen, even if directed against civilians, should be exempt from legal condemnation. No pretext rooted in the causal basis for recourse to violence can exonerate violent methods that amount to terrorism (those that are indiscriminate, fear-inducing, or aimed at civilians). At the same time, it is mere propaganda to argue that these forms of violence should be condemned but that the terrorism of the oppressive side should be ignored. The United States cannot reserve to itself CIA covert operations as "intelligence" while insisting that liberation violence be declared off-limits. A far higher degree of consistency among policymakers is indispensable if the law itself is to command nonpartisan respect. For law to regain legitimacy, it is essential that antagonists be engaged in "low-intensity" warfare under a common and legal regime. Such a step does not extend necessarily to the related broader issues of high-technology military tactics, including, in the final analysis, reliance on nuclear weapons.

Sofaer's criticism of United Nations support for armed struggle to achieve self-determination is nowhere balanced by either comparable limitations on the violent means of their oppressive adversaries (and friends) or any indication of support for a realistic process of peaceful change. His assessment of the failure of law is suggested by the contention that United Nations resolutions and debates are "a clear signal to all that those groups deemed by the majority to be oppressed will be free legally to use force, and therefore cannot be fairly called terrorists."[9] A possibly willed confusion here is to treat recourse to force by oppressed groups as tantamount to terrorism. The whole effort of legal analysis should be to acknowledge a limited option of force, but only within the framework of international law as applicable to both sides.

And here arises a complementary problem for legalizing counterterrorism. Whereas all force constitutes terrorism if it is used by the revolutionary side, no amount of force, however excessive or indiscriminate, is terrorism if it is mounted by functionaries, particularly those operating out of the White House.[10] Demonizing the enemy attempts to shift the exemption from legal accountability with respect to the use of force to the counterrevolutionary or functionary side.[11] Even this degree of coherence is undermined by the Reagan Doctrine and its commitment of support to revolutionary groups battling governments identified as Marxist-Leninist regimes, no matter how reprehensible the tactics of these groups from the standpoint of the law of war.

Such a contention dissolves the very possibility of law in international relations. If each government feels free to give its interpretation of legal rights and duties a higher weight than that of the procedures and institutions of the community, then the law must rely on self-serving procedures of self-help and becomes a test of sovereign wills, but even more so, of destructive capabilities. It amounts to a refusal by the United States to resolve terrorist issues by deference to consensus and community procedures, including those of negotiated settlement of disputes. To the degree that such a military and paramilitary approach is adopted it defies law instead of supporting its growth and evolution. To contribute positively requires an acknowledgment of the legitimacy of the other side and a willingness to limit claims to use violence to situations *generally regarded* as self-defense, that is, those occurring in response to an armed attack across a frontier.

As the United States government has been developing its counterterrorist policy in recent years, it is itself both terroristic and illegal: engaged in indiscriminate violence and often directed at civilian targets. The renunciation of terrorism, to be convincing, must not ignore those patterns of conduct on our side that resemble in essential features the conduct on theirs. Until self-scrutiny becomes part of the antiterrorist drive in law and elsewhere, legalist claims will be dismissed by those actors with different political agendas as propaganda by an international top dog—no more, no less.

As of now, there are several contributions to international legal order that can be made:

1. Demystifying one-sided legal approaches.
2. Finding common ground.
3. Proposing specific recommendations to strengthen international order.

The fundamental standoff, as far as law is concerned, is not between revolutionaries and functionaries as such. It is rather the antagonisms between different forms of state-sponsored violence and the extent to which particular states are prepared to establish legal limits on particular forms of political violence. More concretely, it is the willingness of the Soviet Union and the United States to sponsor different forms of "revolutionary" violence, whether by "national liberators" or "freedom fighters," that assures incoherence at the level of norm and practice. As we have suggested, one means to create a semblance of coherence, but only a semblance, is to win the semantic war by exclusively associating the other side's forms of "terrorism" with legal/moral stigma while somehow exempting one's own from legal scrutiny.

But the international legal order is not so susceptible to one-sided appropriation as formerly. The United Nations, especially the International Court of Justice, is more evenhanded. It is this loss of control that frustrates United States officials. For instance, the current legal adviser, Abraham Sofaer, seems convinced that "the failure" of international law results from the frustration of the will of "civilized nations," which is a code reference to the Western alliance.[12] This frustration of the will is the work of the Third World and its Soviet bloc backers and their endorsement of "the legitimacy of struggles against colonial and racist regimes and other forms of alien domination." Sofaer charges that many of these states "continue to believe that 'wars of national liberation' justify or excuse terrorist acts."[13]

In contrast, the United States, while acknowledging "oppressed people are sometimes justified in resorting to force, but only if properly exercised . . . such uses of force must be consistent with the laws of war and should not be directed at innocent civilians, including hostage-taking, or involve torture."[14] So far so good, and truly, to neutralize the terrorism of the civilized nations, there has been an unacceptable effort on the Third World side to create an exemption for the political violence they support to match the exemption enjoyed by the political violence they oppose.

Here is the rub for the United States version of "the law." It can win the semantic war by successfully associating terrorism mainly with indiscriminate tactics of revolutionaries calculated to produce fear, so that the indiscriminate violence of functionaries is not drawn into the orbit of terrorism. Beyond that, invoking "law" against the practice of torture effectively condemns low-technology forms of unacceptable violence but preserves the option of high-technology tactics (retaliatory bombings directed at civilian centers of population) and weaponry (including nuclear weapons).

These tactics and weaponry induce fear, cause gross harm to the innocent, and have no convincing rationale in either moral or legal tradition. That is, terrorism at the upper end of the violence spectrum is deliberately exempted. Indeed, the United States government has actively resisted general efforts to restate the law of war so as to encompass such weaponry, using its leverage to oppose stigmatizing the greatest terror armory ever conceived. For instance, while participating in the negotiations leading up to the Geneva Protocols of 1977, the United States delegation formally declared that in its view nuclear weaponry was excluded from the coverage of the general rules of prohibition. Such an exclusion seems strained, given the policy objective of such provisions of Protocol I as Article 35 and 36.

Article 35—Basic rules

1. In any armed conflict, the right of the Parties to the conflict to choose methods or means of warfare is not unlimited.

2. It is prohibited to employ weapons, projectiles and materials and methods of warfare of a nature to cause superfluous injury or unnecessary suffering.

3. It is prohibited to employ methods or means of warfare which are intended, or may be expected, to cause widespread, long-term and severe damage to the natural environment.

Article 36—New weapons

In the study, development, acquisition or adoption of a new weapon, means or method of warfare, a High Contracting Party is under an obligation to determine whether its employment would, in some or all circumstances, be prohibited by this Protocol or by any other rule of international law applicable to the High Contracting Party.[15]

A normal reading of these provisions would assume that they are, above all, applicable to weapons of mass destruction.

The cost to the rule of law incurred by this kind of selective approach is the loss of legitimacy for the regime of international law as a whole, especially as it relates to counterterrorism. No genuine consensus is required for a coherent approach that seeks to elicit cooperation among governments. The statist bases of international law have enabled governments to negotiate a series of treaty instruments that appear to condemn terrorist challenges associated generally with acts of political extremism by revolutionary and anarchist groups and even individuals.[16] The prohibitions create a foundation for *voluntary* patterns of cooperation among governments, but they do not mandate any specific action. And because even Western governments are divided on tactics, the majority preferring a low-profile to a prominent role as coenforcer, the tendency is to be lax or worse in interpreting and enforcing the treaty arrangements. In concrete terms, this means that suspected offenders under these treaty arrangements are, with rare exception, not prosecuted or extradited and, if they are punished at all, are punished lightly.

Such a pattern is independent of the political tensions that arise from regarding some treaty offenders as political allies in worthy causes. Hence, although the offenses qualify as terrorism, the perpetrator may be spared as "friend," "agent," or even "hero." The support by the U.S. government given various Cuban exiles who have engaged in violent acts against Castro's Cuba is by now notorious, and well documented.[17] These Cuban extremist groups have staged numerous bombings in this country and have attacked those alleged to be supporters of Castro. As well, early hijackings and aerial explosions of civilian planes seem to have been the work of these groups, but little public reaction occurred. The U.S. government ignored these instances of political violence and the media regard them as worth only of low-profile treatment. Such is the ideological politics of revolutionary terrorism.

Of course, Qaddafi has been vividly explicit in this regard, contending that pro-American groups are CIA terrorists, while according an official welcome to those who engage in the most blood-chilling violence against Israeli or United States persons and property. The most notorious instance was the heroes' welcome he extended to the Palestinians who shot and killed Israeli Olympic athletes at the 1972 games held in Munich.

It weakens the legal approach to treat liberation groups who rely on violent tactics, including those of a terrorist character, in dramatically contradictory ways. The PLO and the anti-Khomeini *Mujaheddin* in Iran (not to be confused with antiregime resistance groups in Afghanistan) have relied on similar tactics based on political violence (assuming the correctness of the worst allegations against the PLO), yet Washington treats the PLO as a terrorist organization and the *Mujaheddin* as a political group that can open information offices and spread its message in the United States.[18]

Despite the depreciation of international law through its manipulation, some positive contributions to the goals of constructive counterterrorism are being made by law and lawyers. In order to reach any agreements at all, governments have been induced to condemn terrorism unconditionally, as well as to regard torture as a species of terrorism. As is often the case, this positive role for international law is achieved indirectly or incidentally, in relation to the larger purposes of developing law in relation to human rights and the conduct of war.

The negotiation under United Nations auspices of the 1984 Convention Against Torture and other Cruel, Inhuman or Degrading Treatment or Punishment is a major normative contribution.[19] It acknowledges state responsibility for inflicting pain upon enemies and establishes the unconditional responsibility of functionaries even to the extent they do no more than carry out orders and follow the policy directives of the day. Article 2(2) of the Draft Convention is worth quoting:

> No exceptional circumstances whatsoever, whether a state of war, internal political instability or any other public emergency, may be invoked as a justification of torture.

And Article 2(3):

> An order from a superior officer or a public authority may not be invoked as a justification of torture.

Members of the convention undertake to implement its basic prohibition, including the prosecution of violators, modes of redress for those claiming to be victims of torture, and cooperation with other foreign governments with regard to extradition and exchange of evidence relating to prosecution of those accused of torture. There is, as well, established within the treaty framework a Committee Against Torture consisting of ten experts selected, in the language of Article 17(1), for their "high moral standing and recognized competence in the field of human rights, who shall serve in their personal capacity." The committee is responsible for receiving and evaluating reports on implementation from the states that are parties to the treaty. As well, parties to the treaty can go further if so inclined. They can declare their willingness to allow the committee to receive complaints about failures to implement from other parties to the treaty, and even from individuals.

The Torture Convention creates the formal potential for innovation without any assurance it will be realized in practice. Sovereignty is still the presiding political force. Governments nominate those elected to serve on the Committee Against Torture, prepare their own compliance reports, and are subject to complaints by other governments or individuals only to the extent that they agree to be. It can be assumed that governments that engage in torture will be the last to participate and, if they do so at all, only in a nominal, public relations manner.

Nevertheless, the Torture Convention helps set a normative climate. To the extent ratified or taken into the body of international law it establishes a "no exceptions" duty to refrain from torture, and it places a burden of legal responsibility on those who set policy or carry it out, regardless of what "superior orders" are given. As a result, it gives victims or human rights adherents a principled basis of objection to torture.

The Torture Convention sets a desirable precedent for an approach to the broader issues of terrorism. Torture is a type of terror—often carried on in secret, designed to instill fear among a wide target audience, and entailing a form of violence that lacks moral or legal mandate. And torture is characteristically, although not exclusively, a species of crime of state. The activity of torture is now condemned as terrorist, and direct or indirect support for a regime that relies on torture as illegitimate. Furthermore, if the torture of a single individual is prohibited, even if there exists an instrumental justification (gaining information), then inflicting death or injury on those who are "innocent" is totally unacceptable even if undertaken in the name of counterterrorism. That is, any resort to political violence with such characteristics seems to be normatively precluded. Such a trend toward condemning political violence that is not limited, proportionate, and defensive is relevant to the worldwide effort to prohibit threats or uses of nuclear weapons and to oppose their further development, and eventually even their possession.[20]

To the extent that the Convention Against Torture repudiates the absolute pretensions of the state in the domain of national security it brings the functionary under the sway of law and morality and thus opposes the kind of unconditional claims to use violence that are expressed by the cult of counterterrorism or by an acceptance of nuclear deterrence. True, this repudiation of terrorism is made by governments and is largely dependent at this stage on self-enforcement and the sanctions of public opinion. But the other, more optimistic reading is that *even* governments have had to acknowledge limits on their discretion to use violence for the ends of state security even in time of war and national emergency, and that citizens can invoke these limits. In this regard the Convention Against Torture revives the enterprise of Nuremberg to impose criminal liability on those who act for the state. It remains to be seen whether these efforts at accountability can overcome the impression of victors' justice, and move on to be rules of general applicability.

Such a repudiation of state-sponsored terrorism of all varieties is clarified in the important UN document of 1970, Declaration on Principles of International Law Concerning Friendly Relations and Co-Operation among States in Accordance with the Charter of the United Nations. This document establishes a basic framework for relations among states and is explicit about several issues bearing on current international law controversies. Principle 1 of the declaration contains the basic prohibition of the use of force in international relations; its commentary asserts that "States have a duty to refrain from acts of reprisal involving the use of force." That is, unless a state can claim self-defense against an armed attack it cannot legally engage in transborder uses of force as part of a forward or preemptive counterterrorist strategy. Further, "Every State has the duty to refrain from organizing or encouraging the organization of irregular forces or armed bands, including

mercenaries, for incursion into the territory of another State."
And closely connected, "Every State has the duty to refrain
from organizing, instigating, assisting or participating in acts
of civil strife or terrorist acts in another State or acquiescing
in organized activities within its territory directed toward the
commission of such acts."[21] If such legal guidelines were applied with some degree of uniformity, then the phenomenon
of state sponsorship would be likely to disappear, but so long
as the accusation of state sponsorship is a propaganda ploy
that exempts scrutiny of one's own behavior by common standards, the law remains an empty manipulator of hostile symbols with very little legitimacy to its claims.

There is a third extremely helpful set of developments
in the area of international law pertaining to international
terrorism—an extension of the law of war to the kind of armed
conflicts in which terrorist practices are most associated in the
contemporary world. In one sense, this extension acknowledges the reality of "low-intensity warfare" and "wars of national liberation." It refuses, in other words, to give functionaries
"a blank check" and to convert revolutionaries into a species
of depraved criminality without any legal protection. The most
relevant developments occurred in relation to the negotiation
of the 1977 Protocol I addition to the 1949 Geneva Conventions on the Protection of Victims of International Armed
Conflicts.[22] Protocol I is itself an elaborate proposed treaty
that sets forth the contemporary law of war in comprehensive
terms responsive to the real currents of international conflict.
What is most encouraging about the protocol is that it reflects
the outcome of complex, sustained intergovernmental negotiations that have built their notions about legal restraint largely
on the basis of the parity between revolutionaries and functionaries with respect to the rules of combat. In other words,
the law pertains to violent practice, regardless of the status
or identity of the political actor.[23] This breakthrough reflects
the shift in the balance of opinion among states to one of
limited support for certain revolutionary causes and is attributable to the legitimacy associated with the rise of the Third

World in the aftermath of colonialism. This extension of coverage is explicitly granted to "peoples fighting against colonial domination and alien occupation and against racist regimes in the exercise of their right of self-determination as enshrined" in the UN Charter. Two features of Protocol I are of especial note: first, the granting of POW status to members of liberation movements; second, the overall reaffirmation of limits on violence that are based on absolute respect for the principle of civilian innocence. In other words, Protocol I is genuinely antiterrorist in its essential character.

There are some technical rules surrounding prisoner of war status, mainly pertaining to an obligation that fighters be distinguishable from civilian populations. But even here the influence of Third World viewpoints is evident. Article 44(3) recognizes "there are situations in armed conflicts where, owing to the nature of the hostilities an armed combatant cannot so distinguish himself;" he shall retain status as combatant, provided only that in combat and preparations for attack "he carries his arms openly." To be a combatant means to be entitled to prisoner of war status, the rights and duties of which are set forth in an earlier 1949 Geneva Convention III Relative to the Treatment of Prisoners of War. When captured, someone entitled to this treatment can only be detained for the duration of hostilities. He cannot be validly punished for taking part in the armed conflict, although he can be prosecuted for specific breaches of the laws of war. Also, a POW cannot be legally subjected to questioning. Once captured, a combatant whether associated with the state or its revolutionary opposition, largely re-acquires the attributes of "innocence."

Another notable feature of Protocol I is its elaboration of a commitment to antiterrorist rules of engagement and combat. In Article 48 the international agreement is very definite about the duty of all Parties "at all times to distinguish between civilian population and combatants and between civilian objects and military objectives." Article 51(2) reads as follows: "The civilian population as such, as well as individual civilians, shall not be the object of attack. Acts or threats of violence, the primary purpose of which is to spread terror among the civilian population are prohibited." A stance of selective violence as part of a legitimate armed struggle is illustrated by charges the South African commissioner of police, General Johan Coetzee, made against the African National Congress. Coetzee contended that the ANC committed 275 acts of "terrorism" between 1976 and 1985 consisting of the following incidents: sixty-one attacks on police; 125 attacks against the economy; fifty-six attacks on military-, police-, or apartheid-related public buildings; and thirty-five attacks on informers or collaborators. These violent undertakings, while possibly the occasion of incidental civilian damage, generally qualified as nonterroristic because the targets of attack were noninnocent, that is, associated with the South African governing structure and the apartheid system.[24]

Other provisions have apparently been drafted with retaliatory violence in mind, especially patterns of reprisal raids associated with Israeli operations against Palestinians or aimed at targets in Arab countries that provide aid and comfort to the Palestinians. For example, indiscriminate violence is forbidden, and an attack is considered indiscriminate if "by bombardment" it "treats as a single military objective a number of clearly separated and distinct military objectives located in a city, town, village," or if "an attack . . . may be expected to cause incidental loss of civilian life . . . excessive in relation to . . . military advantage anticipated" [Article 51(7)]. And in Article 51(6), "Attacks against the civilian population or civilians by way of reprisals are prohibited." Again, the repeated Israeli attacks on Palestinian refugee camps seem to be prohibited by any fair application of the rules contained in Protocol I. Yet even more clearly repudiated is the claim often advanced for liberation groups, especially in the setting of the antiapartheid struggle, that anything goes if it arises as a reaction to oppression and is undertaken in the name of self-determination. Protocol I rejects unequivocally the claims of "liberation terrorism."[25] Protocol I as a whole steers a course around those who would give their unconditional blessings to either functionaries or revolutionaries and is thus a real contribution to an antiterrorist conception of both world order and legitimate armed struggle. Although not enthusiastic about the attempt to extend humanitarian protection to revolutionary groups, the Carter administration concluded negotiations carried on during the Nixon and Ford years and signed Protocol I, indicating its intention to submit the treaty to the U.S. Senate for ratification in good faith. Actually, so far, forty of the more than one hundred signatories, including Denmark, Norway, Belgium, and Italy, have ratified the protocol. Those who have announced opposition, besides the United States, include Israel and France.

The Reagan administration, objecting to certain provisions that might raise the status of revolutionary groups, has decided not to submit Protocol I for ratification.[26] In a letter to the Senate Foreign Relations Committee, President Reagan called Protocol I "fundamentally and irreconcilably flawed" on the ground that it gives recognition and status to liberation groups by granting their combatants POW status. Reagan wrote that "we must not, and need not, give recognition and protection to terrorist groups as a price for progress in humanitarian law."[27] There has also been some bureaucratic opposition to the role that might be assumed by regional organizations such as the Arab League and the Organization of African Unity in deciding the scope of coverage. But as Douglas Feith, a former deputy assistant secretary of defense for negotiations, accurately put it, "President Reagan's decision is a victory for anti-PLO diplomacy."[28]

Perhaps more significant than the predictable attitude of the Reagan administration, given its version of antiterrorism, was the general consensus for rejecting Protocol I. *The New York Times* in an editorial agreed that Protocol I "would improve protection for prisoners of war and civilians, but at the price of new legal protection for guerrillas and possible terrorists." The editorial writer echoed the official line by regarding the assurances about liberation struggles in Protocol

I as "nice words, but also possible grounds for giving terrorists the legal status of P.O.W.'s." The editorial regarded Reagan's repudiation of Protocol I as "a judgment that deserves support."[29]

This reaction to Protocol I suggests the hold of "the cult of counterterrorism" (compare chapter 2) over American mainstream opinion. As a respected Red Cross official, Hans-Peter Gasser, has written, it is a profound misunderstanding of Protocol I to regard that its content relating to liberation activity "legitimizes terrorism." On the contrary, the protocol "is characterized by an elaborate set of prohibitions of terrorist acts" that apply *in toto, to wars of national liberation"; "the* new law should be seen rather as an attempt to achieve stricter, humanity-oriented control over wars of national liberation, such wars being, as experience shows, characterized by particularly severe outbreaks of violence."[30]

This battle over symbols goes to the core of our argument. Protocol I is constructed around the regulation of violent practices, not assuming any necessary link between actor and illegal violence. The United States position, in effect, is to retain the inherent connection between terrorism and liberation activity, so that any violence by such a group as the PLO is dismissed as inherently terrorist, and any response as inherently counterterrorist. Such an appropriation of "law" is an attempt to use it as an ideological instrument of struggle in a divided world, or, if not of struggle, at least of political mobilization among the like-minded. My claim is that this is a misuse of law and that we need the sort of common framework of respect for civilian innocence that Protocol I sets forth with such admirable clarity.

We need, as well, a framework for application that is genuinely antiterrorist. Protocol I moves tentatively in that direction by setting up an International Fact-Finding Commission of independent individuals (Article 90) and by imposing an obligation on parties to pay compensation in the event of any violation (Article 91). These efforts are tentative because participation by states in this part of the framework is essentially voluntary. Sovereign rights are respected; therefore, Protocol I is a basis for the sanctions of public opinion and the ethos of self-enforcement, but not necessarily much more. Nor, however, could more be expected at this time.

From time to time there have been some proposals for an international criminal court empowered to assess allegations of terrorist activity as committed by either revolutionaries or functionaries.[31] Such a supranational proposal gives permanent institutional expression to ideas about individual responsibility of everyone, including government officials, for crimes, especially crimes of state. Terrorism, as has been argued here, is a prime instance of criminality.

But appropriateness does not imply feasibility. Governments remain unwilling to be judged, especially in matters of national security. Besides, leading governments have adopted terrorism as an instrument of state policy in dealing with actual and potential enemies, either by counterterrorist indiscriminate violence or by deterrent threats of annihilating violence in the form of nuclear attack. Without a real transformation of the basis of state power, it seems utopian to imagine governments' tying their hands beyond establishing a new code for the ruler of the game, and even this runs into difficulties because some countries (such as the United States) want those rules to coincide with their foreign policy goals.

What might be possible, however, is for "law" to be removed from the exclusive control of governments. Such a process has started and represents one area of success of social movements trying to reinvent democracy and effective means for expressing popular sovereignty. For instance, the Permanent Peoples' Tribunal is a European citizen-based group, without official sanction, that claims the mantle of "law" to inquire into the commission of crimes of state, including terrorism. Such a body exerts some influence in the struggle to legitimize and stigmatize particular political actors and their methods of behaving. If anything, such a group as the tribunal reverses legitimacy presumptions and is more favorable to revolutionary than to functionary claims.[32] In any event, an encouraging *legal development* is the emerging legalist claims by those who act on the basis of conscience and convictions, as citizens of an inchoate global community, to identify crimes of state including recourse to terrorism.

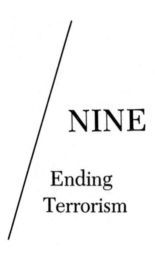

NINE

Ending
Terrorism

A program for ending terrorism must be rooted in a process of self-examination. It is connected with the establishment of limits upon the pursuit of political goals by all actors. Those who repudiate these limits are inclined toward terrorist methods. State actors are the most important source of both limits and their abuse, and especially the leading state actors at any given moment in history. The outer limit of terrorism is omnicide, and reliance by governments on nuclear weapons as potential instruments of conflict represents a total embrace of the ethos of terrorism. The persistence of this reliance in the face of nuclear winter findings, however much scientists debate their implications, expresses a willingness to protect interests and values by recourse, as necessary, to ultimate forms of terrorism. This dependence seems also connected, on the American side, with an absence of effort, even a refusal, to take advantage of denuclearizing opportunities. These opportunities seem to have increased greatly during the period of Gorbachev's leadership in the Soviet Union.

The more graphic imagery of terrorism is associated with violence at close range or by dispossessed elements of society. Let us stereotype this type of terrorism by machine-gun fire directed at tourists in an international airport or by seizure of children as hostages who are threatened by murder if the government in power does not satisfy blackmail demands. This kind of political violence is totally unacceptable. It has to be opposed, prevented, and protected against and its perpetrators captured and punished. At the same time, violence of this depraved sort may rest on a ground of legitimate, even compelling, grievance and an overall setting may provide no alternatives to terrorism. Just as terrorism is unacceptable, so is it unacceptable to impose political frameworks that deny fundamental rights and provide no reasonable means of challenge. When, as in contemporary South Africa, the state oppresses and terrorizes its majority African population, violent responses must be understood as essentially derivative and reactive, not isolated phenomena. The use of violence against those who are innocent or in ways calculated to cause intense fear in the target and others is unacceptable, but its occurrence should be appreciated in relation to contexts of sustained frustration and mass cruelty orchestrated by the state and ruthlessly carried out by official institutions and their representatives. If, as in South Africa, the overwhelming number of casualties are black, then the racial character of violence seems evident and it is possible to apportion degrees of responsibility for violence. Perhaps a single incident could be explained on other grounds, but pervasive patterns of losses from direct encounters cannot. There is, of course, the further reality of shorter life expectancies for the oppressed blacks, an outcome of what the Norwegian social scientist Johan Galtung has called "structural violence." Although these forms of violence take a greater toll than direct violence and afflict the innocent, it is difficult to regard them as terrorism per se because the outcome is an unintended side effect of policy.

The notion of state sponsorship of terrorism embraces its own agencies and agents, as well as groups in the private sector, whether at home or abroad. In this regard, the death squads that have operated in Argentina (1976–1983) and El Salvador are exemplary instances of state-sponsored terrorism. It is misleading and self-serving to claim, as has been repeatedly done by the Reagan presidency, to confine the idea of state sponsorship of terrorism to the training, financing, and encouragement of revolutionary nationalist movements in the Third World.

To end terrorism does not necessarily mean to renounce political violence altogether. A rejection of terrorism does require the acceptance of a framework of moral and legal limits to assess all claims to use violence, regardless of the identity of the political actor. Ending terrorism also does not imply an unconditional acceptance of legality as the outer limit of legitimate political conduct whether of government or of social and political movements. Civil-disobedience concepts, as well as various natural law and Nuremberg arguments based on ideas of "higher law," can apply valid arguments in support of political violence, but not those forms of violence directed at innocent targets.

A program to end terrorism must concern itself equally with both revolutionaries and functionaries if it is to rise above the level of propaganda. If it is exclusively a program to suppress revolutionary violence, then claims that such policies represent a genuine antiterrorism effort are false. If it is a program designed only to discredit states, or particular forms of government, calling them totalitarian or imperialist, then the language of terrorism is being enlisted in the service of partisan causes that lie at the root of geopolitics and give rise to the main patterns of international conflict. Only an inclusive approach based on the character of the violence offers any prospect of an effective, principled, and coherent program to end terrorism.

Such an undertaking is difficult. We have become victims

of partisan language for so long that it seems almost impossible to construct impartial categories. It is an aspect of a conflict-laden manner of perceiving political reality: them against us. The years of cold war rhetoric have deepened this divide. The dominance of political discourse by the interests and outlook of particular states is an even more fundamental explanation of the confusion about the character of terrorism. The effort in recent years has been to connect our enemies with a form of violence we call "terrorism" and to oppose this violence from a higher plateau of actions and behavior called "antiterrorism" or "counterterrorism."

In the Reagan years, this campaign has intensified and focused on Third World, especially Middle Eastern, perpetrators of violence, portrayed as fanatical adherents of extreme behavior, whose actions are being cynically orchestrated by the Soviet government to score foreign policy gains in a world made too dangerous for more traditional forms of expansionism. There is a measure of accuracy in this portrayal, given the turmoil and fundamentalist passions set loose in the Middle East and considering the degree to which the United States is regarded as the enemy of these political forces and responsible for their deep-seated sense of frustration. Disturbing patterns of anti-American terrorism have ensued, but to blame the Soviet Union for these developments or to associate the overall problem of terrorism with this specific category of terrorist behavior is to make it impossible either to end terrorism or to accept a measure of responsibility for the wider situation.

The policy that follows from such an unbalanced approach to antiterrorism is to act as effectively and directly as possible against hostile forces and their patrons. As is frequently supposed in the mainstream antiterrorist writing, the struggle against terrorism is a special species of modern warfare, with the terrorist challenge conceived as an extension and special application of Maoist thinking on guerrilla warfare. Such an enemy must be destroyed to achieve victory; neither negotiations nor accommodations can diminish the terrorist threat.

To back down under pressure or to be humiliated and ineffectual is to suffer "defeats" at the hands of terrorism. The U.S. retreat from Lebanon in 1983 and the long ordeal of the Iranian hostage seizure are, in this understanding, prime instances of defeats at the hands of terrorism.

On the revolutionary side, there is also a tendency to dehumanize the enemy and to make anyone associated with or even living under the protection of the prevailing order a suitable target for violence. The isolation of revolutionary groups, their discipline and underground life-style, make them perceive the world and act in a very fundamentalist style— only *their* truth matters, and if society doesn't yet grasp it, then so much the worse for society and its members. All those who don't join the revolutionary cause lose their innocence, regardless of whether they play an official role in supporting the government in power. Also, the hopelessness of the revolutionary project, especially in relation to well-organized states, can create an ethos of blood for the sake of blood. There is often no feasible political end in view beyond provoking fear and anguish. Such rupturings of civic order induce the citizenry to accept, and even demand, governmental protection and counterviolence of a punitive kind whether the source of political violence is at home or overseas. "Nuke the Ayatollah!" was a popular rallying cry during the hostage crisis even though punitive violence against Iran would have menaced the lives of the hostages. The hatred of the terrorists generally takes precedence over protective concern for their hostage victims.

The current breakdown of relations evident in the practice of terroristic forms of violence is an affliction of modernity that threatens both humane forms of politics and the overall survival of international order and the human species. A program for ending terrorism must address itself to these underlying concerns, seeking to combine the practical requirements of the present situation with the search for real solutions. This latter quest goes deep into the subsoil of politics, ethics, and conflict and will require time and patience, but without it, the spirals of terroristic violence are likely to persist, and even to engulf our culture.

A program of constructive counterterrorism would seek to realize these objectives:

Integrity of language. Refrain from any reference to terrorism that tends to restrict the term to adversary tactics and behavior. Relate terrorism to all forms of political violence that induce fear, that cannot be validated by societal traditions of law and morality, and that do not respect limits on the pursuit of public policy goals. The political violence and the operating milieus of both revolutionaries and functionaries must be encompassed, with no exemptions made for sacred causes or unconditional claims. Neither the revolutionary nor the functionary can waive the restraints of law and morality so as to pursue more effectively a series of political objectives.

Identify prevailing practices of terrorism associated with both revolutionaries and functionaries in order to promote their repudiation. Abstractions about terrorism do not help, nor do self-serving formulations. Characterizations of terrorism must not be confined to its "otherness" and the policy challenge being to devise tactics "to fight back." We seek something more objective and, in the end, more effective and self-enhancing than a military strategy for dealing with enemies who use political violence to induce fear and havoc.

The essence of an objective approach is to lift the discourse above the level of contending conceptions of "the good"—battles of ideas about democracy and liberation. Accordingly, terrorism is identified here by three elements:

■ actual or threatened violence for primarily political ends.

■ reliance on means that in themselves (that is, that can not be justified by the end to be served) seem immoral and illegal.

■ effects that generate fear beyond the victims of violence, suggesting that the acts of violence are coded with symbolic messages.

Less central is the secret or conspiratorial element that is usually associated with such forms of political violence. On the basis of this conception, several practices can be unconditionally condemned as forms of terrorism:

- seizure of hostages.
- torture and assassination of political opponents, including "disappearances" and "kidnappings."
- hijacking of planes, ships, trains.
- use of explosive devices in places of civilian use such as stores, restaurants, and cultural and recreational centers.
- bombing (from air or sea) of inhabited areas, especially places associated with civilian presence, including hospitals, churches, refugee camps, and undefended towns and cities.
- reliance on weaponry of mass destruction, especially nuclear weapons but also chemical, biological, radiological ones.
- covert operations, including acts of violence, designed to destabilize a constitutional order, assassinate officials and political opponents, and alter the character of government by interference with self-determination.
- covert operations, including acts of violence, designed to overcome popular opposition and stabilize the governing process of a foreign country despite its commission of gross abuses of human rights on a systematic basis.

There are some unavoidable ambiguities. If the target of violence is reasonably apprehended as a source of terrorism, then the action may not be objectionable: for instance, using violence against foreign troops or agents who have themselves engaged in terrorism. When revolutionaries identify and capture someone who is responsible for the torture of political prisoners, then his subsequent execution is not an act of terrorism, unless carried out in a gruesome way to induce fear. All claims of justifiable violence should be scrutinized carefully; the burden of persuasion rests heavily upon the perpetrator. Even if it is undertaken in the name of antiterrorism, the selectivity and discriminate character of the violence must be apparent and must impress informed and impartial persons as reasonable, given the overall circumstances.

In this regard, murdering a secret agent who has engaged in cruel abuses is not itself terrorism, nor is placing a bomb at a military facility of a foreign occupying power. But if the territorial government is legitimate and there exist democratic means to change official policies, then recourse to the tactics of private warfare is disruptive of constitutional order and terroristic in its character. The identification of certain instances of practice as terrorist or not is partially linked to context and interpretation. The roots of objectivity involve the moral and legal status of the violence relied upon and its relation to the existence of alternative means. We cannot identify what is terrorism without passing judgment about the reasonableness of a given claim to act violently to achieve some political end.

Nuclear weaponry complicates the picture. The primary role of nuclear weapons is to threaten massive violence, especially in the form of credible threats that will be carried out under certain circumstances. The threats themselves induce a generalized fear of catastrophe and annihilation and produce "a balance of terror" in the circumstance of each superpower's relying on the threat to destroy the other utterly if it launches a nuclear attack. The status of this weaponry is dubious from both moral and legal perspectives, especially to the extent that first-use options and notions of extended deterrence are retained.

At the same time, deterrence is embedded in the security systems of the nuclear weapons states. The Catholic bishops allowed in their 1983 pastoral letter that relying on nuclear weapons to a limited degree is acceptable, but only for a potential retaliatory role, and then only if accompanied by good faith and diligent efforts to achieve nuclear disarmament. Even under this doctrine of conditional acceptance, it seems reasonable to conclude that the United States government, at least, has sustained its embrace of nuclearism, retaining first-use options and postures of extended deterrence and, arguably, increasing its reliance on nuclear weaponry by seeking a first-strike option under the guise of "weapons modernization programs" and "strategic defense initiative" (SDI). And what is worse, the U.S. government has seemed to reject many negotiating possibilities for denuclearizing forms of arms control. Even if the United States and the Soviet Union do reach agreement on the elimination of intermediate-range missiles, the basic story remains one of lost opportunities.

Adhere to normative guidelines that are congruent with prevailing societal understandings of law and morality. The burden of justification is always upon perpetrators of violence, especially if the violence is in pursuit of political goals. At the same time, official doctrines of law and morality are not decisive in all instances, especially in a political setting in which gross patterns of human rights violations exist and in which democratic procedures do not operate to provide citizens with reasonable opportunities to challenge state policies and practices.

FUNCTIONARIES

War is not necessarily, or even normally, a species of terrorism, yet threats and belligerent practices may be. Recourse to war is governed by international law, as well as by the constitutional structures of domestic society. The basic notion embodied in the United Nations Charter and recently given an extensive interpretation by the World Court in the setting of allegations by Nicaragua against the United States role in Central America is that uses of force are "illegal" unless undertaken in "self-defense" against a prior "armed attack." An illegal use of force may constitute both a violation of international law and a "crime against peace" in the Nuremberg sense that could result in individual criminal liability for the leading policymakers, yet this is not terrorism.

The issue of terrorism arises when leaders and bureaucrats plan and execute policies designed to threaten indiscriminate destruction; aim weapons at nonmilitary targets; carry out policies that deliberately cause cruel and unusual suffering for civilians, prisoners of war, or combatants; and engage in deeds and disseminate propaganda calculated to induce fear in nonmilitary elements of the enemy society. United States tactics in Vietnam involved many instances of terrorism in war. Among the most notorious of these was reliance on "free-fire zones" (anything that moves in wide areas of the countryside treated as a target) and the Phoenix Program (assassination of the civilian infrastructure of villages alleged to be under Vietcong control). There were also terroristic tactics employed by the North Vietnam/National Liberation Front side in the war but not of a character that in any way mitigated the violation of civilian innocence by the United States/South Vietnam side in the war. Adherence to the laws of war as embodied in several Hague and Geneva treaties relating to the conduct of hostilities is necessary to avoid introducing a terrorist dimension into warfare.

The more problematic and relevant issue of terrorism by government pertains to the internal and external use of force during periods of peace. Governments are sovereign within territory and are not precluded from executing individuals for the commission of serious crimes. Governments and their representatives are forbidden to violate fundamental human rights, but such violations do not normally qualify as terrorism unless of a severe and systematic character that is calculated to induce fear, eliminate opponents by extralegal means, rely on excessive and cruel violence to sustain order, employ torture as a punitive or enforcement technique, and seek as official policy to eliminate an ethnically or religiously distinct element in the population (genocide).

Thus, if enforcement officials shoot or torture alleged terrorists who are in prison, this is a species of state terror. If the government incites, guides, and otherwise encourages private or semiprivate groups to kidnap, torture, and execute opponents, this is a species of state terror, as illustrated by the operation of "death squads" in Videla's Argentina or over the years in El Salvador. On some occasions, the civilian leadership may not be able to control military and intelligence subunits or former government networks that engage in such terrorist practice. The issue of responsibility is one of factual connection and capability. Tolerance or encouragement of terror against enemies of the regime, especially if law enforcement is possible, leads to an accessory responsibility for terrorism. A government owes its citizenry, at a minimum, protection against official and semiofficial practices of terrorism. Functionaries unable to secure this obligation of government have a normal minimum obligation to resign and, depending on the setting, to do so in such a way as to make public the occurrence of state terrorism.

The existence of secret police that engage in covert operations at home or abroad presents special problems. Such an arm of government is inherently more difficult to constrain within limits of law and morality, especially if the state, as is characteristic of modern states, views internal and national security in absolute terms and as shrouded by secrecy. As Americans, we grasp the terrorist core at the operation of such organizations of state power as the KGB and the Shah's Savak. Their main roles are inducing fear, intimidating opposition, and punishing any expressions of dissent severely.

It is more difficult to reach a similar clarity about our own police and intelligence operations. Because the security rationale is so persuasive with the citizenry and media, organs of the state such as the FBI and CIA are accorded a generally favorable status in public discourse. When unfavorable practices come to light there is a tendency to explain the disclosures as anomalies or as the outcome of actions by zealous or disturbed individuals and to respond to the symptoms of official wrongdoing by presidential commissions and congressional investigations that provide a measure of reassurance. At the same time, structures of secrecy are relegitimated and the mandate to engage in covert operations confirmed, subject only to the imposition of a greater degree of presidential and legislative "oversight."

If one takes account, however, of the links and practices, the approval of covert operations is tantamount to an endorsement of terror. In the Iran/Contra investigations there has been attention to the bureaucratic dynamics that got out of hand and to a series of functionaries (and their private sector contacts) who may have acted improperly, even illegally. The Tower Commission has recommended more oversight by Congress and the president and a greater reliance on the CIA (as distinct from the NSC) in covert operations but fails in its recommendations even to preclude the NSC from acting in exceptional circumstances. The congressional hearings seem to have been designed to extend the narrative of who knew what and what became of the money. Such a process gathers evidence that might create the factual basis for criminal indictments or political disgrace of a number of public figures. But there is no evident substantive effort to challenge governmental prerogatives to engage in political violence of a terroristic character.

As a consequence, the effects of sustaining the Contra resistance movement are ignored altogether even if such support is coupled with compelling evidence of crimes against humanity directed at the people of Nicaragua. There has been no effort by Congress or the president to constrain the CIA and other branches of government to the limits of international law. President Reagan in his speech on the Iran/Contra developments given after the issuance of the Tower Commission report said only this:

> I wanted a policy that was justifiable and understandable in public as it was in secret. I wanted a policy that reflected the will of the Congress as well as the White House. And I told them that there'll be no more freelancing by individuals when it comes to our national security.[1]

At most, such a posture promises coherence (we won't say in public that we will not trade arms for hostages and then do so secretly) and respect for a greater balance between Congress and the presidency. It does not provide reassurances against illegal and immoral uses of force, promising only that if disclosed they would likely be popular with the public. Because uses of force are popular when they are directed at targets associated with allegations of Third World terrorism or Marxism-Leninism, there are no effective or operative limits on United States policy. Assassinations; bombings of cities, even refugee camps; abuse of captives can all be justified as secret policies that are not antagonistic to American values. They can be made to fit within the notion of strategic assets. Terrorism is an instrument of state policy given other names so as to disguise its character, but regarded as useful, even necessary, and treated as legitimate. Once the mood of outrage subsides, and the sense of scandal dims, official recourse to terrorism again becomes an acceptable means of pursuing foreign policy.

If terrorism is to be ended, then this mandate must be unconditionally withdrawn and the capability dismantled. The United States government, if it is to be an antiterrorist actor, that is, responsive to American values (regardless of short-term interests), must limit its options to those allowable by law and morality. Any given claim to use force must be assessed by its reasonableness and defensive character within context, but no context can justify governmental reliance on torture or terror.

REVOLUTIONARIES

Recourse to political violence is always characterized as illegal if undertaken by opponents of a prevailing political order. But as in the case of functionaries it is not necessarily "terrorism" unless it ignores the constraints of law and morality in its violent practices.

At the same time, there is a greater presumption of terrorist orientation, especially if violent opposition is initiated in a political atmosphere where a constitutional arrangement operates and does not exclude important segments of the population.[2] That is, political violence per se in a democratic society has a terrorist quality.

That quality is intensified to the extent that the targets of violence are selected to be transmitters of fear to the general populace and are innocent of wrongdoing or have no official status. When a resistance group shoots police, soldiers, or prison officials it is not necessarily engaged in terrorism if those who resort to political violence have sustained the burden of persuasion incumbent upon them to justify their reliance on armed struggle to achieve their goals. In this regard, the ANC and the PLO seem justified from legal and moral perspectives in their recourse to political violence in relation to South Africa and Israel, respectively, but this does not exempt such organizations from their responsibility to refrain from political violence directed indiscriminately, excessively, or intentionally designed to harm the innocent. If they do not constrain their violence within these guidelines, then their practices can be suitably regarded as terrorist and punished accordingly.

Revolutionaries, even less than functionaries, are never free from the constraints of law and morality. Indeed, revolutionaries have the additional taint of illegitimacy, reacting against formal governmental authority, whereas functionaries start off with a favorable identity as the legitimate institutional expression of political community. To the extent the government rules by violence and fear and does not allow dissent and free elections, it loses, or compromises, its legitimacy.

As chapter 8 argues, normative guidelines exist and are fairly clear in most applications. Their effectiveness would be enhanced by the broad acceptance and implementation of the two 1977 Geneva Protocols Relating to the Protection of Victims of International and Non-International Armed Conflicts. These protocols clearly and concretely reinforce the general limits endorsed here and impose responsibility on the political leadership for military undertakings, whether covert or overt.

On these bases, some recommendations for public policy can be set forth. President Reagan has been unusually adept at manipulating the rhetoric of foreign policy to censure opponents while clothing United States action of a comparable character in the protective clothing of national security. When the Soviet Union engages in surveillance within the American embassy in Moscow it is reprehensible "espionage"; when the United States does the same thing it is "an intelligence coup." More to the point, Reagan has tried to present the covert operations dimension of foreign policy, especially as carried out in Central America, as beyond legitimate scrutiny, even by American citizens.

The lack of limits and accountability associated with covert operations is evident. One of the reasons to select a covert approach is to evade public scrutiny of controversial policies, especially if the policies are unpopular at home or contravene stated goals. In effect, intelligence operations are given a virtual blank check, and their performance often discloses a lack of regard for human rights, including fundamental principles of self-determination and nonintervention, respect for laws of war, and prohibitions on crimes against humanity. For this reason it seems to me that a serious antiterrorist policy is incompatible with the retention of a covert operations capability of a generalized character.

Such an extension, to be practical, is complicated and requires some fine tuning. Those covert operations involving direct and indirect uses of military and paramilitary force should be prohibited unless connected directly with undertakings explicitly sanctioned by the United Nations Security Council or General Assembly as furthering peacekeeping or human rights goals. Even then, as otherwise, such operations should be constrained by the norms of international law governing the conduct of hostilities. These norms can never be suspended for the sake of expediency. The reliance on internal secrecy in relation to Congress should be completely abandoned, and in relation to the American people secrecy should only be allowed if the government can sustain a heavy burden of persuasion in the course of an explanation to the congressional oversight committee.

The arguments that others engage in covert activities, or that if such activity is not performed by the CIA, then the

locus will merely be shifted to a more pliable part of government or farmed out to the private sector, are not convincing.
If the United States opposes terrorism, it must cease its practice no matter what the consequences. If the practical effects
are taken into account, every political actor, including especially private groups, possesses the basis for advancing a comparable rationale. Shultz's acknowledgment that revolutionary
terrorism can be effective is not meant to provide a justification, but, on the contrary, to stiffen the opposing will.

Besides, the pragmatic record of terroristic practice by
government is not very clear. United States interventions in
Third World countries have certainly influenced political outcomes in the short run, but they have often generated very
intense anti-American backlashes over time and have made
Americans and their property prime targets for political violence. The Iran story is a good case history of the cycle that
ran from perceived success (restoring the Shah to power in
1953) to perceived failure as a consequence of the Islamic
revolution. Similarly, the Soviet use of the KGB to influence
politics abroad has had a mixed record. To the extent the
Soviet Union has gone with the anticolonial flow in the Third
World it has enjoyed a better record and image than the
United States. As soon as Soviet covert or overt violence
supports a political status quo at odds with the popular will
in a foreign country, then an anti-Soviet backlash has been
evident as in Eastern Europe and Afghanistan. Soviet encouragement of revolutionary forms of terrorism would be
more subject to genuine censure if the United States renounced such practices and committed itself to a code of conduct that included adherence to moral and legal norms
applicable to reliance on political violence.

There are two issues here: (1) a renunciation of secrecy
as the basis of foreign policy initiatives involving the use of
force; (2) the acceptance as unconditionally binding of the
moral and legal limits pertaining to any use (overt or covert)
of political violence, whether as an aspect of official policy or
of resistance politics.

To carry out these two goals it would be necessary to constrain much more effectively than now the covert operations side of existing intelligence agencies, including especially the CIA. Such a policy constraint would have to be coupled with unqualified legislative prohibitions, including a prohibition on the privatization of covert activities through reliance on soldiers of fortune, arms dealers, and the operatives of organized crime. As necessary, a new division of the CIA or a separately constituted agency could be created to deal with defensive and legitimate counterterrorist situations, including hostage rescues and the possible destabilization of governments engaged in severe, systematic commission of crimes against humanity or genocide in the event such patterns were identified and censured by the United Nations or the investigative reports of such independent nongovernmental organizations as Amnesty International, the International Commission of Jurists, or the Permanent Peoples Tribunal. Intelligence gathering and espionage cannot be called terrorism even in those instances when the techniques relied upon violate the law of the target country.

The essence of ending state-sponsored terrorism in a democratic society such as the United States is the effective extension of constitutionalism to the conduct of foreign policy. Among other effects, accountability implies adherence to law, including international law. Any deliberate recourse to terrorist practice, direct or indirect, covert or overt, active or reactive, must be prohibited unconditionally. Giving citizens and courts a mandate to enforce international law directly would provide a powerful check upon governmental tendencies to promote short-term and ideological goals without respecting applicable limits of law.[3] Limits associated with moral considerations (respect for innocence, for diversity, for self-determination) are most effectively implemented by an antiterrorist political culture, which is now lacking in the United States, a country beset by partisan passions and by a generally indulgent attitude toward excessive violence, especially as deployed against enemies.

The effort to bring normative guidelines to bear on revolutionary activities is complex and cannot realistically hope to have immediate results. Part of the effort must be to associate political legitimacy of resistance claims with adherence to operative moral and legal limits. This can be encouraged by extending the benefits of law and morality to conflict so that a reciprocal structure exists. Political education, diplomatic practice, and policies of international institutions can all contribute. All revolutionary movements aspire to the recognition of their legitimacy. The symbolic quest for status is often as important to political prospects as the search for money and weapons. To the extent that terrorism is consistently renounced it will be possible to develop some credibility for procedures that make adherence to normative guidelines an indispensable prerequisite to international recognition and support and hence to political effectiveness.

It is arguable that the main factions of the PLO, once their demands had become salient on an international level, appreciated that the terroristic image of the organization was a liability. As of 1974 the PLO formally renounced terrorism, and, in fact, its principal leaders and more moderate diplomats have themselves been frequent targets of political violence by more extremist Palestinian factions. This Palestinian renunciation of terrorism can be challenged as only tactical and partial, but the antiterrorist posture struck by Arafat seems connected with the pragmatic judgment that diplomatic respectability could not be achieved by the PLO if it continued to be directly associated with spectacular instances of terrorism as in the manner of its pre-1974 exploits. This kind of realization gives governments considerable leverage, especially if conflict-resolution mechanisms are available to provide a nonviolent alternative.

Develop a positive foreign policy toward social and political change and radical forms of nationalism in other countries. Recourse to revolutionary terrorism is often, but not always, a delayed reaction to some circumstance of injustice, perceived or actual. When that circumstance is so regarded by an important element of the population and the prevailing arrangements of power provide no effective democratic procedures for peaceful challenge, an explosive, violence-generating situation is created. If the existing government is supported by major outside forces—especially if it has been installed by these forces—there arises a temptation to blame local suffering on outsiders and to legitimate acts of violence as resistance. It is important to distinguish situations in which foreign troops and military bases are present as a result of the constitutional processes of the country and express its free will from those in which a foreign military presence can be best explained by coercion, either through intervention or conquest. The issue of legitimacy is partly perception, partly historical circumstance. Some instances are difficult to distinguish. United States military forces in the Federal Republic of Germany were there in the aftermath of war, but their continued presence seems to be a legitimated expression of an alliance based on mutual respect for sovereign rights. Under such circumstances, radical groups are fully entitled to criticize harshly the role of NATO forces in Germany, but they have no acceptable basis for recourse to violence against them. But what of NATO's reliance on a strategic option of nuclear first use? The case for resistance is strong here, and the argument against violent resistance is mainly pragmatic and prudential, namely, that it induces a result opposite to its goal.

In this historical period this general condition of conflict and domination is influenced by a strong current of nationalism that exists as a faith worth dying for in many regions. Whatever gets in the way of this nationalist momentum is regarded as illegitimate, an expression of a colonial or neo-colonial international order. From these experiences, ideas about just wars of national liberation have emerged, receiving a certain blessing from the political organs of the United Nations, especially the General Assembly. Violence on behalf of these nationalist causes, especially in the Third World, is bound closely to the perception of revolutionary terror and to the castigation of countries as sponsors of those forms of terrorism.

Here arise the ambiguity and complexity of the overall setting. The nationalist claim, especially as opposed to foreign domination, enjoys considerable political legitimacy even in its reliance on armed struggle. But the character of the encounter often pits a well-armed state against a disorganized, rural-based revolutionary opposition. Furthermore, the issues become entwined with geopolitics. The United States has generally perceived nationalist tendencies as a threat, to be linked in its underlying reality to the normative challenge of socialism and leftist radicalism, and the overarching geopolitical rivalry with the Soviet Union. It has sided with the established order, giving increasing support to British and French efforts in the 1950s to defend their colonial interests against alleged radicalism and Soviet expansion.

Such imagery has induced the U.S. government to attempt a series of interventions to thwart the outcomes of nationalist movements in the Third World. As a result nationalist victories are experienced as United States defeats, and even more, frustrated nationalists explain their failures and frustrations by reference to the United States as the constabulary force supporting the old oppressive order. The Palestinian instance is central, with the United States seen by most Arabs as a major factor in Israel's will and capability.

Nationalist forces often cannot openly challenge the structures that exist, and yet to accept them would be to accept the humiliations of defeat. On both sides of this impasse, the appeal of terrorist tactics is great. The revolutionaries seek to convey the standard message of symbolic violence. The functionaries are equally determined to crush the will of a broadly based civilian opposition. Neither side is inclined to focus on the military capability of the other. Governing by terror is then sometimes challenged by those who rely on terror; terror can beget terror, but not necessarily. Some forms of state terror produce high degrees of domestic stability despite cruelty and mass discontent. Sustaining armed resistance may not be easy if the society is strictly regimented and penetrated by informers. The Solidarity movement in Poland has explored some avenues of nonviolent resistance, seeking to erode the sphere of governmental effectiveness while not risking encounters of a military or quasimilitary character.[4]

What is worse, as we have noted, the geopolitical lens distorts the nature of the violence. It is only "terror" if it is performed by the other side in the underlying either/or portrayal of world political forces. Sandinistas are them, Contras are us; Sandinistas are engaged in terrorism, whereas their opponents are freedom fighters. The whole debate as to policy is conducted on the confusing basis of a mixture of ideological labels and pragmatic assessments. They are our enemies. These enemies are linked to the Soviet Union. What is the most effective action? The issue is narrowed to one of tactical choice— can intervention succeed? is it strategically worth trying? The intelligence agencies and the military, as specialists in tactics, tend to win these debates, or at least to put opponents on the defensive. As a result, terrorism is tacitly endorsed as state policy, but not explicitly or with entirely open eyes; hence, secrecy is crucial. This endorsement has taken many doctrinal forms—counterinsurgency in the 1960s, counterrevolutionary wars in the 1970s, and low-intensity warfare in the 1980s. But the essential result is the same: making use of high-technology weaponry deployed to kill those directly and indirectly associated with radical nationalism and a reflex effort to disrupt the illusion of control that is tied up with state power. The greater the mobilization of popular forces, the more severe the response in support of state power, and the more desperate the reactions from below.

In this regard, although it is difficult to tie the causal knots, symbolic violence of a disruptive character becomes very appealing to the revolutionary side. It often seems the only viable option: inflict pain by shocking acts of symbolic violence whose impact is achieved through media emphasis and shock effect. Terrorism can achieve an effect far out of proportion to the actual losses inflicted.

The standard reflex is punitive—inflict actual pain on the civilian constituency represented by the terrorists. If revolution is waged for the sake of the future, then counterrevolution seeks to cause immediate civilian suffering disproportionate to any calculus of expected gains. The intention is to break the will of those who give support.

Breaking the terrorist spiral means accepting nationalist dynamics as legitimate. It means adopting a noninterventionary diplomacy. It means exploring every avenue of peaceful settlement and mutual reconciliation. And, above all, it means respecting the autonomy of nationalist movements and refusing to reduce nationalism to the abstractions and formulas of geopolitics.

For the United States, this kind of antiterrorism would require a rejection of efforts to prevent radical political outcomes in foreign countries and a corresponding willingness to accept radical governments as legitimate if they are accepted as such by appropriate regional and global institutions. Such a reorientation of outlook does not mean that these various nationalisms will produce desirable political outcomes, or that they in turn cannot be censured, even opposed, because their patterns of practice include indiscriminate violence against persons and property. It does mean renouncing an interventionary option when our government dislikes the political outcome in another country. It means coexisting with Khomeini's Iran and Castro's Cuba.

A positive foreign policy also must respect the sovereign rights of the small and the weak. An ingredient here is golden rule diplomacy—don't claim what you don't concede to others with comparable status. When the U.S. government proposes preemptive raids to disrupt terrorist preparations, it must be construed as conceding the same option to others similarly situated. If it is actively related to specific cases, the sense of mutuality will introduce self-restraint and discipline into the process by which violence is used by a government to combat hostile activity by others, including terrorists, and will enable the perception that action against terrorism is itself a species of terrorism.

Improve media treatment, public understanding, and anti-terrorist policy. There is an important nexus between media attentiveness and governmental responses to various forms of political violence. A government can emphasize its own preoccupations in such a way that the media are turned on or off, especially in issues having security implications.

It is possible that a government unintentionally inflames a terrorist challenge by calling attention to its impotence. This happened during the response by the Carter presidency to the embassy seizure in Iran over the 1979–1980 period. Motivated by concern for the American hostages being held, and possibly feeling some responsibility for their suffering as a consequence of the White House decision to admit the Shah to the United States despite threatened repercussions, the Carter leadership focused the media on this event as a test of wills between Tehran and Washington. As a consequence, the United States was challenged to act in a situation where action would likely fail or lead to an even worse situation. The rescue attempt, bungled in the Iranian desert by a series of technical failures, might have made matters much worse had it "succeeded," leading either to the death of the hostages or to serious repercussions for other Americans in Iran.

In contrast, the aftermath of the 1986 Iran/Contra disclosures has been to push the American hostages being held in Lebanon off the front pages. These hostages have no inherent importance to their captors. If a firm and consistent policy of giving no concessions and no excess publicity is accorded, such undertakings lose some of their appeal for revolutionary groups. Media exaggeration creates a major incentive to rely upon terrorist spectaculars.

Sometimes, however, a terrorist threat is deliberately exaggerated by public officials for reasons of domestic politics. There was a proclaimed shift in emphasis early in the Reagan administration from human rights to terrorism. This focus on terrorism seemed to be an effort to mobilize widespread support at home and abroad for uses of military power overseas, especially in the Third World. As the efforts by Washington to stabilize the government in El Salvador were being thwarted and inhibitions on intervention remained strong ("the Vietnam allergy"), the call to oppose terrorism was a search for some common ground.

This call, however, created prominence for terrorism but frustrated understanding. It was disoriented by the basic attempt to identify terrorism with ideological adversaries in the Third World. It was also confused with an overall effort to promote more militarist approaches to revolutionary nationalist movements in the Third World. The media were responsive and receptive, exhibiting a tendency to pass onto the public whatever is accented by the government, especially if it can be presented in vivid images. As a consequence, most of public opinion became a captive of this highly selective presentation of terrorism, and the policy discourse in the United States focused on means to punish or destroy these challenges rather than on the upsurge of indiscriminate violence on all sides of political conflict, including especially the governmental side.

To help end terrorism, the media must be encouraged to shift their critical attention to the outbreak of indiscriminate forms of violence. Academic and other sources of political analysis should also be encouraged in the same direction. Such a refocus would certainly include contending with what revolutionaries do, but it would likewise extend policy concern to what functionaries do in the name of state policy.

Inhibit recourse to terrorism by peaceful means. Discouraging the state from terrorist practices is associated with strengthening human rights, democracy, and constitutionalism, mainly through internal developments, but, to the extent possible, also through external pressures brought to bear by international institutions, human rights groups, and development of international legal standards and implementation procedures.

Discouraging antistate political groups from recourse to such violence, aside from seeking to meet grievances and to place all forms of conflict within a normative framework, is a matter of attentiveness and prudence. Making it easy to hijack a plane or ship is to invite desperate groups to employ such a tactic. Airport security can discourage hijacking by altering the risk-taking calculus of a revolutionary group. Such reasoning applies with especial vigor to nuclear facilities, materials, and weapons. It is essential that security precautions be thorough at all sensitive targets, including embassies and foreign bases.

Prudence also extends to the avoidance of provocations, especially giving aid and comfort to individuals or interests that have induced suffering elsewhere. Part of the reason that Americans and official property have become preferred targets in several parts of the world is the perception that the U.S. government has contributed to social and political grievances or has made their resolution impossible. To give asylum to deposed foreign dictators and their entourage, especially if associated with their reign of power, is to invite radical retaliation. The patterns are not consistent. The admission of the Shah incited anti-American terrorism in Iran and the Middle East, whereas admission of Marcos has had no comparable consequences. Nevertheless, it seems prudent to examine all sensitive acts and activities so as not to be unduly provocative. The model of principled behavior seems relevant here, although specific applications may be different (for example, off-base restrictions on servicemen stationed in various foreign countries).

Again, as elsewhere, prudence and avoidance of provocation are more than a matter of hardware and paramilitary vigilance. Indeed, militarizing U.S. embassies abroad contributes to their classification as "legitimate" targets in political conflict. At the same time that security precautions are taken, efforts to improve the image of the American presence should be made. Visitors to American embassies abroad normally encounter a U.S. Marine guard, apparently untrained for the role, who tends to be stiff and often hostile, especially to those who seem poor or exotic. Further, he addresses a visitor from behind Plexiglas and over a shrill microphone. The whole experience can be acutely alienating, even for an American citizen.

Another approach is possible: to be hospitable, to make embassies reflect positive American values, and to embed security procedures in a setting that is not aggressive. That is, embassies give the government an opportunity to model relations with others, either to create goodwill or to substantiate hostile stereotypes. There is no reason to contribute to the image that the United States is indeed "the evil empire." Especially given the wealth and power of the United States, sensitivity to the sufferings and struggles of others would tend to undercut the terrorist logic associated with anti-Americanism.

Superpower Code of Conduct in the Third World. Most of the extreme forms of unrestricted violence occur in the Third World. The patterns of superpower rivalry and intervention have extended many conflicts and brought terrorist tactics to play. At the same time, both superpowers endorse the normative ethos of nonintervention relating to support for exiles, arms sales and transfers, covert operations, and military and paramilitary training and guidance. Adherence to such a framework could reduce intervention in many instances. The basis of such a regime of nonintervention is adherence to mutual rules of restraint, mechanisms for consultation and complaint, and an underlying political realization that intervention rarely achieves its goals if it challenges basic nationalist tendencies. If such a regime could be negotiated and established, it would cut many of the links between Third World conflict and outside powers. As a consequence, the temptations to engage in international terrorism would fall away.

In the film *Starman*, when the extraterrestrial observer is asked to assess the most attractive aspect of the human species, he replies: "You are at your very best when things are worst." The pervasiveness of terror as the idiom of conflict and security has created a situation that threatens the worst and already deepens divisions among the peoples of the earth in apparently irreconcilable ways. Each side peers across the terrorist divide and perceives evil on the other side. The spiral of violence and fragmentation in a setting of absolute conviction is what produces terror and also what makes us perceive only the hostile other as the guilty party.

The ultimate expression of this structure is represented by the exchange of threats to use weapons of mass destruction even if there is assumed a risk of extinguishing future generations and the survival of the species itself. This willingness to rely on nuclear weaponry to sustain security involves an unprecedented assault on the protected status of innocent persons in the present and yet unborn. Increasingly, as well, sustaining such reliance in the face of condemnation by religious institutions and international experts is to adopt terrorism as a policy of last resort.

If governments of leading states claim a terrorist option for themselves, then it is difficult to deny the option to their weak and aggrieved opponents. If political ends can justify the suspension of moral and legal means for the strong, then the weak will feel that their choice to fight back can also be made on a purely expedient basis without respect for normative boundaries. Both functionaries and revolutionaries have embraced terrorism as a dominating political creed. This embrace is so pervasive in our world that it has induced despair.

If we want to be hopeful about our destiny, then it is necessary on all sides to believe that security and justice can be achieved without a terrorist option and to commit ourselves to such a future. Not only does this commitment require limited claims to engage in political violence, accepting the constraints of international law and morality, but it means giving greater weight to what Robert Jay Lifton has called our "species self" and what others have identified as "global identity," "human interests," and "human solidarity." Underneath this call is a sense that human unity is real and important, and that differences must be resolved in all circumstances without loss of respect for the ultimate worth of the other.

The radical form of species self would seem to imply a literal embrace of an imperative of nonviolence, even in its drastic version of resisting no evil. Although such normative radicalism involves a repudiation of terrorism in the purest imaginable form, it seems too unconditional given the structures of oppression and exploitation in our world. If fundamentalists spread violence to intimidate and destroy those who believe differently or racist regimes create intolerable conditions for ethnic groups, the option of defensive violence used within normative boundaries cannot be ruled out. Indeed, a counsel of nonviolent resistance may be neither prudent nor even moral in some situations. Peoples so persecuted, societies so threatened must not be denied rights of self-defense, but these rights must be increasingly subjected to some form of impartial scrutiny. The buildup of the role of international institutions is important for this undertaking.

I believe we are living at a time when our feeling of species identity is becoming more widespread and manifest. The emergence of this encompassing frame is confused by the persistence of nationalism and by the rise of fundamentalist cults of all kinds, but it is this emergence that gives the antiterrorist cause its real foundation of hope. When identities change, the process is uneven and rarely acknowledged for decades, possibly centuries, after the new order has been established. We only "discovered" centuries later that the Peace of Westphalia in 1648 was a decisive moment in the passage of feudal Europe to the modern framework of the territorial sovereign state. The participants at the time were, in general, ignorant of this underlying shift, explaining new developments in incremental terms that accepted as fixed the prevalence of the old order.

If the terrorist option is renounced by symbolically important political actors, then the renunciation is likely to spread. I think there is an underlying weariness associated with the terrorist idiom, whoever is making such claims. There is a strong societal consensus against nuclearism in most democratic countries. Even leaders of the nuclear superpowers have recently at their Iceland summit given some hope of attaining the ideal of a world without nuclear weapons. Although a nuclear backlash has shut down this window of opportunity for the time being, there is a cumulative trend toward greater questioning of any dependence on nuclear weapons as instruments of policy.

Similarly, there is greater questioning of the clandestine undertakings of functionaries planning their operations in settings shielded from scrutiny and accountability. There is a growing belief by citizens in democratic societies that creating exemptions from constitutionalism jeopardizes the prospects of a government, even in a democratic society, to act on behalf of the citizenry—its interests and fundamental beliefs. Without the constraints of law and morality, power tends to be deployed in unacceptable ways, especially in the course of conflict and in relation to enemies. Covert operations persist, but under a darkening cloud.

The Soviet moves toward *glastnost,* even if provisional and reversible, are also encouraging. The underlying promise by the state is to encourage democratization and to respect the rights of people and to accept the discipline of law and morality, as well as acknowledge the importance of effective procedures of accountability.

Even revolutionaries have begun to see the antiterrorist light. Of course, as with all aspects of the subject, trends and countertrends, unevenness, and contradictory bodies of evidence prevail. At the same time, there is a growing understanding among radicals that revolutionary struggle that relies on terror will continue to terrorize once in control of the state. Claims of liberation, in other words, are being subjected to normative tests and self-criticism during the process of struggle. Many new possibilities are associated with the theory and practice of liberation theology in many situations of conflict around the world. Such a religious awakening to the suffering of the poor and the crimes of the strong infuses political struggle with moral passion and spiritual sensitivity, but also with an unwavering rejection of any terrorist practice that violates innocence or the sacredness of life.

The fateful moment is approaching when we can divide the world not by color or class or nationality, but by those who claim a terrorist option and by those who refuse it. If the primary ethical call of our time is to resist the intolerable, the place to begin is a renunciation of terrorism in all of its guises.

Notes

PREFACE

1. Cf. "The Dirty War" (a three-part report compiled by various authors), NACLA report on Americas, Vol. 20, No. 3, June 1986, pp. 33–47.

2. Thomas C. Schelling, *Arms and Influence* (New Haven: Yale University Press, 1966), p. 34.

3. Text in *The New York Times*, July 16, 1987.

4. Elaine Sciolino quotes Brian Jenkins, the counterterrorist expert from RAND, in this vein: "The incidence of international terrorism is very high [in 1987], but popular perceptions are based on a handful of spectacular incidents that involve Americans, not by numbers." See generally her piece headlined "For the U.S., a Deceptive Lull in Terrorism," *The New York Times*, September 20, 1987.

1: THE TWO SOURCES OF TERRORISM

1. The Armenian story is told in convincing detail in Gerard Chaliand and Yves Ternon, *The Armenians: From Genocide to Resistance* (London: Zed Press, 1983); see also the proceedings of the Permanent Peoples' Tribunal published as *A Crime of Silence: The Armenian Genocide* (London:

Zed Press, 1985); Turkish sources continue to question the basic contention of genocide—see, for instance, Kamuran Gurun, *The Armenian File: The Myth of Innocence Exposed* (New York: St. Martin's Press, 1985). This Turkish account treats the whole issue as a collision of militant nationalisms with most of the violence up until the present day emanating from the Armenian side. Of course, it is difficult for a nonexpert to assess competing interpretations of complex events that occurred in past generations, and surely partisan accounts are inevitable where national passions are aroused. Nevertheless, the allegation of genocide against the Armenians seems well founded and has yet to be convincingly refuted or somehow acknowledged by Turkish authorities. For an objective account see Leo Kuper, *Genocide: Its Political Use in the Twentieth Century* (New Haven: Yale University Press, 1981), pp. 101–19.

2. Jenkins, "New Modes of Conflict," Santa Monica, Calif., RAND Publication Series R-3009-DNA, 1983, p. v.

3. The most notorious propagator of this conspiratorial imagery of terrorism is Claire Sterling in her various writings. See especially *The Terror Network* (New York: Holt, Rinehart and Winston, 1981). The evidence provided seems largely to emerge from U.S. intelligence sources and may even embody a considerable amount of disinformation. Nevertheless, its thesis is espoused by many conservatives in and out of government and is widely disseminated in the mass media, being treated as gospel by influential newspapers, including *The Wall Street Journal*. My skepticism is not meant to deny opportunistic Soviet support for nationalist causes that are anti-Western and that rely on terrorist tactics. Unfortunately, both superpowers rely on "terrorists" as an instrument of foreign policy when it suits their purposes. Each accuses the other and describes its own sponsored groups and movements in benevolent language. The sad point is that both superpowers have taken the easy step of renouncing the terrorism of its adversary; neither has renounced its own sponsorship of political violence that would qualify as terrorism if perpetrated by adversaries.

2: THE CULT OF COUNTERTERRORISM

1. Such an emphasis has been prominent among all those who have championed the reinvention of the cold war in the years since the Nixon presidency. One particularly perceptive interpretation of this wider process of geopolitics, its dynamics and rationale, is that of Noam Chomsky. See *Towards a New Cold War* (New York: Pantheon, 1982). Also helpful is Leon Wofsy, ed., *Before the Point of No Return* (New York: Monthly Review Press, 1986). For expressions of the counterterrorist outlook on international politics that results see Benjamin Netanyahu, ed., *Terrorism: How the West Can Win* (New York: Farrar, Straus, Giroux, 1986), and Uri Ra'anan et al.,

eds., *Hydra of Carnage: The International Linkages of Terrorism and Other Low-Intensity Operations* (Lexington, Mass.: Lexington Books, 1986).

2. Paul Johnson, "The Cancer of Terrorism," in Netanyahu, *Terrorism*, p. 31.

3. A poignant expression of this unwarranted resistance to scholarly inquiry is to be found in Bruno Bettelheim's assessment of Robert Jay Lifton's *The Nazi Doctors: Medical Killing and the Psychology of Genocide* (New York: Basic Books, 1986). Bettelheim writes: "Dr. Lifton comes dangerously close to the attitude expressed in the French saying, '*tout comprendre c'est tout pardonner,*' an idea I cannot subscribe to where ruthless and callous murderers are concerned. . . . Having devoted much of my life to this problem [of studying the Nazi death camp phenomenon], I have restricted myself to trying to understand the psychology of the prisoners and I have shied away from trying to understand the psychology of the SS—because of the ever-present danger that understanding fully may come close to forgiving. I believe there are acts so vile that our task is to reject and prevent them, not to try to understand them empathetically as Dr. Lifton did." Bettelheim, "Their Specialty Was Murder," *The New York Times Book Review*, October 5, 1986, p. 62. My view is that without understanding, especially of vile acts, there can be no learning, and without learning there is bound to be repetition in some form. And further, that a firm line can be drawn so as to enable full understanding and, at the same time, total condemnation. I believe Lifton successfully drew such a line in his fine study of Nazi doctors, and it is a line that I seek to maintain in this work on terrorists of all persuasions.

4. For an overview see Darrell Garwood, *Under Cover: Thirty-Five Years of CIA Deception* (New York: Grove Press, 1985). Especially helpful is a chronology prepared by Tom Gervasi, appearing as an appendix, pp. 293–99.

3: A STEP TOWARD CONSTRUCTIVE COUNTERTERRORISM

1. For various perspectives on this central issue see James Turner Johnson, *Can Modern War Be Just?* (New Haven: Yale University Press, 1984); Burns H. Weston, ed., *Toward Nuclear Disarmament and Global Security* (Boulder, Colo.: Westview Press, 1984); Avner Cohen and Steven Lee, eds., *Nuclear Weapons and the Future of Humanity* (Totowa, N.J.: Rowman and Allanheld, 1986); F. H. Knelman, *Reagan, God and the Bomb* (Buffalo: Prometheus Books, 1985); and Philip J. Murnion, ed., *Catholics and Nuclear War* (New York: Crossroad, 1983).

On the related issue of the necessarily indiscriminate character of nuclear weapons use as associated with doctrines of deterrence and their equivalent (for instance, the USSR emphasizes, "defense" and "retaliation" and avoids the language of deterrence, but not its essential posture of threat to unleash indiscriminate destruction), and of the incompatibility between such indiscriminateness and international law even within the scope of a use of force that is otherwise permissible as self-defense see Horst Fischer, *Der Einsatz von Nuclearwaffen nach Art. 51 des I. Zusatzprotokolls zu den Genfer Konventionen von 1949* (Berlin: Duncker & Humblot, 1985).

2. Both quotations are from Thomas C. Schelling, *Arms and Influence* (New Haven: Yale University Press, 1966), pp. 17–18.

3. Whether this is avoidable or not, given the strength of technological momentum, is a central issue of controversy between those who insist on repudiating nuclearism and those who insist that it is best to live with nuclear weapons. For contrasting lines of argument see Robert Jay Lifton and Richard Falk, *Indefensible Weapons: The Political and Psychological Case Against Nuclearism* (New York: Basic Books, 1983), and Joseph S. Nye, Jr., *Nuclear Ethics* (New York: Free Press, 1986).

4. Carlos Marighela, *For the Liberation of Brazil* (Middlesex, Eng.: Penguin, 1971), p. 120; on "revolutionary terrorism" see pp. 112f.

5. This is the stress of Michael Walzer in *Just and Unjust Wars* (New York: Basic Books, 1977), pp. 197–206.

6. For a survey of history, see Franklin L. Ford, *Political Murder: From Tyrannicide to Terrorism* (Cambridge, Mass.: Harvard University Press, 1985).

7. Quoted in *The New York Times*, November 24, 1985.

8. "Greater Access to Terrorism Data Is Sought for Immigration Agency," *The New York Times*, February 5, 1987.

9. Richard E. Rubenstein, *Alchemists of Revolution: Terrorism in the Modern World* (New York: Basic Books, 1987), especially pp. 3–16.

10. Ibid., p. 5.

11. Doris Lessing, *The Good Terrorist* (New York: Alfred A. Knopf, 1985).

12. Rubenstein, *Alchemists*, p. 5.

13. This enumeration is relied on in Ronald Reagan's principal speech on terrorism. Speech to the Annual Convention of the American Bar Association, July 8, 1985, text in *The New York Times*, July 9, 1985.

14. Eqbal Ahmad, MERIP (Middle East Report). "Comprehending Terror," Vol. 16, No. 3, May–June 1986, pp. 3–5.

15. *Patterns of Global Terrorism: 1984*, Department of State, Washington, D.C., 1985, inside cover; in 1980 the CIA set forth a slightly different but also nonpolemical definition of terrorism: "the threat or use of violence for political purposes by individuals or groups, whether acting for or in opposition to established governmental authority, when such actions are intended to shock, stun, or intimidate a target group wider than the immediate victims. Terrorism has involved groups seeking to overthrow specific regimes, to rectify perceived national or group grievances, or to undermine international order as an end in itself." Quoted in James Adams, *The Fi-*

nancing of Terror (London: New English Library, 1986), p. 6. The definition associates terrorism especially with fear-inducing political violence and thus seems to exclude assassination; also, it emphasizes violence that disrupts the international order and fails to encompass violence designed to sustain the international order.

16. *Patterns,* p. 1.

17. See Adam Michnik, *Letters from Prison and Other Essays* (Berkeley: University of California Press, 1985); in a Western setting, a complementary perspective, although more religious in its idiom, can be found in James W. Douglass, *Lightning East to West: Jesus, Gandhi and the Nuclear Age* (New York: Crossroad, 1986).

4: THE ROUTINIZATION OF TERRORISM

1. The terminology of "routinization" was suggested to me by Irving Louis Horowitz's stimulating essay, "The Routinization of Terrorism and Its Unanticipated Consequences," in Martha Crenshaw, ed., *Terrorism, Legitimacy, and Power: The Consequences of Political Violence* (Middletown, Conn.: Wesleyan University Press, 1983), pp. 38–51. Horowitz construes the terrorist threat more narrowly than I do, but his line of interpretation is still very relevant to the argument advanced in this book.

2. Cf. report in *The New York Times,* December 12, 1986.

3. Informative and still challenging on this phenomenon of postrevolutionary terrorism is Crane Brinton, *The Anatomy of Revolution* (New York: Vintage, 1957).

4. For a consideration of the connections between gross violations of human rights and resistance politics see Richard Falk, *Human Rights and State Sovereignty* (New York: Holmes and Meier, 1981).

5. Hannah Arendt, *On Revolution* (New York: Viking, 1965); but on the wider problematique of revolutionary process see Arno J. Mayer, *The Persistence of the Old Regime* (New York: Pantheon, 1981).

6. For a helpful short summary see James Adams, *The Financing of Terror* (London: New English Library, 1986), p. 8.

7. Adeed Dawisha, *The Arab Radicals* (New York: Council on Foreign Relations, 1986), p. 14.

8. His role included an alleged secret agreement to provide PLO protection for U.S. diplomats in the Arab world, which as implemented thwarted terrorist plots. See Adams, *Financing of Terror,* pp. 90–92.

9. For background see Yossi Melman, *The Master Terrorist: The True Story Behind Abu Nidal* (New York: Adama Books, 1986).

10. Dawisha, *Arab Radicals,* p. 14.

11. James DeNardo, *Power in Numbers: The Political Strategy of Protest and Rebellion* (Princeton, N.J.: Princeton University Press, 1985), p. 229.

12. See Select Committee to Study Government Operations with Respect to Intelligence Activities [Church Committee]. *Alleged Assassination Plots Involving Foreign Leaders: An Interim Report*. 94th Cong., 1st sess., November 20, 1975. Cf. also evidence of U.S. relationship to the assassination of the Diem brothers in Vietnam in Ellen J. Hammer, *A Death in November* (New York, E. P. Dutton, 1987).

13. This allegation is developed most fully by Seymour M. Hersch in "Target Qaddafi," *The New York Times Magazine*, February 22, 1987.

14. For accounts see Michael King, *Death of the Rainbow Warrior* (New York: Penguin Books, 1986); *The Sunday Times* Insight Team, *Rainbow Warrior* (London: Arrow Books, 1986); and David Robie, *Eyes of Fire: The Last Voyage of the Rainbow Warrior* (Auckland West, N. Z.: Lindon Publishing, 1986).

15. Walter Laqueur, *The Age of Terrorism* (Boston: Little, Brown, 1987), p. 3.

16. Michael Walzer, *Just and Unjust Wars* (New York: Basic Books, 1977), pp. 197–206.

17. Cf. Walzer, *Just and Unjust Wars*, pp. 197–201; also Laqueur, *Age of Terrorism*, pp. 24–71.

18. Cf. voluminous literature on the failure of the United States to adhere to the laws of war in Vietnam. Representative discussion of these varied issues can be found in: Richard A. Falk, ed., *The Vietnam War and International Law*, Vols. 3 and 4 (Princeton: Princeton University Press, 1972, 1976). Peter D. Trooboff, ed., *Law and Responsibility* in *Warfare: The Vietnam Experience* (Chapel Hill, N.C.: University of North Carolina Press, 1975).

19. Walzer, *Just and Unjust Wars*, p. 198.

20. For example, in relation to the CIA's Phoenix Program to kill Vietcong "infrastructure." Cf. Darrell Garwood, *Under Cover: Thirty-five Years of CIA Deception* (New York: Grove Press, 1985), pp. 191–92. More recently, the CIA's role in relation to Contra killing has been documented in numerous places, such as Reed Brody, *Contra Terror in Nicaragua: A Report of a Fact-Finding Mission, September 1984–January 1985* (Boston: South End Press, 1985). Cf. also Philip Agee, *Inside the Company: CIA Diary* (New York: Stonehill, 1975); also, Church Committee, *Alleged Assassination Plots*.

21. Laqueur, *Age of Terrorism*, p. 85; but see p. 83, where Laqueur refers approvingly to a view of premodern Russian revolutionaries as "young terrorists" who were "men and women of the highest ethical standards." And, as such, a direct contrast to their portrayal by Dostoyevski in *The Possessed* as crazed and deluded fanatics. In Laqueur's words: "Any similarity between the 'possessed' and the terrorists of the 1880s is purely accidental" (p. 83).

22. Michael "Bommi" Baumann, *Terror or Love?* (New York: Grove Press, 1977).

23. Nuel Emmons and Charles Manson, *Manson in His Own Words* (New York: Grove Press, 1987), p. 23.

24. Ibid., p. 201.

25. These themes are developed in chapters 7 and 9.

26. Cf. Tim Pat Coogan, *The IRA* (New York: Praeger, 1970); Richard Rose, *Governing Without Consensus* (Boston: Beacon Press, 1972); Conor Cruise O'Brien, *States of Ireland* (New York:, Random House, 1972); and J. Bowyer Bell, *The Secret Army: A History of the IRA 1916–1970* (Cambridge, Mass.: MIT Press, 1974). Interesting interpretations of IRA and Baader-Meinhoff activity can be found in Raymond R. Corrado, "Ethnic and Ideological Terrorism in Western Europe," in Michael Stohl, ed., *The Politics of Terrorism*, 2d rev. ed. (New York: Marcel Dekker, 1983), pp. 255–326, and in Adrian Guelke, "Loyalist and Republican Perceptions of the North Ireland Conflict: The UDA and Provisional IRA," in Peter H. Merkl, ed., *Political Violence and Terror* (Berkeley: University of California Press, 1986), pp. 90–122.

27. Richard E. Rubenstein, *Alchemists of Revolution: Terrorism in the Modern World* (New York: Basic Books, 1987), p. 21.

5: THE TERRORIST MIND-SET: THE MORAL UNIVERSE OF REVOLUTIONARIES AND FUNCTIONARIES

1. Seymour M. Hersch, "Qaddafi Targeted," *The New York Times Magazine*, February 22, 1987.

2. There are, by now, many accounts of this savage encounter between Western, white settler peoples and indigenous, nonwhite peoples. The American experience is characteristic, but certainly not worse than what has occurred elsewhere, including in this hemisphere. For helpful documentation of the American experience, stressing its relationship to violence against those who are innocent, see particularly Michael Paul Rogin, *Fathers and Children: Andrew Jackson and the Subjugation of the American Indian* (New York: Alfred A. Knopf, 1975); Richard Drinnon, *Facing West: The Metaphysics of Indian-Hating and Empire-Building* (Minneapolis: University of Minnesota Press, 1980); Richard Slotkin, *Regeneration Through Violence: The Mythology of the American Frontier, 1600–1860* (Middletown, Conn.: Wesleyan University Press, 1973); and Frederick Turner, *Beyond Geography: The Western Spirit Against the Wilderness* (New York: Viking, 1980).

3. An illuminating reliance on the patterning of melodrama to polarize societal responses to revolutionary violence is developed in Robin Erica Wagner-Pacifici's *The Moro Morality Play: Terrorism as Social Drama* (Chicago: University of Chicago Press, 1986), especially pp. 278–94.

4. Benjamin Netanyahu in "Defining Terrorism" in Netanyahu, ed., *Ter-*

rorism: How the West Can Win (New York: Farrar, Straus, Giroux, 1986), p. 10 (emphasis in original).

5. Typical selectivity as to facts reported and omitted, but relatively moderate in overall tone, is Robert Oakley, "International Terrorism," *Foreign Affairs* 65: 611–29; see especially pp. 616–20.

6. Even the titles used strengthen the illusion that the problems of "nuclear terrorism" are a consequence of revolutionary threats to nuclear facilities and capabilities rather than of the weapons themselves as possible instruments of warfare and threat diplomacy. For example, Louis Rene Beres, *Terrorism and Global Security: The Nuclear Threat* (Boulder, Colo.: Westview Press, 1979). Beres, although elsewhere a critic of nuclearist statecraft, here draws a sharp and, in my view, unwarranted contrast between "nuclear terrorism" and "nuclear war." See pp. 50–58. A more blatant effort to dissociate terrorism from nuclear weapons strategy is to be found in Paul Leventhal and Yonah Alexander, eds., *Nuclear Terrorism: Defining the Threat* (Washington, D.C.: Pergamon-Brassey's, 1986).

7. Albert Speer, *Inside the Third Reich: Memoirs* (New York: Macmillan, 1970), p. 521.

8. Ibid., p. 112.

9. Ibid., p. 113.

10. Robert Jay Lifton, *The Nazi Doctors: Medical Killing and the Psychology of Genocide* (New York: Basic Books, 1986), pp. 418–65.

11. Ibid., p. 418.

12. Ibid., p. 421.

13. E. P. Thompson's extraordinary essay on "exterminism" was initially published as "Notes on Exterminism, the Last Stage of Civilisation," *New Left Review*, No. 121, May–June 1980, pp. 3–31; cf. also "Exterminism Revisited" in Thompson, *The Heavy Dancers* (New York: Pantheon, 1985), pp. 135–52. Also of fundamental importance on this theme is Jonathan Schell's *The Fate of the Earth* (New York: Alfred A. Knopf, 1982).

Perhaps the most careful effort at nuclearist justification is that of Joseph S. Nye, Jr., *Nuclear Ethics* (New York: Free Press, 1986). Nye writes, "We can give survival of the species a very high priority without giving it the paralyzing status of an absolute value. . . . The degree of that risk is a justifiable topic of both prudential and moral reasoning" (pp. 45–46). If human survival is not an absolute, then surely any lesser form of violence is subject to similar canons of "moral and prudential reasoning," and terrorism of all forms is legitimated so long as it is the outcome of conscientious reflection.

14. Nye develops this kind of argument in support of nuclear deterrence throughout his book; see especially pp. 91–132. A similar perspective is well developed in Lawrence Freedman, *The Price of Peace: Living with the Nuclear Dilemma* (New York: Henry Holt, 1986).

15. Wagner-Pacifici, *Moro Morality Play*, p. 291.

16. Ibid., p. 282.

17. The text of the letter is printed in ibid., p. 296.

18. Quoted in Klaus Wasmund, "The Political Socialization of West German Terrorists" in Peter H. Merkl, ed., *Political Violence and Terror,* (Berkeley: University of California Press, 1986), p. 215.

19. This analysis is based on Wagner-Pacifici discussion, *Moro Morality Play,* especially pp. 278–87.

20. Niccolò Machiavelli, *The Prince,* Ch. XVIII (New York: W.W. Norton, 1977), p. 64.

21. Ibid., p. 65.

22. Ibid., p. 66.

23. This view that anything goes in war is, of course, at odds with the international law of war, formal adherence to this law by all governments, the punishment of enemy soldiers and policymakers for violations of the laws of war, and even occasional prosecution of one's own soldiers for their failure to uphold the law of war in combat. The public tensions that arose throughout the United States in relation to the prosecution of Lieutenant Calley for his role in the My Lai massacre illustrated the cultural uncertainty as between "anything goes" and the competing view "there are limits." For background see Richard Hammer, *One Morning in the War* (New York: Coward-McCann, 1970); Seymour M. Hersh, *My Lai 4* (New York: Random House, 1970); and Richard Falk, Gabriel Kolko, and Robert Jay Lifton, eds., *Crimes of War* (New York: Random House, 1971).

24. Among those who have been most prominent in government and find themselves adopting unconditional antinuclearist positions see George F. Kennan, *The Nuclear Delusion,* rev. ed. (New York: Pantheon, 1982); Robert S. McNamara, *Blundering into Disaster: Surviving the First Century of the Nuclear Age* (New York: Pantheon, 1986); also important is Morton H. Halperin, *Nuclear Fallacy: Dispelling the Myth of Nuclear Strategy* (Cambridge, Mass.: Ballinger Publishing Co., 1987).

25. A good survey of antinuclearist thinking is contained in Burns H. Weston, ed., *Toward Nuclear Disarmament and Global Security* (Boulder, Colo.: Westview Press, 1984).

6: THE MYTH OF THE GOOD TERRORIST

1. For example, Bernard Lewis, *The Assassins: A Radical Sect in Islam* (New York: Oxford University Press, 1967); for a wider survey of antecedent forms of terrorism see Walter Laqueur and Yonah Alexander, eds., *The Terrorism Reader* (New York: Meridian, 1987), especially pp. 1–116; particularly interesting on premodern religiously motivated terrorism is David C. Rapoport, "Fear and Trembling: Terrorism in Three Religious

Traditions," *American Political Science Review*, Vol. 38 (1984), pp. 658–77.

2. Working Group on Terrorism (Bruce George, Rapporteur), "Final Report," North Atlantic Assembly, February 1987, p. 10.

3. Ibid.

4. Address to the nation, March 16, 1986, in M. Falcoff and Robert Royal, eds., *The Continuing Crisis* (Washington, D.C.: Ethics and Public Policy Center, 1987), p. 15.

5. Cf., for instance, "The CIA's Nicaragua Manual," published as *Psychological Operations in Guerrilla Warfare* (New York: Vintage, 1985).

6. Cf., Reed Brody, *Contra Terror in Nicaragua: Report of a Fact-Finding Mission: September 1984–January 1985* (Boston: South End Press, 1985), especially chronology, pp. 153–83, and bibliography, pp. 205–06. Cf. also a respected study by Americas Watch, *Violations of the Laws of War by Both Sides in Nicaragua, 1981–85*, published in New York: 1985. Also helpful: Christopher Dickey, *With the Contras* (New York: Touchstone, 1987) and Dieter Esch and Carlos Rincón, *The Contras: Interviews with Anti-Sandinistas* (San Francisco: Synthesis, 1984).

7. See chapter 8, *n. 7.*

8. For discussion of the Nuremberg Principles as an operative part of the domestic legal setting see Francis Anthony Boyle, *Defending Civil Resistance Under International Law* (Dobbs Ferry, N.Y.: Transnational Publishers, 1987), pp. 61–67, 122–25. See generally Bradley F. Smith, *Reaching Judgment at Nuremberg* (New York: Basic Books, 1977).

9. Text of poem as recited, *The New York Times*, May 20, 1987.

10. Ibid., May 21, 1987.

11. Ibid.

12. Note the difference between this situation and that of civil resistance against alleged violations of international law. In civil resistance, the defiance of law is nonviolent and symbolic, and its occurrence is deemed necessary as the harm or threat of harm attributed to government policies is ongoing.

13. For overall background on the Barbie trial and an early assessment of its importance, see Ted Morgan, "Voices from the Barbie Trial," *The New York Times Magazine*, August 2, 1987.

14. Joseph S. Nye, Jr., *Nuclear Ethics* (New York: Free Press, 1986), pp. 45–46.

15. Ibid., p. 100.

16. Much of the deterrence literature proceeds on this assumption of nuclear irreversibility. See the book produced by the Harvard Nuclear Study Group, Albert Carnesale and others, *Living with Nuclear Weapons* (New York: Bantam, 1983). Of course, not all ways of living with nuclear weapons are equal in terms of risks and effects. Members of the Harvard group have tried to connect the unavoidable reliance on nuclear weapons with policies

designed to constrain their use in a period of crisis. See Graham T. Allison, Albert Carnesale, Joseph S. Nye, Jr., *Hawks, Doves, and Owls: An Agenda for Avoiding Nuclear War* (New York: W. W. Norton, 1985).

17. C. Builder and M. Graubard, "The International Law of Armed Conflict: Implications for the Concept of Assured Destruction," Santa Monica, Calif., RAND Publication Series R-2804-FF, 1982.

18. Nye, *Nuclear Ethics, n.* 13, enumerated and explained, pp. 99–132.

19. Analysis along these lines is in Richard Falk, Lee Meyrowitz, and Jack Sanderson, "Nuclear Weapons and International Law," Occasional Paper No. 10, Princeton World Order Studies Program, 1980.

20. For instance, Morton H. Halperin, *Nuclear Fallacy: Dispelling the Myth of Nuclear Strategy* (Cambridge, Mass.: Ballinger Publishing Co., 1987); and Robert S. McNamara, *Blundering into Disaster: Surviving the First Century of the Nuclear Age* (New York: Pantheon, 1986).

7: WHY IRAN? WHY LIBYA? IRAN/CONTRA REVELATIONS AND TERROR NETWORKS

1. Cf. "The Ayatollah's Big Sting," *U.S. News and World Report,* March 30, 1987, pp. 18–28; there are indications of an even more questionable search for a moderate faction in Qaddafi's Libya. See *The New York Times,* August 16, 1987.

2. *The New York Times,* March 19, 1987.

3. By late 1987 perhaps even the Reagan administration had relinquished its room for maneuver on the Contras and Central America. The neoconservative position, so influential in Republican circles, made support for the Contras a litmus test for the Republican nomination. Presidential candidates, including even Vice President George Bush, situated themselves to the right of Reagan, questioning any negotiated settlement with Nicaragua unless it is coupled with high levels of continuing military support for the Contras.

4. William Westmoreland, *A Soldier Reports* (New York: Doubleday, 1976), p. 96.

5. Kermit Roosevelt, *Countercoup: The Struggle for the Control of Iran* (New York: McGraw-Hill, 1979), pp. 199–200.

6. For a first-person account, see General Robert E. Huyser, *Mission to Iran* (New York: Harper & Row, 1986).

7. Private communication with Mansour Farhang, who represented Iran in the United States at the time of the hostage seizure and was in direct contact with Khomeini.

8. This possibility has been the subject matter of persistent rumors told to me by various confidential sources in the media and from the ranks of those formerly serving the Iranian government but now in exile. The rumor

has been given a wider currency by the report of an interview in Paris by Abol-Hassan Bani-Sadr, the former president of the Islamic republic; see Flora Lewis, "The Wilds of Tehran," *The New York Times*, August 3, 1987.

9. Uri Ra'anan et al., eds., *Hydra of Carnage: The International Linkages of Terrorism and Other Low-Intensity Operations* (Lexington, Mass.: Lexington Books, 1986), p. 6.

10. Ibid. (emphasis in the original).

11. Ibid., p. 7.

12. Ibid., p. 13.

13. Ibid., p. 15.

14. Neil C. Livingstone and Terrell E. Arnold, eds., *Fighting Back: Winning the War Against Terrorism* (Lexington, Mass.: Lexington Books, 1986), p. 22.

15. Ibid., p. 23.

16. Cf. "Casey, an Architect of Aid for Contras, Sent Former Aide to Assist, Sources Say," *The Wall Street Journal*, April 2, 1987.

17. *The New York Times*, February 18, 1987.

18. *The New York Times* Special, *The Tower Commission Report* (New York: Times Books/Bantam, 1987).

19. Ibid., p. 64.

20. Ibid., p. xvii.

21. Ibid., p. 64.

22. Ibid., p. xv.

23. Ibid., p. 98.

24. Text in *The New York Times*, March 5, 1987.

25. *Tower Commission Report*, p. 94; emphasis in original.

26. Ibid.

27. Ibid., p. 97; emphasis in original.

28. Ibid., p. 98.

29. Ibid., pp. 98–99; emphasis in original.

30. *The New York Times*, March 5, 1987.

31. See Jonathan Marshall, Peter Dale Scott, and Jane Hunter, *The Iran-Contra Connection* (Boston: South End Press, 1987).

32. *Tower Commission Report*, p. 369.

33. Ibid., p. 370.

34. Cf. enumeration of factors exerting influence, ibid., p. 275.

35. Cf. Marshall, Scott, and Hunter, *n*. 31, pp. 167–186.

36. *Tower Commission Report*, p. 337.

37. Ibid., p. 344.

38. Current Policy No. 783, U.S. Dept. of State, Bureau of Public Affairs, as delivered January 15, 1986, p. 1.

39. Ibid., p. 2.

40. Ibid., p. 3.

NOTES

8: ON RESCUING LAW FROM THE LAWYERS

1. Current Policy No. 783, U.S. Dept. of State, Bureau of Public Affairs, as delivered January 15, 1986, pp. 1–4.

2. Ibid., p. 3.

3. Ibid.

4. Cf., for example, the text of Venice statement on terrorism in *The New York Times,* June 10, 1987.

5. General Assembly Resolution 41/38, November 20, 1986 (vote: 79–28–33).

6. For text of judgment, see Nicaragua v. United States of America, Merits, Judgment of 27 June 1986, ICJ Reports, p. 14.

7. Article 94 of the United Nations Charter reads as follows: "(1) Each Member of the United Nations undertakes to comply with the decision of the International Court of Justice in any case to which it is a party. (2) If any party to a case fails to perform the obligations incumbent upon it under a judgment rendered by the Court, the other party may have recourse to the Security Council, which may, if it deems necessary, make recommendations or decide upon measures to be taken to give effect to the judgment." The charter is a treaty that has been ratified by the United States and is therefore binding on the government. Such an analysis is made to suggest that it would be reasonable for the United States to respect this judgment, not that the United Nations can enforce it nor that the United States is necessarily more delinquent than other member states, several of which have also ignored adverse judgments.

8. Current Policy No. 783, p. 3.

9. Abraham D. Sofaer, "Terrorism and the Law," *Foreign Affairs* 64:906 (1986).

10. Cf. Sofaer, "The War Powers Resolution and Antiterrorist Operations," Current Policy No. 832, U.S. Dept. of State, Bureau of Public Affairs, as delivered April 29, 1986, pp. 1–4.

11. In President Reagan's speech on terrorism delivered to the American Bar Association, he categorized Iran, Libya, North Korea, Cuba, and Nicaragua as "a confederation of terrorist states"; elsewhere Reagan asserts that inasmuch as "these terrorist states are now engaged in acts of war against the Government and people of the United States, any state which is the victim of acts of war has the right to defend itself" (*The New York Times,* July 9, 1985).

12. Sofaer, "Terrorism and the Law," pp. 902–03.

13. Ibid., p. 905.

14. Ibid., p. 906.

15. Adam Roberts and Richard Guelff, eds., *Documents on the Laws of War* (Oxford: Clarendon Press, 1982), p. 409.

16. Convention on Offenses and Certain Other Acts Committed on Board

NOTES

Aircraft, Tokyo, 1963; Convention for the Suppression of Unlawful Seizure
of Aircraft (Hijacking), The Hague, 1970; Convention for the Suppression
of Unlawful Acts Against the Safety of Civil Aviation (Sabotage), Montreal,
1971; Convention on the Prevention and Punishment of Crimes Against
Internationally Protected Persons Including Diplomatic Agents, 1973; International Convention against the Taking of Hostages, 1979.
17. Cf. Edward S. Herman, *The Real Terror Network: Terrorism in Fact
and Propaganda* (Boston: South End Press, 1982), pp. 63–69.
18. Cf. Gary Sick, "The Uses and Abuses of Terrorism," *SAIS Review*, 7,
(Spring 1987): 11–26; on general activity of *Mujaheddin* as armed resistance
to Khomeini's rule, see pp. 19–20.
19. For text, see UN Doc. E/CN.4/1984/72 Annex of 9 March 1984.
20. There is by now a voluminous literature. Some writing is collected in
Arthur S. Miller and Martin Feinrider, eds., *Nuclear Weapons and Law*
(Westport, Conn., Greenwood Press, 1984); also very helpful is Francis
Anthony Boyle, *Defending Civil Resistance Under International Law*, (Dobbs
Ferry, N.Y.: Transnational Publishers, 1987), pp. 51–154.
21. For text, see Ian Brownlie, ed., *Basic Documents in International Law*
(Oxford: Clarendon Press, 2d ed., 1972), p. 35.
22. For convenient text of Protocol I, see Roberts and Guelff, *Documents
on the Laws of War*, pp. 389–446.
23. There is in Protocol I a refusal to accord spies or mercenaries prisoner-
of-war status. See Articles 46(1) and 47(1) .
24. Information based on material in William J. Pomeroy, *Apartheid, Imperialism, and African Freedom* (New York: International Publishers, 1986),
p. 174.
25. The most authoritative discussion of the relationship between terrorism
and Protocol I is contained in Hans-Peter Gasser, "Prohibition of Terrorist
Acts in International Humanitarian Law," *International Review of the Red
Cross*, July–August 1986, pp. 3–15; cf. also Statement of the Independent
Commission on Respect for International Law on U.S. Ratification of Protocol I to the Geneva Convention, June 1, 1987, pp. 1–8 (mimeographed).
26. At the same time the Reagan administration has submitted for ratification the 1977 Geneva Protocol II Relating to the Protection of Victims
of Non-International Armed Conflicts; text reprinted in Roberts and Guelff,
Documents on the Laws of War, pp. 449–63.
27. *The New York Times*, February 16, 1987; for Reagan administration
rationale, see L. Paul Bremer III, "Terrorism and the Rule of Law," Current
Policy No. 947, U.S. Dept. of State, Bureau of Public Affairs, April 23,
1987, pp. 1–4, especially 3–4.
28. Ibid., p. 5.
29. "Denied: A Shield for Terrorists," *The New York Times*, February 17,
1987.
30. Gasser, "Prohibition of Terrorist Acts," p. 13; emphasis in original.

31. Cf. Robert Woetzel, "International Terrorism and an International Criminal Court," 1986 (mimeographed).

32. So far the Tribunal has had thirteen judicial sessions on issues ranging from Turkish responsibility for the massacre of the Armenians in 1915–1916, Soviet intervention in Afghanistan, gross violations of human rights in a series of Third World countries to United States intervention in Nicaragua. For discussion and assessment of approach see Antonio Cassesse and Edmond Jouve, eds., *Pour un droit des peuples* (Paris: Berger-Levrault, 1978).

9: ENDING TERRORISM

1. *The New York Times,* March 5, 1987.

2. For a useful formulation see Conor Cruise O'Brien, "Thinking About Terrorism," *The Atlantic Monthly,* June 1986, pp. 50–66; also O'Brien, "Terrorism Under Democratic Conditions: The Case of the IRA," in Martha Crenshaw, ed., *Terrorism, Legitimacy, and Power: The Consequences of Political Violence* (Middletown, Conn.: Wesleyan University Press, 1983), pp. 91–104. See also Paul Wilkinson, *Terrorism and the Liberal State,* 2d ed. (New York: New York University Press, 1986).

3. This general rationale underlies Francis Anthony Boyle, *Defending Civil Resistance Under International Law* (Dobbs Ferry, N.Y.: Transnational Publishers: 1987); cf. also George Delf, *Humanizing Hell: The Law v. Nuclear Weapons* (London: Hamish Hamilton, 1985).

4. The orientation toward political action is outlined by Adam Michnik, *Letters from Prison and Other Essays* (Berkeley: University of California Press, 1985).

Select Bibliography

NOTE: This Select Bibliography is not meant to be comprehensive, to gather the books that share the outlook of the author, or even to list the works relied upon in footnotes. Inclusion here only expresses the judgment that a particular work is informative, or argumentative in an important way.

ADAMS, JAMES. *The Financing of Terror*. London: New English Library, 1986. Valuable on the neglected issue of the financial base of revolutionary terrorism; objective journalism, yet opinionated along mainstream lines.

BAUMANN, MICHAEL (BOMMI). *Terror or Love?* New York: Grove Press, 1977. A confessional repudiation of revolutionary terrorism (as lifestyle politics).

BERES, LOUIS RENE. *Terrorism and Global Security: The Nuclear Threat.* Boulder, Colo.: Westview Press, 1979. Useful, probing inquiry into mainstream terrorist dispositions toward threatening or causing nuclear catastrophe.

BRINTON, CRANE. *The Anatomy of Revolution*. New York: Vintage, 1957. Although originally published in 1952, still essential background on revolutionary/functionary recourse to terrorist practices.

BRODY, REED. *Contra Terror in Nicaragua: A Report of a Fact-Finding Mission, September 1984–January 1985*. Boston: South End Press,

1985. Documentation of anti-Contra allegations; the darkest side of mainstream counterterrorism.

CAMUS, ALBERT. *The Rebel: An Essay on Man in Revolt.* New York: Vintage, 1956. A passionate critique of terrorist politics.

CHOMSKY, NOAM. *Pirates and Emperors: International Terrorism in the Real World.* New York: Claremont Research and Publications, 1986. A powerful indictment of functionary terrorism with a focus on the Mediterranean caldron.

COHN, NORMAN. *The Pursuit of the Millennium.* Fair Lawn, N.J.: Essential Books, 1957. Influential on the fundamentalist thrust toward limitless political violence.

CORDES, BRIAN, ET AL. *A Conceptual Framework for Analyzing Terrorist Groups.* Santa Monica, Calif.: RAND, 1985. A typical think-tank contribution to mainstream counterterrorism.

CRENSHAW, MARTHA, ED. *Terrorism, Legitimacy and Power: The Consequences of Political Violence.* Middletown, Conn.: Wesleyan University Press, 1983. A valuable collection: highly intelligent essays, diverse perspectives.

DAWISHA, ADEED. *The Arab Radicals.* New York: Council on Foreign Relations, 1986. Useful on the relationship between radical politics and reliance on terrorist methods.

DELF, GEORGE. *Humanizing Hell: The Law v. Nuclear Weapons.* London: Hamish Hamilton, 1985. A genuine antiterrorist polemic in the context of nuclearism. Passionate, provocative, impressive.

FANON, FRANTZ. *The Wretched of the Earth.* New York: Grove Press, 1967. A powerful rationale for revolutionary violence, and also for terrorism.

FORD, FRANKLIN L. *Political Murder: From Tyrannicide to Terrorism.* Cambridge, Mass.: Harvard University Press, 1985. Useful on terrorism as discriminate political violence and on historical evolution; opinionated.

FREEDMAN, LAWRENCE, ET AL. *Terrorism and International Order.* London: Routledge & Kegan Paul, 1986. Valuable series of essays; mainstream, but moderate and thoughtful.

FURET, FRANCOIS, ANTOINE LINIERS, AND PHILIPPE RAYNAUD. *Terrorisme et Démocratie.* Paris: Fayard, 1985. Important on political effects of Left terrorism in France.

GARWOOD, DARRELL. *Under Cover: Thirty-Five Years of CIA Deception.* New York: Grove Press, 1985. Comprehensive indictment.

HACKER, FREDERICK J. *Crusaders, Criminals, Crazies: Terror and Terrorism in Our Time.* New York: W.W. Norton, 1976. A psychological perspective; wide-ranging, thoughtful, not conceptually rigorous.

HERMAN, EDWARD S. *The Real Terror Network: Terrorism in Fact and Propaganda.* Boston: South End Press, 1982. Turns the tables on mainstream counterterrorism; scholarly, engaged, shocking material on right-wing political violence condoned by the U.S. government.

KOVEL, JOEL. *Against the State of Nuclear Terror*. Boston: South End Press, 1983. Reliance on nuclear weaponry as functionary terrorism.

LAQUEUR, WALTER. *The Age of Terrorism*. Boston: Little, Brown, 1987. Synoptic; mainstream interpretation of revolutionary terrorism; valuable historical background.

LAQUEUR, WALTER, AND YONAH ALEXANDER, EDS., *The Terrorism Reader*. New York: Meridian, 1987. Useful background; mainstream.

LESSING, DORIS. *The Good Terrorist*. New York: Alfred A. Knopf, 1985. Fictive insight into the personality disorders of revolutionary terrorists in modern capitalist societies.

LEWIS, BERNARD. *The Assassins: A Radical Sect in Islam*. New York: Oxford University Press, 1967. A valuable study of origins, but not if appropriated in support of anti-Arab, anti-Islamic counterterrorism.

LIFTON, ROBERT JAY, AND RICHARD FALK. *Indefensible Weapons: The Political and Psychological Case Against Nuclearism*. New York: Basic Books, 1983. Some connections between functionary terrorism and nuclear deterrence.

LIVINGSTONE, NEIL C., AND TERRELL E. ARNOLD, EDS. *Fighting Back: Winning the War Against Terrorism*. Lexington, Mass.: Lexington Books, 1986. Aspires to be the manual for mainstream counterterrorism.

MAAS, PETER. *Manhunt: The Incredible Pursuit of a CIA Agent Turned Terrorist*. New York: Random House, 1986. The outer limits of functionary terrorism operating in the private sector; investigative journalism.

MCGEHEE, RALPH W. *Deadly Deceits: My 25 Years in the CIA*. New York: Sheridan Square Publications, 1983. Devastating critique of functionary mind-set by former insider.

MACHIAVELLI, NICCOLÒ. *The Prince*. New York: W.W. Norton, 1977. Underlies it all!

MARIGHELA, CARLOS. *For the Liberation of Brazil*. Middlesex, Eng.: Penguin, 1971. Influential, insider advocacy of revolutionary armed struggle.

MARSHALL, JONATHAN, PETER DALE SCOTT, AND JANE HUNTER. *The Iran-Contra Connection*. Boston: South End Press, 1987. Devastating exposé of the underpinnings of Iran/Contra disclosures; well documented; raises important unanswered questions.

MERKL, PETER H., ED. *Political Violence and Terror*. Berkeley: University of California Press, 1986. Conceptually liberating and suggestive at its best, but uneven; informative on European varieties of revolutionary terrorism.

MURPHY, JOHN F. *Punishing International Terrorists: The Legal Framework for Policy Initiatives*. Totowa, N.J.: Rowman and Allenheld, 1985. Mainstream, but solid and useful.

NETANYAHU, BENJAMIN, ED. *Terrorism: How the West Can Win*. New York:

Farrar, Straus, Giroux, 1986. The bible of counterterrorism; influential, one-eyed.

NEWHOUSE, JOHN. "The Diplomatic Round: A Freemasonry of Terrorism," *The New Yorker*, June 8, 1985, pp. 47–63. A good journalistic account of mid-1980s mainstream concern about the terrorist menace.

NYE, JOSEPH. *Nuclear Ethics*. New York: Free Press, 1986. An influential effort to reconcile nuclear deterrence with mainstream adherence to ethical standards.

PARRY, ALBERT. *Terrorism: From Robespierre to Arafat*. New York: Vanguard, 1976. Useful, mainstream, journalistic.

PRADOS, JOHN. *Presidents' Secret Wars: CIA and Pentagon Covert Operations Since World War II*. New York: William Morrow, 1986. Helpful background on functionary terrorism.

RA'ANAN, URI, ET AL., EDS. *Hydra of Carnage: The International Linkages of Terrorism and Other Low-Intensity Operations*. Lexington, Mass.: Lexington Books, 1986. Influential mainstream counterterrorist perspectives.

RANELAGH, JOHN. *The Agency: The Rise and Decline of the CIA*. Rev. ed. New York: Simon & Schuster, 1987. Comprehensive, useful, journalistic, sympathetic to the agency.

RUBENSTEIN, RICHARD E. *Alchemists of Revolution: Terrorism in the Modern World*. New York: Basic Books, 1987. Wonderfully illuminating; objective, wide-ranging.

SCARRY, ELAINE. *The Body in Pain: The Making and Unmaking of the World*. New York: Oxford University Press, 1985. The wider landscape brilliantly construed; difficult, but worth it.

SCHELLING, THOMAS C. *Arms and Influence*. New Haven: Yale University Press, 1966. Unwitting rationale for functionary terrorism in the guise of using force effectively in international relations; lucid, suggestive; influential.

SCHMID, ALEX P., AND JANNY DE GRAAF. *Violence as Communication: Insurgent Terrorism and the Western News Media*. Beverly Hills, Calif.: Sage Publications, 1982. Excellent on the media; informative, illuminating, innovative; an important contribution.

SCIASCIA, LEONARDO. *The Moro Affair and the Mystery of Majorana*. Manchester, Eng.: Carcenet, 1987. Brilliant reflective essay on the kidnapping and execution of Aldo Moro by the Red Brigades.

SENART, ROGER, AND NOEL HAUTERIVE. *L'Expansion Fanatique et Ses Crimes*. Paris: Editions L'Harmattan, 1987. Wide-ranging, somewhat journalistic survey of fanaticisms emergent in the contemporary world; makes useful connections relevant to terrorist upsurge.

STERLING, CLAIRE. *The Terror Network*. New York: Holt, Rinehart and Winston, 1981. Influential; purports to link cold war and upsurge of anti-West revolutionary terrorism; a poorly evidenced tract; alleged to be based partly on "misinformation."

STOCKWELL, JOHN. *In Search of Enemies: A CIA Story*. New York: W.W. Norton, 1978. Valuable on the functionary mind-set; an embittered critique.

STOHL, MICHAEL, ED. *The Politics of Terrorism*. 2d rev. ed. New York: Marcel Dekker, 1983. Useful, diverse, academic.

THOMPSON, E. P., AND MARY KALDOR, EDS. *Mad Dogs: The U.S. Raids on Libya*. London: Pluto, 1986. A critique of U.S. counterterrorist foreign policy with a focus on the European outlook.

U.S. SENATE SELECT COMMITTEE TO STUDY GOVERNMENTAL OPERATIONS WITH RESPECT TO INTELLIGENCE ACTIVITIES [CHURCH COMMITTEE]. *Alleged Assassination Plots Involving Foreign Leaders: An Interim Report*. Washington, D.C.: U.S. Government Printing Office, 1975. Source material on functionary terrorism, United States style.

WAGNER-PACIFICI, ROBIN ERICA. *The Moro Morality Play: Terrorism as Social Drama*. Chicago: University of Chicago, 1986. Fascinating, brilliant, significant, but difficult reading.

WALTER, E. V. *Terror and Resistance: A Study of Political Violence*. New York: Oxford University Press, 1969. Seminal, conceptually imaginative; academic yet indispensable.

WALZER, MICHAEL. *Just and Unjust Wars*. New York: Basic Books, 1977. An important, influential study, wide-ranging and conceptually valuable.

WELLMER, ALBRECHT. "Terrorism and the Critique of Society." In *Observations on "The Spiritual Situation of the Age,"* edited by Jurgen Habermas. Cambridge, Mass.: MIT Press, 1985, pp. 283–307. Exceptionally valuable essay on revolutionary terrorism.

WILKINSON, PAUL. *Terrorism and the Liberal State*. 2d ed. New York: New York University Press, 1986. Useful, wide-ranging, mainstream; vulnerabilities and dilemmas of a constitutional democracy faced with a revolutionary terrorist challenge.

WOHLSTETTER, ALBERT. "The Delicate Balance of Terror," *Foreign Affairs* 38:211–34 (1959). Extraordinarily influential article on the degree to which the exchange of nuclear threats by the superpowers constituted terrorism, sustained peace, and seemed unstable.

WRIGHT, ROBIN. *Sacred Rage: The Wrath of Militant Islam*. New York: Simon & Schuster, 1985. Insight into the fundamentalist and religious foundations of terrorism, either revolutionary or functionary.

INDEX

Speer, Albert, 81–82
Splitting of personality, terrorism and, 81–82
Stalin, Josef, 81
Stallone, Sylvester, 112–13
Star Wars. *See* Strategic Defense Initiative (SDI)
State interests, terrorism and, 6–8
State terror, 77, 171–72
State-sponsored terrorism, 18, 32–33
Stauffenberg, Count, 55–56, 102–3
Sterling, Claire, 193*n*3
Stimson, Henry, 25
Strategic Defense Initiative (SDI), counterterrorism and, xviii
Student protests, in France (1968), 45
Sullivan, William, 115–16, 120
Support of terrorism, by U.S.S.R., 7–8, 165
Symbionese Liberation Army, 9

Talleyrand, Charles Maurice de, xx
Territorial locus, of terrorism, 29–30
Terror,
media and victims of terror, 78–79
nuclear weapons and, 108–9
state terror, 77, 171–72

Terrorism,
antecedents of, 41–45
definition of, xiv, 26–27, 167, 195*n*15
forms of, 168–70
governmental forms. *See* State-sponsored terrorism
inhibition of recourse to, 185–87
as instrumental violence, 50–52
selective sense of term, 16–17
U.S. State Department definition of, 33–35
Terrorists,
good terrorist and political violence, 103–4
label as tool in political conflict, 27–28
mind-set of, 75–93
Terry, Fernando Belaúnde, xv
Tet offensive, xx–xxi
Thatcher, Margaret, 68
Thompson, E. P., 83
Torture, 152–54
Committee Against Torture, 152–53
Convention Against Torture and other Cruel, Inhuman or Degrading Treatment or Punishment (1984), 152–54
Torture Convention. *See* Convention Against Torture and other Cruel, Inhuman or Degrading Treatment or Punishment